THE LAW, SOCIETY, AND POLITICS OF ENTERTAINMENT IN BRITAIN

This open access book examines the rules shaping British political entertainment.

Satire is a powerful tool for exposing political hypocrisy. It can be offensive and provocative, sparking debates about the limits of freedom of expression and the harm in humour. The book focuses on broadcasting restrictions born from the quaintly named rules on taste and decency, and impartiality, assessing the potential damage to democracy when rules are misinterpreted. In examining the historical and legal context, it traces how regulatory frameworks have evolved and impacted on the creative industries.

Through interviews with industry professionals including comedians, writers and executive producers, the book challenges the idea that regulation dictates editorial choices and creates a 'cancel culture'. It reveals how broadcast practitioners decide the ethical and legal limits of offensive humour, and how the misinterpretation of the impartiality requirement can undermine satire's role. Performers and writers discuss how self-censorship and social pressures influence what we see and hear in the media.

Much of British political satire has been 'smoothed out' due to fears of offending audiences or because of a timid approach to programme making. This has left the audience unchallenged, uninformed, and politically disengaged. The book argues for a policy change to broadcast regulation. The impartiality requirement should be dropped for satire, and broadcasters should be more robust in defending their output.

This book is essential reading for policy makers, lawyers, and both media students and academics keen to understand the editorial process and the effect of 'cancel culture'.

The Law, Society, and Politics of Entertainment in Britain

Regulation or Self-Censorship?

Jennifer Young

•HART•
OXFORD • LONDON • NEW YORK • NEW DELHI • SYDNEY

HART PUBLISHING

Bloomsbury Publishing Plc

Kemp House, Chawley Park, Cumnor Hill, Oxford, OX2 9PH, UK

1385 Broadway, New York, NY 10018, USA

Bloomsbury Publishing Ireland Limited, 29 Earlsfort Terrace, Dublin 2, D02 AY28, Ireland

HART PUBLISHING, the Hart/Stag logo, BLOOMSBURY and the Diana logo are trademarks of Bloomsbury Publishing Plc

First published in Great Britain 2026

A catalogue record for this book is available from the British Library.

A catalogue record for this book is available from the Library of Congress.

ISBN: HB: 978-1-50998-866-2
ePDF: 978-1-50998-868-6
ePub: 978-1-50998-869-3

Typeset by Compuscript Ltd, Shannon

This book is dedicated to my father Ken who loved comedy, my fabulous husband Brian and children Felix and Tobias, and my darling mother Irmgard.

PREFACE

This book is based on my PhD, itself inspired in part by the Victoria and Albert Museum's exhibition 'Censored! Stage, Screen, Society at 50'.[1] The exhibition marked the 50th anniversary of the Theatres Act, which abolished state censorship of the theatre. Originally work created for the stage had to be approved by the Lord Chamberlain and there were examples of scripts with comments illustrating what had been cut or rejected by the Lord Chamberlain's office before the plays could be performed in public. From the exhibition I drew comparisons between the work done by the Lord Chamberlain's office, censoring plays before granting them licences, and my time as an editorial compliance adviser for various broadcasters. Working in compliance I had to make decisions about programme content for broadcasting, checking that it complied with the regulations and the law, and considering the level of offensive content which might be deemed justifiable, or appropriate by audiences.

This book traces the beginning of state censorship using historical sources, and brings the arguments for and against state regulation up to the present day through interviews with modern practitioners. The book includes quotes and language which may be deemed offensive or discriminatory to illustrate themes around harm and offence (once called 'taste and decency'). The book also considers the thorny issue of the regulations on impartiality and the impact that has on political entertainment.

I am indebted to the wide range of people who contributed to the interviews in this book. I purposely recruited a proportion of contributors who do not reflect my own political leanings or ideologies. It should be noted that I do not necessarily agree with the political or ideological beliefs some participants hold but do not feel that it would be right, especially in a book which discusses censorship, self-censorship and social censure, to exclude their voices from this conversation. In fact, I believe it gives a more rounded representation of the times because it includes opinions from this wide range of people.

[1] www.vam.ac.uk/exhibitions/censored-stage-screen-society-at-50.

ACKNOWLEDGEMENTS

First, I want to thank the participants in the interviews who were all incredibly generous, giving their time and expertise for free.

Thanks too to Professors Michael Harker and Paul Bernal, Professor David Mead and Dr Sabine Jacques who were good enough to read various versions of this book and for their advice and support throughout. I also greatly appreciated my Research Fellowship awarded by the University of Liverpool School of Law, giving me access to their fine library during the polishing of this book.

I must thank the Southeast Network for Social Science for funding my PhD, the Dutch Research Council (VI.Vidi.201.111, NWO Talent Programme Vidi SSH 2020) and my PI Dr Alberto Godioli and finally UKRI for the open access publishing funding, SENSS grant number ES/P00072X/1.

TABLE OF CONTENTS

Preface.......... vii
Acknowledgements.......... ix
List of Interview Participants.......... xv
Table of Cases.......... xix
Table of Legislation.......... xxi

1. Introduction **1**
I. Scope.......... 7
II. Defining the 'Political' in Political Satire.......... 8
III. Outline of Chapters.......... 9
A. Chapter Two – Satire and the Law.......... 9
B. Chapter Three – Regulating and Repressing Information, Ideas and Entertainment.......... 9
C. Chapter Four – Politicians as Entertainment and Entertainers.......... 10
D. Chapter Five – The Groundwork for the Interviews.......... 10
E. Chapters Six and Seven – The Interviews.......... 10
F. Chapter Eight – Conclusion.......... 11

2. Satire and the Law **12**
I. Introduction.......... 12
II. The Roots and Role of Satire.......... 12
III. The Definition and Importance of Satire.......... 17
IV. Regulating Political Expression.......... 19
V. A Challenge Too Far?.......... 23
VI. Laughing All the Way to Court.......... 24
A. Humour, Hate Speech and Free Speech.......... 24
B. The Strasbourg Court and Political Punchlines.......... 27
C. Ofcom.......... 32
D. The Meta Oversight Board.......... 35
VII. Conclusion.......... 38

3. Regulating and Repressing Information, Ideas and Entertainment **42**
I. Introduction.......... 42
II. Regulating the Printed Word.......... 44
III. The Stage Licensing Act 1737.......... 47
IV. Press Freedom and Theatre Censorship.......... 49

V. The Arrival of Moving Pictures and World War I 55
VI. Progression on the Stage and Post-War Booms 57
VII. The Permissive Age 60
VIII. Abolition of Lord Chamberlain as Censor 65
IX. The Arbiters of Taste and Decency 66
X. Conclusion 69

4. Politicians as Entertainment and Entertainers 71
I. Introduction 71
II. Politicians as Entertainment 78
III. Keeping Control – Editorial Ownership 81
IV. Rules of Coverage 86
V. One Step Further, Politicians as 'Entertainers' 90
VI. Regulating Current Broadcast Media 91
VII. Digital Democracy 94

5. The Groundwork for the Interviews 96
I. Introduction 96
II. Aims and Questions 99
III. Approaches to Data Gathering 100
IV. Participants and their Status 101
V. Ethical Considerations 104
VI. A Snapshot in Time 105

6. The Interviews on Harm and Offence 107
I. Introduction 107
II. Holding the Line 108
III. Key Rules and Principles 108
A. Not a Blueprint but a Framework 113
B. Compliance and Legal 116
C. The Chain of Worry 119
D. Just Because Someone is Offended by Something doesn't Mean they are Right 128
E. Inclusivity Creates an Exclusivity 134
F. Broadcasting the Taboo. Are you *Really* Going to Go There? 137
G. The Court of Public Opinion 140
H. The Minefield of Social Media and (Self) Censorship 146

7. The Interviews on Due Impartiality 150
I. Introduction 150
II. Key Rules and Principles 153
A. Impartiality is a State of Bliss 155
B. Right Wing Comedians 164

C. Upsetting the Apple Cart 166
D. An Existential Threat 172
E. Her Majesty's Loyal Opposition 174

8. Conclusion 177
I. The Courts 181
II. Media Regulation: Restricting Information and Ideas 182
III. Social Censure 182
IV. Power and Protection 183
V. Policy Solutions 186
VI. Towards a Satire Exception 187
VII. Once More Unto the Breach 188

Bibliography 190
Index 201

LIST OF INTERVIEW PARTICIPANTS

Anonymous (Compliance Consultant 01)

Anonymous (Compliance Consultant 02)

Anonymous (Executive Producer)

Anonymous (Producer 02)

Anonymous (Writer and Performer 09)

Anonymous (Writer and Performer 11)

Anonymous (Lawyer)

Shane Allen (Controller of Comedy)

Steve N Allen (Writer and Broadcaster)

Ric Bailey (Chief Adviser Politics BBC)

Trevor Barnes (Compliance Consultant)

Jo Bunting (Producer)

Simon Evans (Stand-up Comic and Broadcaster)

Dominic Frisby (Stand-Up Comic and Broadcaster)

Michael Grade, Lord (Chair of Ofcom)

Laura Grimshaw (Radio Producer)

Jon Holmes (Producer and Writer)

Robin Ince (Writer and Broadcaster)

Leo Kearse (Stand-Up Comedian)

Graham Linehan (Writer)

John Lloyd (Executive Producer)

Andrew Newman (CEO, Spelthorne Community Television)

Steve North (General Manager UKTV)

Andy Parsons (Writer and Performer)

Jon Plowman OBE (Executive Producer)

Christine Rose (Writer)

Jolyon Rubinstein (Writer and Performer)

Alexei Sayle (Writer and Broadcaster)

Charlie Skelton (Writer and Script Editor)

Jon Thoday (Co-Executive Chairman, Avalon)

Neil Webster (Writer and Producer)

Richard Wilson (Executive Producer)

Please note this book contains offensive and discriminatory language.

TABLE OF CASES

Boyle v MGN Ltd [2012] EWHC 2700 (QB) 34, 131
Campbell v MGN [2004] UKHL 5
De Libellis Famosis (1606) 5 Co Rep 125a, 77 ER 250 45
GB News v Ofcom [2025] EWHC 460 (Admin) 79, 91
R (Autonomous Non-Profit Organisation TV- Novosti) v The Office of Communications [2020] EWHC 689 (Admin) 151
R (Gaunt) v Office of Communications [2010] EWHC 1756 (QB) (13 July 2010) 32
R v Penguin books LTD [1960] [1961] 1 WLUK 17; [1961] Crim LR 176 61
Redmond-Bate v DPP [1999] 7 BHRC 375 .... 35, 143
Whitehouse v Gay News and Lemon [1979] AC 617; [1979] 2 WLR 281 68

European Cases European Court of Human Rights

Alves da Silva v Portugal App no 41665/07 (20 October 2009) 6, 23, 26, 28
Bonnet v France App no 35364/19 (25 January 2022) 31–32
Egill Einarsson v Iceland (No.2) App no 31221/15 (17th October 2018) 32
Eon v France App no 26118/10 (14 March 2013) 15, 19, 26, 28, 111
Gachechiladze v Georgia App no 2591/19 (22 July 2021) 30
Gaunt v the United Kingdom App no 26448/12 (6 September 2016) 32
Handyside v The United Kingdom App no 5493/72 (7 December 1976) 3, 25, 29–30, 97
Kuliś and Różycki v Poland App no 27209/03 (6 October 2009) 23
Le Pen v France App no 45416/16 (28 February 2017) 31–32
Lingens v Austria App no 9815/82 (8 July 1986) 3, 16, 28, 38, 89
M'Bala M'Bala v France App no 25239/13 (20 October 2015) 27
Otto-Preminger-Institut v Austria App No. 13470/87 (20 September 1994) 30

Patrício Monteiro Telo de Abreu v Portugal App no 42713/15 (7 June 2022)....28–29, 31, 147, 181
Perincek v Switzerland App no 27510/08 (15 October 2015) 26
Sekmadienis v Lithuania App no 69317/14 (30 January 2018)....30
Sousa Goucha v Portugal App no 70434/12 (22 March 2016)....31
Vereinigung Bildender Künstler v Austria App no 68354/01 (25 January 2007) 25, 28–30
Z.B. v France App no 46883/15 (2 September 2021) 27
Ziembiński v Poland (no. 2) App no 1799/07 (5 July 2016)....26

Other Jurisdictions

Erdoğan v Böhmermann 7 U 34/17 (15 May 2018)....15
Lex Iulia de adulteriis coecendis[1] (c.18 BC)....42
M.T.C v Public Prosecutor Cass Pen.N 320/2022 10 January 2022....33

[1] Part of the Julian Laws legislating moral behaviour.

TABLE OF LEGISLATION

Statutes

An Act for preventing the frequent Abuses in printing seditious treasonable and unlicensed Bookes and Pamphlets and for regulating of Printing and Printing Presses (Charles II, 1662) 46
Bull Exurge Domine (Pope Leo X, 1520) 45
Communications Act 2003 .... 6, 8, 25, 32, 40, 91–92, 100, 108, 110, 113, 151, 153, 177
Copyright, Designs and Patents Act 1988 .... 17, 87–88
Criminal Libel Act 1819 (60 Geo III & 1 Geo IV c 8) 49
De Libellis Famosis 1606 (5 Co Rep 125a, 77 ER 250) 45
Human Rights Act 1998 ....22–24, 98
Licensing Act 1737 (10 Geo 2 c 28) 47–48, 57, 64, 180, 182, 185
Newspaper Stamp Duties Act (60 Geo III c 9) 49
Obscene Publications Act 1959 60–61
Royal Charter for the continuance of the British Broadcasting Corporation (December 2016) Cm 9365 S.6 (1) and (2).... 154, 172
Scandalum Magnatum 46
Sexual Offences Act 1956 .... 61, 69
Stage Licensing Act 1737, *see* Licencing Act 1737
Television Act 1954 ....65, 70, 74–75, 77, 151
Theatres Act 1843 (6 & 7 Vict c 68) 50–51, 57–58, 63–64

Other Legislation

Charter of Fundamental Rights of the European Union [2012] OJ C 326/02 29
Council of Europe's Committee of Ministers Recommendation No R (97) 20 on Hate Speech. (adopted 30 October 1997) 26

1

Introduction

ridiculum acri fortius et melius magnas plerumque secat res[1]

From the first scratch of a stylus in wax to ink rolled on panel and press, from fingers striking a keyboard to silent movies, spoken words weaving through airwaves and across nations, writers have used humour to poke at the powerful. Humour is an effective critique of those in authority, highlighting contradictions and hypocrisy. Political entertainment is a powerful tool for exposing pomposity and duplicity. With a long tradition of holding politicians to account, it challenges the orthodox. It can be offensive, distasteful, and unkind. It creates disputes over the limits to freedom of expression. There is always someone, somewhere who decides what can and what cannot be said. People, regulations and laws constantly struggle to navigate these limits.

This book discusses political satire, freedom of expression and what decides the audience's ability to discover innovative and challenging information and ideas through entertainment. By examining the historical and legal context of political entertainment, it provides insights into how regulatory frameworks governing political satire evolve, and how these impact on democratic debate. By understanding the effects that those historical restrictions had on creativity it considers the present and future implications on today's writers and producers.

The book reveals the current regulatory impact through the eyes and experiences of practitioners. It demonstrates how they interpret and apply rules, regulations and laws to the creation and curation of 'traditional' television and radio satire. This book determines the factors influencing today's decisions on political entertainment, to write or not to write, to broadcast or not. There are interviews with writers and editors, from self-styled 'right wing' comedians to those in editorial positions, including Lord Michael Grade and the BBC's Chief Adviser Politics. The interviews focus on socio-political content that has the potential to breach The Ofcom Broadcasting Code (with the Cross-promotion Code and the On Demand Programme Service Rules) (the Code) regulations of Harm and Offence and Due Impartiality.[2]

[1] Horace, *Satires* 1.10 (trans: Ridicule cuts through power swiftly and more deeply than bitterness).
[2] The Ofcom Broadcasting Code (December 2020), ss 2 and 5.

This book concludes that much of the satire which remains on British traditional broadcast media, and there is little at the moment, has been smoothed out and left toothless. Two reasons for this came to light: one being a concern of offensive content creating an audience or media backlash, and the other through practitioners (mis)interpreting the Code and editorial guidelines. Editorial control and self-censorship leave the audience unchallenged, unprovoked, and less informed politically. The impartiality requirement is especially damaging to political satire. Satire is a form of democratic communication which should be protected and defended as vigorously as serious political speech.

Whilst the focus is on political entertainment, we trace the historical influences, social mores, laws, regulations and policies which led to the censorship of socio-political entertainment. This is to understand the obstacles which stymie the creation of political satire and to promote its importance both as artistic expression and political speech, because of its democratic value to society.

Echoes of old laws still affect the modern-day satirist. This is reflected through the interviews in the final chapters of this book. Here people who write, perform and produce political entertainment broadcasts in the United Kingdom (UK) explain their thought processes behind getting their work to air, or their reasoning for self-censoring their writing. They consider how today's legal and social constraints influence what is written and/or performed on broadcast media or what might be diluted down, removed from scripts or performances, by whom and why.

These interviews discuss how freely they believe they can produce political satire about the subjects and people they judge to be deserving of ridicule. For some, more than a curbing of their freedom of expression right might be at stake when satirising their targets. Social censure for overstepping an invisible boundary and causing offence can result in writers, performers or editors losing their livelihood or reputation, being 'cancelled'.

To put these interviews into the context of the right to freedom of expression, this book looks at the history of the regulation and the creation of socio-political content focussing in on the audio-visual medium of political entertainment. This is not only to draw the readers' attention to the way laws and rules developed through time leading to the current broadcast regulations, but also to consider whom these rules might ultimately protect. This then culminates with the thoughts and opinions of contemporary broadcast satirists and those with the powers to influence television and radio programming output.

Regulations might repress progressive ideas in a democratic society, even when it is done in the name of audience protection. In some cases, laws and rules and regulations which were, and still are, put in place to protect the audience serve rather to protect powerful figures and institutions. Historically powerful people and institutions controlled political information and progressive ideas by restricting news and political entertainment. This control benefitted the powerful, protected their reputations and kept any scandalous behaviour and dubious policies from scrutiny. This made a mockery of democracy. Banning political entertainment which ridiculed those in power or refusing to allow minority viewpoints which could widen societal interests, limits democratic understanding and engagement. It restricts the opportunities for debate, and it curbs political speech.

Echoes of historical laws and regulation, and concerns of repercussions from crossing invisible boundaries, still linger today in writers' rooms and production offices. Content which could be created and produced sometimes never makes it to air. This is because of the way in which regulations are interpreted, or the way in which the production team believes an audience might interpret programme material. Audience reactions to provocative material can lead to concerns about cancellation, and this then gags gag writers.

As the European Court of Human Rights (ECtHR) says, '[F]reedom of political debate is at the very core of the concept of a democratic society'.[3] Whilst this book does not argue for unfettered freedom of expression, it considers that shocking events may call for creative people to have the ability to use shocking content to challenge a government and to provoke the audience too. To this end there is a discussion on rules which encompass content that can offend the quaintly-coined old rules of taste and decency, how these evolved into the modern concept of harm and offence, and how this is now interpreted by practitioners.[4] Without the ability to challenge an audience, the ability to discuss contentious issues openly and progress as a society may be lost. As the ECtHR stated:

> Freedom of expression constitutes one of the essential foundations of such a society, one of the basic conditions for its progress and for the development of every man.
>
> … it is applicable not only to 'information' or 'ideas' that are favourably received or regarded as inoffensive or as a matter of indifference, but also to those that offend,
>
> shock or disturb the State or any sector of the population. Such are the demands of that pluralism, tolerance and broadmindedness without which there is no 'democratic society'.[5]

Whilst freedom of expression rights and current broadcast regulation are balanced enough not to restrict broadcast political entertainment, it is not always interpreted by practitioners in this way. Those traditional boundaries and legacy rules have left a mark on people who make editorial decisions. These boundaries will be explored in the following chapters. They stop work being produced, as sometimes a satirist decides it is just not worth it, that 'the juice isn't worth the squeeze'.[6]

One of the inspirations for this book was an exhibition at the Victoria and Albert Museum in London called *Censored! Stage, Screen, Society at 50*. It marked 50 years since the Theatre Act of 1968 abolished state censorship of British theatre

[3] *Lingens v Austria* App no 9815/82 (8 July 1986), para 42.
[4] The Ofcom Broadcasting Code (December 2020), s 2.
[5] *Handyside v The United Kingdom* App no 5493/72 (7 December 1976), para 49.
[6] Charlie Skelton, writer, in interview.

productions. The displays of scripts, marked with comments indicating where the office of the Lord Chamberlain had cut lines or censored whole plays, brought into focus how traditional broadcasting compliance editors and producers now take the place of the Lord Chamberlain and the theatre producers. Compliance teams, editorial policy departments, executive producers and producers check scripts or view or listen to programmes and advise producers to make cuts or confirm the content as compliant to the editorial policies or broadcast codes. The Lord Chamberlain and previous laws and guidance had a substantial chilling effect on innovative political entertainment, could this still be the case today?

Another motivation for writing this book was a disquiet that over-regulation of broadcast content was stifling creativity, leading to a lack of challenging programming which could engage audiences politically through the lens of satire. It was a concern that over-regulation caused a censorship by omission, writers might not create hard-hitting, socio-political commentary in the form of comedy because they felt restricted by regulatory boundaries and so produced softer content, unlikely to challenge the audience. Alternatively, a misinterpretation of the regulations might mean producers would over-reach and, by doing so, omit or remove content which was within the remit of the Code, or their decisions were made on a subjective, rather than a legal, basis.

Finally, how real is cancel culture? Are those who write and perform comedy being silenced by the court of public opinion? Some argue there is a deadening of political debate based on the concept that people, including comedians, writers and performers are 'too scared' to say anything, or the state is taking away the right to free speech and no one 'is allowed' to say anything anymore. However, as the interviews show, regulatory boundaries are sometimes misinterpreted or rarely considered in editorial decision making, except by people who work in editorial compliance roles and/or act in an advisory capacity.

Whilst a writer or performer can initially control what they write, they do not have complete control over the material they write for traditional television and radio. How much must they conform rather than innovate so as not to rock the boat of broadcasting? When they self-censor it creates empty spaces. These empty spaces are the artistic works which go uncreated, and examples are documented later in this book.

When existing work is sanctioned by the law, or by society, it has repercussions in the form of a chilling effect on expression, writers self-censor work they would have otherwise produced, creating further empty spaces where there should be innovative artistic output.[7] These gaps in output are explored through both a retrospective examination of the evolution of the laws which developed around audio-visual content, and in how those laws affect socio-political entertainment in the present day. Any disruption, beyond that prescribed by law, to the free flow of accurate information and ideas interferes with the audiences' ability to navigate the political landscape, make an informed opinion and therefore, an informed

[7] Here and throughout 'speech' encompasses all types of expression including verbal and visual.

choice at the ballot box. Freedom of satirical expression keeps a check on governmental powers, and promotes tolerance and diversity, and this is reflected through the case law discussed later.

Britain has a long tradition of political comedy. In the 1960s, often considered the golden age of British satire, it was rarely so afraid of criticising those in power. It excelled in rebelling against the orthodox, bringing new ideas to challenge the public and that needs to continue. Satirical programming can cause offence and court controversy but restricting satire and socio-political entertainment impacts on democratic debate, stripping the audience of the chance to access new and engaging ideas and the ability to see the world from a different angle.

Whilst the importance of satire is widely acknowledged, the process of its curation (by whom, why and with what outcome) before it is released to the public is an important but neglected area of research in the United Kingdom. The less creative people feel able to challenge the orthodox, the fewer opportunities exist to inspire social change and promote critical thinking.

Creative people need to be able to use contentious material that offends, shocks and disturbs an audience to convey offensive, shocking, disturbing and socially unacceptable behaviour. Such content raises awareness of the unpleasantness and hostility that bigoted political ideologies create and gives audiences the information and arguments to counter it. Without the ability to challenge an audience, to discuss controversial issues openly, to counter the arguments of the intolerant, ultimately the ability to progress as a society is diminished. These arguments are often nuanced, and humour gives the opportunity for audiences to see and appreciate these nuances.

This is not to say that there should be unfettered freedom of expression, there should be a considered approach to using offensive language and situations. There is a need for some speech to be restricted, and as political entertainment is there to expose and ridicule the powerful, it should not be discriminatory or attack vulnerable sections of society. Expression which courts controversy by being purposely gratuitously offensive or incites discrimination or violence is rightly not protected by laws in many countries.

Whilst the media may have the power to shape how politicians are portrayed; the politicians have the power to shape what the media are able to do by drawing up these laws. When political entertainment is suppressed, by law, regulation, or political pressure influencing and amplifying public outcries and social censure, then this has an impact.

> The free exchange of information and ideas on matters relevant to the organisation of the economic, social and political life of the country is crucial to any democracy. Without this, it can scarcely be called a democracy at all. […] Artistic speech and expression is important for similar reasons, in fostering both individual originality and creativity and the free-thinking and dynamic society we so much value.[8]

[8] Lady Hale in *Campbell v MGN* [2004] UKHL 22 [2004] AC 457, para 148.

As Lady Hale says, access to information about the economic, social and political life of the country is crucial to democracy. Political entertainment is a form of artistic speech and political expression which informs the economic, political and social life of a country and fosters originality and creativity. Political satire is extraordinarily important as a way of sharing information and ideas and, as a form of political speech, there should be few restrictions placed on it. Comedy is an attractive and popular form of entertainment to a wide audience, especially a younger audience, more so than 'hard news'. It is an effective tool to aid critical thinking and an important source of political information for those who may not engage with serious news programmes. Any restriction of expression affects the right of the audience to receive different ideas. This right should only be restricted when it is prescribed by law, pursues a legitimate aim and is necessary in a democratic society, or inter alia, for the protection of health or morals and for the protection of the reputation or rights of others. The ECtHR, like Lady Hale, states that political speech deserves the highest protection and additionally any interference with satire, as a form of artistic expression, should be examined with particular care.[9] The Council of Europe has recognised that satirical artistic expression can be purposely contentious when exposing the failings of those in the public eye, and that it can be difficult to judge a line of acceptability for content which is offensive.[10] This is the line which writers, performers, producers and editorial executives must tread when considering what content is appropriate for broadcast. This line is blurry and fuzzy and sometimes difficult to track. When legal or regulatory breaches occur, they illustrate how courts and regulators consider applying sanctions on creative content. These sanctions, especially when coupled with the changing attitudes in society, can influence the writing and broadcasting of innovative socio-political content which is balancing on the edges of that blurry line.

On drawing up the Communications Act 2003 the Government required Ofcom to set down a code for broadcasters. The most relevant sections of the Code, or at least those that most affect political entertainment production, are Section 2, Harm and Offence and Section 5, Due Accuracy and Due Impartiality. Whilst these regulations can be interpreted as reasonable enough not to restrict broadcast political satire, the production community regularly felt they should produce content less likely to upset their audience. This was often to do with a concern that a few audience complaints would be blown out of proportion by certain media outlets which would then create a media storm, or as one contributor put it 'a fuss'.[11]

[9] See *Alves da Silva v Portugal* App no 41665/07 (ECtHR, 20 October 2009), para 27.
[10] Council of Europe, *Free to create – Artistic freedom in Europe* (Council of Europe Report, 2023) 12.
[11] Jon Plowman, independent producer, and former BBC Head of Comedy in interview.

As Barendt said,

> An argument that it is right to ban offensive language to protect the sensitivities of the audience would substantially undermine freedom of expression. The general public, or perhaps the particular audience, would in effect be able to impose a veto on the language used by speakers. The implications for freedom of political speech and the arts would be considerable.[12]

Such vetoes create a gap in public conversation, impact on artistic impression, and lead to a less informed electorate. The interviews later in the book broach the subject of the audience reacting through the medium of social media, and certain elements of the mainstream media amplifying this, to try to veto content or get those involved sacked. Similarly, this amplification of a Heckler's Veto can be used by those in Government, especially when criticising public service broadcasting, to shut down public debate.

I. Scope

The media effects of satire, for example as a driver of policy change, are not discussed in any detail. Although political entertainment, especially satire, is important as an indicator of a healthy democracy, there is a minimal discussion on scholarly arguments regarding political satire effects which might influence the electorate or make no mark upon it. Greater consideration is given to what has, and still might, either restrict or influence creators to write or self-censor political entertainment.

The Ofcom Code does not give a definitive definition for either harm or offence and none is given here because of the shifting and subjective nature of both. Ofcom guidance points to health and wealth claims being potentially harmful but neither financial nor medical harms are under discussion in this book.[13] Rather the focus of the book is on the legal and regulatory decisions which affected, both now and in the past, decisions about what content is shared with the population and how this influences writers' and performers' decisions to push boundaries or to potentially self-censor, or those in editorial roles not to broadcast certain material. The emphasis is on how and why people make editorial decisions which restrict information and ideas; to edit out or to retain material, to write something unorthodox or to conform and self-censor. The focus is on traditional broadcast material where there are or have been editorial gatekeepers, where work must be approved before publication or broadcast, such as by an institution, an editor or a producer. Therefore, whilst there is some discussion on the moderating of social

[12] E Barendt, *Freedom of Speech*, 2nd edn (Oxford, Oxford University Press, 2005) 296.
[13] Ofcom Guidance Notes Section 5: Due Impartiality and Due Accuracy and Undue Prominence of Views and Opinions: Issue Six (Ofcom, 22 March 2017).

media platforms, there is no detailed discussion about the opportunities that the internet has created for comedians to produce and broadcast their own content, or the effects that the internet might have on traditional broadcasting.

II. Defining the 'Political' in Political Satire

Often 'political' has been interpreted as simply parliamentary, this is too narrow for the purposes of this book.[14] Politics has been described as 'a concept that we employ as part of the models, or mental frameworks, through which we interpret and try to understand the world around us'.[15] This interpretation is over-broad for the purposes here, given it could capture almost every subject. To set boundaries around the concept of political content, it will be content which engages the special impartiality requirements in the Communications Act 2003, s 320(2).

> '(2) Those matters are—
> (a) matters of political or industrial controversy; and
> (b) matters relating to current public policy.'

Ofcom further defines these 'matters' as 'political or industrial issues on which politicians, industry and/or the media are in debate'.[16] It applies to national and international issues. Therefore, 'political' within this book is not a narrow definition of parliamentary politics, concerned specifically with politicians or public policy, but more generally socio-political programming content which might include discrimination or other material which could be considered as harmful or offensive depending on the context.

In terms of defining satire and political satire, the scholar George Test describes satire as having four basic elements, 'attack or aggression, laughter or humor, play, and judgment'.[17]

Political satire does not need to produce laughter, or be funny, but rather create a feeling of discomfort. It is an effective way to promote critical thinking.[18] Additionally, humour is defined here as speech which the speaker and at least some of the audience find amusing.[19] This concept of humour includes discriminatory jokes which many may rightly find harmful or offensive.

[14] P Keighron, 'The Politics of Ridicule: Satire and Television' in M Wayne (ed), *Dissident Voices the Politics of Television and Cultural change* (London, Pluto Press, 1998) 133.

[15] G Ponton and P Gill, *Introduction to Politics*, 3rd edn (Oxford, Blackwell, 1993) 9.

[16] Ofcom Guidance Notes Section 5: Due Impartiality and Due Accuracy and Undue Prominence of Views and Opinions: Issue Six (Ofcom, 22 March 2017).

[17] GA Test, *Satire: Spirit and Art* (Tampa, University Press of Florida 1991) x.

[18] K McDermott, 'You Gotta Laugh: Teaching Critical Thinking via Comedy' (2019) 19(2) *Pedagogy: Critical Approaches to Teaching Literature, Language, Composition, and Culture* 339 and A Kilby, 'Provoking the Citizen' (2018) 19 *Journalism Studies* 1934.

[19] J Holmes and M Marra, 'Over the Edge? Subversive Humor Between Colleagues and Friends (2002) 15(1) *Humour: International Journal of Humor Research* 65.

III. Outline of Chapters

A. Chapter Two – Satire and the Law

This chapter begins by examining the roots of satire and why it is an important genre to protect. It illustrates how socio-political entertainment in its various forms is believed to stimulate democratic debate and participation in democracy. Satire has been 'important in the development of European liberal democracies as a way of critiquing entrenched elites, abuse of power, and the status quo'.[20] It considers the important role satire has as a watchdog to hold both the government and the media to account.

It then discusses jurisprudence encompassing satire, artistic expression, freedom of expression and the high level of protection the courts afford to political expression. This is illustrated through domestic case law and supranational court case law which deals with political entertainment. These cases include offensive content and partiality and illustrate how humour can be used to mask content which could be discriminatory, harmful or offensive, and the on-going arguments around the legal limitations to freedom of expression. It considers how the courts judge humour, political expression, and discriminatory jokes to draw parallels with how those in broadcast production similarly must consider where the acceptable boundaries of expression lie. It highlights the concerns that the courts have with restricting political speech and artistic expression because of the potential chilling effect of intervention.

B. Chapter Three – Regulating and Repressing Information, Ideas and Entertainment

Here the laws which historically bound political entertainment are examined. The focus is on socio-political entertainment, to understand what stopped writers and performers from weaving political themes or risqué topics into their work. It illustrates how those laws and rules restricting the creation of political entertainment influence beliefs around modern regulations. It follows the legal history of the regulations and laws applied to the written word, theatre, and cinema through to the creation of the Ofcom Code. It proves that no matter how audio-visual media technology adapts to escape censorship it is always followed by regulation and that regulation can have a chilling effect on creative material. It illustrates how there has always been a person, or an institution, making editorial

[20] T Lewis, 'At the Deep End of the Pool: Religious Offence, Debate Speech and the Margin of Appreciation before the European Court of Human Rights' in J Temperman and A Koltay (eds), *Blasphemy and Freedom of Expression: Comparative, Theoretical and Historical Reflections after the Charlie Hebdo Massacre* (Cambridge, Cambridge University Press, 2017) 273.

decisions about access to political knowledge, information and progressive ideas and shows how these decisions are not always based in law. Entertainment was not only censored because of fears of insurrection and incitement but also powerful people who were fearful of ridicule and, by being ridiculed, having their power undermined.

C. Chapter Four – Politicians as Entertainment and Entertainers

The arguments and debates about reporting Parliament and eventually televising Parliament are discussed here, to illustrate how politicians on both sides of the House of Commons were worried about their reputation. Some were keen to ensure that if the cameras entered the House, tight rules of coverage could be drawn up so that the House would keep editorial control. These rules are explained here and how politicians influenced them, and threatened any broadcasters who fell foul of the rules with punitive action.

The process is seen through the debates in Parliament leading up to the broadcast of sound recordings and the televising of proceedings in 1989. The chapter incorporates the changing attitudes towards the media and traces how opinion amongst the Honourable Members has shifted so far that some politicians now appear in reality shows and become television presenters.

D. Chapter Five – The Groundwork for the Interviews

The second half of this book focuses on the effect of regulations on modern-day decision production and practitioner experiences. These sections study the rationales of the practitioners when making editorial choices which allow or restrict broadcast material.

E. Chapters Six and Seven – The Interviews

Chapter six explains the roles of the participants and, alongside the following chapter, delves deeper into how editorial decisions are made and the reasoning behind editing content, or why certain material is never created through the rationales behind self-censorship. These two chapters clarify the two very different sections of the Ofcom Code which are most likely to affect the writing and disemination of political satire on a broadcast medium. Chapter six describes the regulations and the findings which relate to participants' interpretation and understanding of the Ofcom Code on Harm and Offence, whilst chapter seven does the same with regard to the Due Impartiality requirement.

F. Chapter Eight – Conclusion

On the surface, this book explores how, throughout history, powerful people and institutions control both the medium and method of information distribution to the general population. What is novel is the examination of how the legacy of rules and regulations impact on modern day broadcast satire. Broadcast practitioners, writers, performers, and those in editorial control, discuss how their work is affected (or not) by the Code and broadcasters' in-house editorial policy.

Impartiality, or the interpretation of the rules of impartiality, is problematic when applied to political entertainment. The interviews reveal that applying the impartiality rule to political entertainment does not necessarily protect the electorate, the audience, or enhance political debate. Sometimes it can be used to protect the image of the politician, the dignity of the Houses of Parliament, the reputation and/or the income of broadcasters and content producers. There is a tension throughout history between powerful people and the media of the day. There have been many laws and rules laid down which might seem incomprehensible now, many of which were done to protect those in power from ridicule and from scrutiny. Yet, as illustrated, we can sometimes still feel the ripples of their effects centuries later.

2

Satire and the Law

> Freedom of speech and religion are core values that make our country great. They are, indeed, protected in law. What is or is not a joke, or what constitutes satire, is, I believe, in the eye or ear of the beholder and is not, perhaps, for Government to opine on.[1]

I. Introduction

This chapter explains the foundations and purpose of the satirical genre and tradition. It defines and emphasises the importance of satire, illustrating how satire was, and is still, seen as a threat to authority around the world. Then follows a brief explanation of the rules around political entertainment, alongside examples of case law, where the courts recognise the important role that satirical and political entertainment plays in a democratic society.

Looking at the pros and cons of regulating political satire, it focuses on the Broadcasting Code's due impartiality requirement which is particularly difficult to navigate when writing and producing socio-political entertainment for broadcast in the United Kingdom. This will set the scene for the later interviews where media practitioners discuss impartiality and harm and offence standards in relation to their work. These sections raise the issues which come with interpreting humour and bring in similarities and comparisons with social media platform moderation by drawing on decisions made by the Meta Oversight Board.

There is a body of literature which discusses the effects of humour on society by humour studies scholars. In some cases, these overlap with socio-legal approaches to humour and the law, but to date there has been little consideration of the legal and regulatory effects on humour production or the chilling effects of editorial policy or social censure. To understand why these effects are problematic we should first establish why satire is such an important part of political speech.

II. The Roots and Role of Satire

The freedom to express new ideas and challenge those in power through satire has always been an important way to inform, entertain and educate. Some academics

[1] Freedom of Expression (Religious Satire) Amber Rudd, HC Deb 5 December 2016 Vol 618 col 13.

argue that the word satire originates from 'Satyr'. Satyrs were those mythological half-human and half-horse hybrids first appearing in ancient Greek plays to bring some comic relief. They were bawdy, drunken and playful, galloping around with erections, chasing nymphs and generally misbehaving like an early incarnation of the 1970s comic Benny Hill. They were more burlesque than political and one of their roles was to parody the tragedy of the play.

As Satyric interludes progressed these turned into their own full-length plays. Some believe that they held an important political purpose, to challenge the tyranny of Government, but this argument seems etymologically impossible.[2,3] The prevailing belief is that modern British political satire is derived from the Roman tradition, from the Latin *satura*, meaning mixed dish or medley. This was considered a more erudite form of entertainment than the lampoons of those Greek Satyrs.

Political satire has always had to tread carefully around choosing a target. Even in ancient Rome no satirist could attack powerful people without considering the chance of life-changing repercussions. They needed the advantage of an influential patron: the more influential the patron, the greater freedom of expression a writer might have. For example, the satirist, Gaius Lucilius, who wrote his satires in around 133BC, was a wealthy knight. He lived in the Roman republic under the patronage of the powerful Scipio family. Therefore, he was ensured a greater level of protection than the later and more famous satirists Juvenal, Persius and Horace. Lucilius' freedom to write contrasts with the chilling effect that contemporary society had on those later, better known satirists.

> Lucilius fills the negative space around the texts of Horace and Persius and Juvenal. He is what they avoid or fail at. He is what has been edited out. He is the promise, or the threat, of a version of satire that is never realized, a weapon that might be, but never is, brought to bear.[4]

This negative space is important to acknowledge because its existence is reflected in modern satire. Modern satire is edited, or goes unwritten, because of a fear of reprimand from the regulator, or a fear of being cancelled through social censure, or a misapplication of the rules.

It is, of course, difficult to illustrate the impact of those negative spaces, to show an effect because something does not exist. This is where the interviews discussed later in this book come into their own. The interviews can show where there are still negative spaces around today's satirists and what can be done to address the issue so the audience does not lose out.

[2] NB Reynolds, 'Features of Greek Satyr Play as a Guide to Interpretation for Plato's Republic Polis' (2012) 29(2) *The Journal of the Society for Greek Political Thought* 234.

[3] N Rudd, *The Satires of Horace and Persius* (London, Penguin Books, 1976) 2.

[4] B Breed, E Keitel and R Wallace (eds), *Lucilius and Satire in Second Century BC Rome* (Cambridge, Cambridge University Press, 2018) 37.

Like Lucilius, today's comedians and comedy producers who have a more secure work environment or are more famous and/or successful have more power to perform what they want. They can be experimental or daring in their satirical output and express themselves more freely than those lower down the comedy ranks. Like the satirists of the ancient world, many satirists live and have lived under authoritarian regimes and have obvious reasons to self-censor, a principal one being self-preservation.

Comedians who live in authoritarian states are imprisoned, their livelihoods or even their lives endangered because of ridiculing those in power. It has been claimed that the ability to produce cutting political satire is a measure of how well a democracy is functioning.

> It [political satire] is an expression of free speech, of peaceful dissent, and thus a bellwether of the extent of openness in a society. Among the several tests by which we measure the extent of individual freedom, the right to ridicule must be included.[5]

It is well known that the Nazis banned satire in Germany and Czechoslovakia, and by 1933 Hitler criminalised jokes criticising the Reich. Those who used comedy as a form of political protest were imprisoned and some killed, yet this did not have the desired effect of silencing dissent. The practice of trying to silence comedians with the law is still happening around the world.

In 2008 the Burmese regime imprisoned the comedian Zargana, a vociferous opponent to the military Government.[6] Tunisian satirist Wassim Lahrissi was arrested for 'offending the president' in 2015 when he impersonated him. In 2018 Saudi Arabia introduced a law where those who create or share online content 'which mocks, provokes or disrupts public order, religious values and public morals' are subject to a five-year prison sentence and a large fine.[7]

More recently the Sri Lankan comedian and activist Nathasha Edirisooriya was arrested for incitement to hatred following jokes she had made about Buddhism; it made no difference that she was raised as a Buddhist. In China the promoter for the comedian Li Haosh was fined over £1.6 million and suspended from holding any performances in Beijing. Haosh was dropped from their books, and his account was removed from China's Weibo Social Media Platform. This happened because he had told a joke likening the People's Liberation Army to his dogs chasing a squirrel, and by doing so had broken a law banning insults against military personnel.[8]

[5] L Freedman, *The Offensive Art: Political Satire and Its Censorship Around the World from Beerbohm to Borat* (ABC-CLIO, 2008) 165.

[6] P Bramham and S Wagg (eds), *The New Politics of Leisure and Pleasure* (Basingstoke, Palgrave Macmillan, 2010) 187.

[7] 'Saudi Arabia to punish online satire "mocking public order"' (*BBC Online*, 4 September 2018) www.bbc.co.uk/news/world-middle-east-45410676.

[8] J Young, 'China Cracks Down on Stand Up' (*Forhum*, 13 June 2023) www.forhum.org/blog/china-cracks-down-on-stand-up/.

It is not just authoritarian countries which have laws which stifle rebellious humour. In 2018 in Germany, Turkish president Erdoğan brought a charge for insult against the German satirist and comedian Jan Böhmermann under a rarely used provision prohibiting insulting foreign heads of state dating from 1871 (the provision was repealed by Germany after the trial was concluded).[9]

Other European countries still have laws which stop politicians and powerful figures being targeted by political humour.[10] The Italian television channel RAI suspended the satirical programme *Raiot* after Silvio Berlusconi's TV company sued for defamation.[11] Could this mean that Governments believe satire can influence public opinion so much that it is a serious threat to their authority?

Whilst writing this book Donald Trump is in his second term as President of the United States and appears extraordinarily thin skinned when he is the target of humour. An indication that Trump would not take a joke at his own expense was when Stephen Colbert's *The Late Show* was cancelled by CBS swiftly after he had made a joke criticising the network's parent company Paramount for settling a lawsuit with Trump. He called this a bribe, as Paramount needed approval from the Federal Communications Commission (FCC) for a multi-billion-dollar merger with Skydance Media.[12] CBS insisted it was a financial decision, but Trump celebrated the cancelation on his Truth Social platform saying, 'I absolutely love that Colbert got fired'.[13] He said that it would be Jimmy Kimmel too, and that happened after Kimmel made a comment about the murder of the right-wing American activist Charlie Kirk. His network, ABC crumbled in the face of a threat from the Chairman of the FCC who said, 'These companies can find ways to change conduct and take action, frankly, on Kimmel, or there's going to be additional work for the F.C.C. ahead.'[14] Whilst this might not be considered as direct Government action against a satirist, much like with the Chinese comic Li Haosh, if the corporation behind the comedian is threatened then the comedian is more likely to be silenced. This is not the first time that an American President has interfered with satirical programming. During his interview, the joint founder and Co-Executive Chairman of the television production and talent management company Avalon which produces the satirical show *Spitting Image* described how, when *Spitting Image* was on NBC in the 1980s, '[I]t was allegedly cancelled because

[9] *Erdoğan v Böhmermann* 7 U 34/17 (15 May 2018).

[10] For example, see *Eon v France* App no 26118/10 (14 March 2013).

[11] DE Popa and V Tsakona, *Studies in Political Humour: In Between Political Critique and Public Entertainment* (Amsterdam, John Benjamins Publishing Company, 2011).

[12] S Cain, 'The Late Show with Stephen Colbert to end in 2026 as CBS cancels show' *The Guardian* (8 July 2025) www.theguardian.com/tv-and-radio/2025/jul/18/the-late-show-with-stephen-colbert-to-end-in-2026-as-cbs-cancels-show?CMP=share_btn_url.

[13] JQ Nelson, 'Trump celebrates Colbert getting booted by CBS in gleeful Truth Social post' *Fox News* (18 July 2025) www.foxnews.com/media/trump-celebrates-colbert-getting-booted-cbs-gleeful-truth-social-post?msockid=04a5f175b6e667b033dee4bdb7c166ca.

[14] J Koblin, MM Grynbaum and B Barnes, 'ABC Pulls Jimmy Kimmel Off Air for Charlie Kirk Comments After F.C.C. Pressure' *The New York Times* (17 September 2025) www.nytimes.com/2025/09/17/business/media/abc-jimmy-kimmel.html.

Ronald Reagan called the president of NBC because he didn't like his puppet'.[15] The First Amendment does not always protect satirists from Governmental overreach. These types of reaction from powerful people cause an impact on democratic speech.

Whilst there are opposing views on how effective satire might be as a dynamic force for democratic change, it is often acknowledged as playing a valuable part within political debate. Satire influences political knowledge and participation and can significantly strengthen oppositional movements.[16] Political humour is a vital part of a democracy and needs to be protected as fervently as political speech.

In research carried out by The Office of Communications (Ofcom) which regulates British broadcasters, contributors include satirical commentary on current events within the definition of current affairs. They recognise satire's critique of those in power fulfils a democratic purpose.[17] It can be as effective, if not more so, than traditional news media, acting as a fourth estate against both the authority of the media and those in political power.[18] Research indicates it reaches audiences that would not necessarily usually watch traditional news programming, encouraging them to engage with current affairs.[19] Political satire, or 'news satire' is a means to engage people and to 're-invigorate their political interest'.[20] Thus satire is an important form of political discourse.[21]

Media practitioners also appreciate that satire plays a useful communicator of news. During his interview for this book, the Chief Adviser Politics at the BBC described satire as part of the 'smorgasbord of scrutiny' of politicians. International courts recognise the importance of freedom of the press. It is a 'means of discovering and forming an opinion of the ideas and attitudes of political leaders'.[22] The impartiality rule and rules on harm and offence can restrict the ways in which satirists might lay out this 'smorgasbord' in the UK. Ofcom agrees that the right to freedom of expression is of major importance whilst equally acknowledging the Code does restrict broadcast content.

Whilst there are legitimate restrictions on certain types of expression, humour, even humour which some audience members might find offensive, can promote

[15] Interview with Jon Thoday, Avalon.

[16] DL Collinson, 'Leadership, Humor, and Satire' in RA Couto (ed), *Political and Civic Leadership: A Reference Handbook* (Thousand Oaks: SAGE Publications, Inc., 2010) 1075.

[17] Ofcom Report on: The Current Affairs Audit 2005, s 4.10.

[18] G Meikle, '"Find Out Exactly What to Think – Next!": Chris Morris, Brass Eye, and Journalistic Authority' (2012) 10 *Popular Communication* 14.

[19] AB Becker, MA Xenos and DJ Waisanen, 'Sizing Up The Daily Show: Audience Perceptions of Political Comedy Programming' (2010) 18 *Atlantic Journal of Communication* 144, See also V Luckerson, 'How the "John Oliver Effect" Is Having a Real-Life Impact' *Time.com* (10 July 2015) www.time.com/3674807/john-oliver-net-neutrality-civil-forfeiture-miss-america.

[20] I Katsirea, '"Fake news": reconsidering the value of untruthful expression in the face of regulatory uncertainty' (2018) 10(2) *Journal of Media Law* 159.

[21] Collinson (n 16).

[22] *Lingens v Austria* App no 9815/82 (8 July 1986) para 42, whilst not a case about satire, is often cited within ECtHR jurisprudence in cases where politicians have been the target of satire.

tolerance and broadmindedness. It does this by enabling a discussion of subjects normally considered taboo.[23] This capacity is echoed by writers and producers in the interviews. It is well established in free speech theory that having the ability to argue contentious issues in the public sphere can act as a safety valve to relieve social tensions. However, this type of safety valve might be bad for effective democratic engagement if it leads to political apathy.[24] Rather than encouraging the electorate to take an active role in democracy, political satire might simply increase feelings of disdain for politics and politicians.[25] Ridiculing politics and politicians through political entertainment might create cynicism and this can actively disengage the audience from politics.[26] This is an argument which is strengthened when we see the ramifications of an impartiality requirement in broadcast satire, when programme makers believe they need to create politically balanced programming. An audience might be led to believe that each political party is as bad as each other and conclude 'why vote?'.

On the other hand, political entertainment can educate, inform and stir people to engage better with politics and it is for this reason that the reduction of satire currently commissioned in the UK broadcast industry is troubling. Satire has the specific purpose of delivering a critique of media attitudes and/or public policy and political opinion.[27] This ultimately benefits the audience.

III. The Definition and Importance of Satire

The Oxford English Dictionary defines satire as

> A poem or (in later use) a novel, film, or other work of art which uses humour, irony, exaggeration, or ridicule to expose and criticize prevailing immorality or foolishness, esp. as a form of social or political commentary.[28]

It is this definition of satire, a tool with which to critique social or political immorality or foolishness, which best suits political entertainment.

Whilst there is a Parody Exception in law protecting the genre from certain legal actions pertaining to copyright infringements, satire is a stand-alone genre.[29] Parody and satire can be used together and some scholars define satire which employs parody in the form of a traditional broadcast news framework, as 'fake

[23] JP Emerson, 'Negotiating the Serious Import of Humor' (1969) 32 Sociometry 169, cited in J Palmer, *Taking Humour Seriously* (London, Routledge, 1994).
[24] Freedman (n 5).
[25] A Kilby, 'Provoking the Citizen' (2018) 19(13) *Journalism Studies* 1934.
[26] RP Hart and EJ Hartelius, 'Critical Forum The Political Sins of Jon Stewart Critical Studies' (2007) 24(3) *Media Communication* 263.
[27] P Alonso, 'Sacha Baron Cohen and Da Ali G Show: A Critique on Identity in Times of Satiric Infotainment' (2016) 49 *The Journal of Popular Culture* 3.
[28] *Oxford English Dictionary*, 3rd edn (Oxford, Oxford University Press, 2013).
[29] The Copyright, Designs and Patents Act 1988, s 30(a).

news' or 'news parody'.[30] Obviously satirical 'fake news' is very different from 'fake news' which purposely distributes disinformation or misinformation, although there have been times when the two have been confused. In interview, a producer of the satirical panel show *Have I Got News For You*, describes how political satire on British broadcast television and radio is checked for 'pinpoint accuracy' before it is transmitted. Bizarrely this means that broadcast satire can be more accurate than some politicians participating in television and radio interviews.

British programmes which used the format of US late night satirical 'fake news' were *The Day Today*, *Brass Eye*, *The Mash Report* and *Unspun*, none of which have been recommissioned. These take the form of a traditional news programme with an 'anchor' delivering a script to camera. Such programmes might contain vox-pops or 'expert' interviews, and the content often critiques social and political issues.[31] They expose 'the machinery of news but in its more piercing forms also can confront the broader machinery of public discourse'.[32]

These programmes are especially important to provoke critical thinking, to focus an audience on ideas of 'self-deception, pretence and hypocrisy', and can have the dual purpose of both entertaining an audience and exposing the double standards of governments.[33] These programmes provide 'a vital counterbalance to the arrogance of power and the tyranny of unquestioned authority'.[34] Satire does not need (or necessarily aim) to be popular but rather to explore 'important cultural matters of the day'.[35] It can be 'a form of comedy which ridicules its subject […] with a view to encouraging change', created 'to laugh people out of their follies'.[36] By encouraging change, satirists offer an alternative view, challenge the orthodox and question those in power.

Although socio-political satire might lack mass popular appeal it does serve a more important purpose than just being entertaining. Unfortunately, lacking mass appeal makes it unattractive to television and radio commissioners. Drawing a large audience is essential to broadcasters, especially those which rely on advertising revenue. This lack of appeal can be exacerbated by uncomfortable viewing, created by risk-taking which pushes at the boundaries of good taste, or the rules on harm and offence.

The controversial programme *Brass Eye* is an example of this. It often sailed close to the boundaries of offence. Channel 4 argues this type of satire exists to 'expose pretensions and vanities', the dishonesty of the media and 'political

[30] Meikle (n 18).
[31] ibid.
[32] G Baym, and JP Jones, 'News Parody in Global Perspective: Politics, Power, and Resistance' (2012) 10 (1–2) *Popular Communication* 2.
[33] J Morreall, 'Humour and the Conduct of Politics' in S Lockyer and M Pickering (eds), *Beyond a Joke: the limits of humour* (Basingstoke, Palgrave Macmillan, 2005) 72.
[34] Freedman (n 5)166.
[35] S Kumar and K Combe, 'Political parody and satire as subversive speech in the global digital sphere' (2015) 77(3) *The International Communication Gazette* 211.
[36] K Suter, 'The British Satirical Revolution' (2004) *Contemporary Review The Free Library* 161.

hypocrisy'.[37] Pushing at the boundaries of offence to shock and provoke a reaction is often part of a satirist's technique. A common misconception is that satire needs to be funny, it does not. Often, satirists *want* their satire to leave the audience feeling uncomfortable.[38] It is there both to entertain and to challenge an audience, to make them think about their own bigotry or intolerance.[39] This was the reasoning behind the racial content in one of the early British situation comedies, *Till Death Us Do Part*. The main character was bigoted and used discriminatory language, his beliefs around race and sexuality were supposed to repel the audience, to make them realise how dated these views were. Although the programme is an example of how satire can be problematic, when it does not always hit its mark, it can instead bolster prejudice. Some of the audience did not see the satire and took the programme at face value, making the character into their hero. We will return to this idea later.

IV. Regulating Political Expression

State regulation of broadcasting can be considered an interference with the right of an artist. As stated by the European Court of Human Rights (ECtHR), it should be examined with particular care.[40] This is especially true if its aim is to bring about positive societal change by raising issues in the public interest. As an example, satire can be used as a form of activism; there are American political entertainment shows which have directly encouraged audiences to engage in political issues. The *Daily Show* and *The Late Show with Stephen Colbert* have had a direct political effect. There is also the 'John Oliver effect', so named after the British political entertainer John Oliver who fronts his own show in the US, *Last Week Tonight with John Oliver*. John Oliver's report on net neutrality crashed the FCC's website after he urged viewers to submit comments to support the protection of an open internet. The reason that this is possible is that unlike in the UK, American television shows do not require impartiality, due or otherwise. Whilst the FCC had imposed the Fairness Doctrine on broadcast licensees in 1949, which worked in a similar way to Ofcom's Due Impartiality requirement, it was ended in 1987 as it was decided it violated the First Amendment.[41] This may be one of the reasons that

[37] BSC Finding, '*Brass Eye Special*, Channel 4 and S4C, 26 and 27 July 2001, 2235–2310 and 0010–0045' www.webarchive.nationalarchives.gov.uk/ukgwa/20090905130645/http:/www.ofcom.org.uk/static/archive/bsc/pdfs/bulletin/brasseyespecialfinding.htm.

[38] This feeling of discomfort was thought to be more important than 'preaching to the converted' by some participants in the interviews.

[39] See for example Sacha Baron Cohen's keynote speech to the Anti-Defamation League, youtu.be/ymaWq5yZIYM.

[40] *Eon v France* App no 26118/10 (14 March 2013) para 60.

[41] C Caldera, 'Fact check: Fairness Doctrine only applied to broadcast licenses, not cable TV like Fox News' *USA Today* (28 November 2020) eu.usatoday.com/story/news/factcheck/2020/11/28/fact-check-fairness-doctrine-applied-broadcast-licenses-not-cable/6439197002/.

during interview, the BBC's Chief Adviser Politics considered that satire is more successful as part of the political landscape in the US.

UK broadcasters must comply with the impartiality rules stipulated in Section Five of the Ofcom Code. Over 20 years ago Tambini and Cowling discussed how the UK's broadcast media's due impartiality regulations might be applied in a digital future. It was considered that the regulatory framework might not be effective in a multi-channel environment.[42] Concerns were raised about impartial news being threatened by the commercialisation and fragmentation of the broadcast news market, and the changing face of politics. However, the rules on impartiality remain the same now as existed then.

The polarisation caused through newscasting in the US illustrates that it is important to regulate factual output for accuracy, and present broadcast news with impartiality. This ensures the audience can access information about politics, scientific matters and social issues without bias. They can then make informed decisions and participate in democracy without being influenced by the government or media owners. Impartiality might prevent the belief that there is only one correct point of view on important matters.[43] Cushion and Lewis describe unbiased news as 'a critical issue in maintaining a healthy and democratic public sphere.'[44] Research indicates that the current framework of interventionist regulation improves balance and accuracy, and that tougher regulation enhances media content for news.[45] There is a belief that where a wide range of views are reflected in the media, citizens feel included in the democratic process.[46] However, neutral reporting can sometimes hinder the audience's understanding of complex matters. For example, the lack of analysis and interpretation of issues during the British Referendum on the European Union in 2016 gave an undeserved comparable weight to the evidence on both sides of the campaign, especially when opinion and conjecture was presented as fact.[47] An important part of political discussion should be contextualising information and opinions, but in this case, as Seaton pointed out, 'the definition of balance was stretched to damaging limits: it corrupted rather than informed public understanding'.[48]

Satire, when impartiality is interpreted by production teams as balance, may confuse or mislead the audience when opinion and fact are given the same weight.

[42] D Tambini, 'Introduction and Summary: broadcast news under threat' in D Tambini and J Cowling (eds), *New News?:Impartial Broadcasting in the Digital Age* (London, IPPR, 2002) 1.

[43] T Gibbons, *Regulating the Media*, 2nd edn (London, Sweet & Maxwell, 1998) 96.

[44] S Cushion and J Lewis, 'Impartiality, statistical tit-for-tats and the construction of balance: UK television news reporting of the 2016 EU referendum campaign' (2017) 32(3) *European Journal of Communication* 208.

[45] S Cushion, J Lewis, M Wren and GN Ramsay, 'The impact of interventionist regulation in reshaping news agendas: A comparative analysis of public and commercially funded television journalism' (2012) 13(7) *Journalism* 831.

[46] J Rowbottom, 'Extreme Speech and the Democratic Functions of the Mass Media' in I Hare and J Weinstein (eds), *Extreme Speech and Democracy* (Oxford, Oxford University Press, 2009) 614.

[47] Cushion and Lewis (n 44).

[48] J Seaton, 'Brexit and the Media' (2016) 87(3) *The Political Quarterly* 335.

At times there may only be one correct position amongst the range of voices used to create a balance of views. There is an argument that the 'due' in the impartiality requirement enables politicians to control broadcast media so that broadcasters cannot criticise political systems.[49] For broadcasters it puts

> substantive constraints on the content of their programming and, regulating for openness and diversity of viewpoint cannot be achieved when the state's interest dominates the context of debate. Broadcasting, therefore, is neither as independent nor as fair as might be inferred from the standard of impartiality.[50]

And this is particularly true when it comes to broadcast satire, an impartiality requirement in satirical programming may disengage the viewer from political debate. Allaina Kilby addressed the difficulties which satire in the UK faced because of the due impartiality rule during election times.[51] This issue of due impartiality and its impact on satire has been addressed by the BBC's Chief Adviser Politics, Ric Bailey who argues:

> constraints felt by British satirists are not imagined but rooted in the sub-conscious cultural media atmosphere; however, they often stem from a misunderstanding of impartiality and actual regulatory practice and should not prevent satire – during these disruptive periods in US and UK politics – from playing its rightful role as one of the essential components in holding the powerful to account.[52]

As the interviews with political entertainment writers and producers in the later chapters of this book illustrate, Ric Bailey is correct, not everyone who works in the production industry always understands the rules and regulations which bind the broadcast media. This means that sometimes there is an over-reach, and producers and writers force unnecessary restrictions upon themselves. This is problematic as editorial choices impact on audience knowledge and that in turn impacts on political engagement and understanding. If those in editorial positions are over-reaching in their decision making which then affects audience's awareness of political matters, this needs to be recognised and addressed.

Whilst for the speaker the rationales for freedom of expression include self-fulfilment, development and individual autonomy, the rights of the audience should not be overlooked. Enshrined in Article 10 of the ECHR, the audience has the right to hear and receive information and ideas. These ideas help in the discovery of truth and participation in public debate, leading to informed democratic engagement. Recently there have been very few Ofcom breaches which involve satirical programming, indeed there are now very few satirical programmes being

[49] Gibbons (n 43) 109–10.

[50] ibid.

[51] A Kilby, 'The Problem with Satirising the Election' (2019) UK Election Analysis, www.electionanalysis.uk/uk-election-analysis-2019/section-8-personality-politics-and-popular-culture/the-problem-with-satirising-the-election/.

[52] R Bailey, 'When journalism and satire merge: The implications for impartiality, engagement and 'post-truth' politics – A UK perspective on the serious side of US TV comedy' (2018) 33(2) *European Journal of Communication* 200.

commissioned and broadcast. This may underline the argument of many of the interviewees in this book, that people in the industry are playing it safe by not commissioning satirical programmes.

Currently British broadcasters enjoy the right to freedom of expression under the Human Rights Act 1998, but British broadcast satirists are subject to more insidious, invisible forms of censorship. These include self-censorship or censorship by omission because writers are concerned about the consequences of their jokes if there is an audience backlash. There are concerns of access by broadcasters, writers second guess policy or regulatory limits and these all affect what is written and what is edited out.[53]

Finally, there are the 'culture wars' fuelled by political players, and 'cancel culture' which exposes writers and performers to the whims of social media users' opinions and creates those negative spaces.

Cancel culture has been defined as

> a performative phenomenon characterized by collective action directed at individuals in ways that result in them being punished through shaming, silencing, boycotting, or banning their work, and sometimes through loss of employment and career opportunities.[54]

Comedians referred to this as the court of public opinion during interviews. No legal boundaries have been reached for what can and cannot be said, but rather social limits. This is rather where society or the audience sets the threshold to comedy.

Regulators prior to Ofcom referred to 'taste and decency', and whilst this has been replaced in the regulatory codes by Harm and Offence, the echoes of taste and decency still ring in the ears of many people who worked in broadcasting. If a person broke these limits and created an audience backlash to the extent that they were cancelled, this affects those around them. Writers, performers and producers are much more likely to pay attention to headlines or a company or a person being publicly shamed through social media platforms than they are to be encouraged by the national courts or the European Court of Human Rights giving political satire a high level of protection.

There should be a balance between saying the unsayable and raising awareness using comedy. Comedians need to be able to dive into unchartered territory, to be bold and brave and tackle taboo subjects. Sometimes using humour is the best way to do this and society needs to face up to, and to discuss, uncomfortable subjects.[55]

[53] There were concerns about targeting politicians and the Royal Family because broadcasters need access to them for other programming (as per email from Richard Wilson Executive Producer of *Have I Got News for You* (3 July 2019).

[54] G Watt, 'Making Mistakes: Trial by Twitter and Cancel Culture' in *The Making Sense of Politics, Media, and Law: Rhetorical Performance as Invention, Creation, Production* (Cambridge, Cambridge University Press, 2023) 252–83.

[55] ibid.

V. A Challenge Too Far?

It is in this territory of challenging the audience where broadcast satire can potentially fall foul of the legal limits around harmful and offensive language and breach the Ofcom Broadcasting Code. A writer might wish to use extremely offensive and discriminatory language to shock an audience and, by doing so, provoke a counterargument around a discriminatory and shocking subject. However, some of the dialogue or narrative might be considered too provocative by a producer. This then leads to creative content being cut from broadcast, not only because of broadcasting rules but also because those in editorial positions worry that it might be taken at face value by the audience and judged as being harmful and deliberately upsetting. This may be the case even when the purpose of the work is to expose racism, misogyny, political hypocrisy or promote the positives of a pluralist society.

Using shock or provocation as a tactic to promote critical thinking can be problematic generally and because of this it needs a strong contextual argument to defend its inclusion in a television or radio programme. As the practitioners explained in the interviews, some broadcasters might be unwilling to defend contentious content for fear of alienating their audience, some in editorial control may not feel that controversial content is worth the time and effort it takes to get clearance from line managers.[56] Where the intention or contextual factors surrounding a piece of satire are not clear then this material can be more problematic to transmit. Although, if it must be explained to an audience why a joke is not discriminatory but rather targets discrimination, then the target has likely been missed. Ultimately it is easier to cut it out. Those involved in the production of contentious satire, writers and comedians, constantly need to consider how to justify their content. They must judge where they should draw the line and potentially (self) censor their output because of a fear of offending their audience or breaching regulations. It should be remembered that Ofcom is acting as a state authority in its role of regulating the broadcast media and so must judge content under the standards of Article 10 of the European Convention on Human Rights, the right to freedom of expression.

The courts often emphasise the damaging chilling effect when state authorities seek to repress satirical expression. The European Courts have ruled that some humorous expression, especially political satire, should be afforded a high level of protection under Article 10.[57] The domestic protection of such expression is similar, the Ofcom Code is

> drafted in the light of the Human Rights Act 1998 and the European Convention on Human Rights … the right to freedom of expression, as expressed in Article 10 of the Convention, encompasses the audience's right to receive creative material, information

[56] The processes are explained in further detail in ch 6, in s III 'Chain of Worry'.

[57] See eg *Kuliś* and *Różycki v Poland* App no 27209/03 (6 October 2009) and *Alves da Silva v Portugal* App no 41665/07 (20 October 2009).

> and ideas without interference but subject to restrictions prescribed by law and necessary in a democratic society.[58]

The audience needs the media to publish information and news in order to be informed and know if Government and/or private enterprises are acting in a lawful and democratic manner.[59] Therefore, Ofcom too should afford satirical expression, which deals with public interest debate, a high level of protection.

This chapter now turns to both the courts and Ofcom to explain how they approach the subjective and difficult issue of balancing freedom of expression with restricting contentious humorous speech including speech which some would consider harmful and offensive.

VI. Laughing All the Way to Court

A. Humour, Hate Speech and Free Speech

Freedom of expression is a qualified right; this means it can be restricted on certain grounds for certain reasons. This is applicable under international law, supranational law and on a national level. On an international level the United Kingdom is subject to Article 19(2) of the International Covenant on Civil and Political Rights (the Covenant) and restricted by Article 19(3)(a) and (b) and Article 20(1) and (2). For the restrictions in Article 19 to be legitimate, they must be provided by law, pursue a legitimate aim for the rights or reputations of others, or the protection of national security, public order, or public health and morals and be necessary. Article 20 of the Covenant prohibits propaganda for war and any advocacy of national, racial or religious hatred which incites discrimination, hostility or violence. These restrictions are incorporated into Article 10 of the European Convention on Human Rights, with the test of necessity being interpreted as responding to a pressing social need, necessary in a democracy, and proportionate to the aim pursued. This is commonly referred to as the three-part test.

On a national level this test has been incorporated into the Human Rights Act 1998 by virtue of the United Kingdom being subject to the European Convention on Human Rights. This is an important factor when considering the freedom of expression of broadcasters. Whilst broadcasters have a right to freedom of expression, the power to regulate them is bestowed on Ofcom, by the British Parliament. This gives Ofcom the power to impose sanctions on channels which do not comply with the Code.

[58] The Ofcom Broadcasting Code (with the Cross-promotion Code and the On Demand Programme Service Rules) December 2020 (last updated 12 June 2023) www.ofcom.org.uk/tv-radio-and-on-demand/broadcast-standards/legislative-background.

[59] T Baumbach, 'Chilling Effect as a European Court of Human Rights' Concept in Media Law Cases' (2018) 6(1) *Bergen Journal of Criminal Law and Criminal Justice* 92.

Article 10 states that the right to freedom of expression includes the freedom for audiences to receive and broadcasters to impart information and ideas without interference by public authorities. Ofcom is considered a public authority in this context and therefore must balance the requirements of the audience's and the broadcaster's right to freedom of expression as set out in Article 10 of the European Convention on Human Rights. The BBC also 'may be treated as a public authority when engaged in at least some of its activities'.[60] Therefore, the due impartiality and harm and offence regulations as specified by the Code, and which this book will go on to discuss in some depth, restrict broadcaster output but can be legitimate in law under The Communications Act 2003.

In the courts there is a hierarchy of protection regarding different types of speech. Political speech and matters in the public interest are supposed to be given the highest level of protection followed by artistic expression.[61] As political satire is both artistic expression and a genre of political speech it follows that it should be provided with the highest protection in law. Satire's value to public debate has been acknowledged internationally, and so it should be protected from illegitimate interference from a public authority in all its forms – including broadcasting.

The ECtHR's judgments on satirical expression repeatedly state:

> satire is a form of artistic expression and social commentary which, by its inherent features of exaggeration and distortion of reality, naturally aims to provoke and agitate. Accordingly, any interference with the right of an artist – or anyone else – to use this means of expression should be examined with particular care.[62]

The Court considers that the right to openly discuss controversial issues and sensitive subjects is important to society and distinguishes a democratic society from a dictatorship.[63] According to the court, such issues do not have to be expressed in a congenial manner. An often-quoted ECtHR judgment regarding this is from *Handyside v United Kingdom*.

> Freedom of expression constitutes one of the essential foundations of such a society, one of the basic conditions for its progress and for the development of every man. […] [I]t is applicable not only to 'information' or 'ideas' that are favourably received or regarded as inoffensive or as a matter of indifference, but also to those that offend, shock or disturb the State or any sector of the population. Such are the demands of that pluralism, tolerance and broadmindedness without which there is no 'democratic society'.[64]

Although it has limits, and expression around controversial or sensitive subjects should not be a 'direct or indirect call for violence or as a justification of violence,

[60] H Fenwick and G Phillipson, *Media Freedom under the Human Rights Act* (Oxford, Oxford University Press, 2006) 124.

[61] J Rowbottom, 'To Rant, Vent and Converse: Protecting Low Level Digital Speech' (2012) 71(2) *Cambridge Law Journal* 355.

[62] *Vereinigung Bildender Künstler v Austria* App no 8354/01 (25 January 2007) para 33.

[63] Baumbach (n 59).

[64] *Handyside v The United Kingdom* App no 5493/72 (7 December 1976) para 39.

hatred or intolerance'.[65] The right to freedom of expression is a qualified right, and as per Article 10(2) carries with it 'duties and responsibilities'. This creates tensions between conflicting rights but several cases concerning satire have come before the ECtHR, highlighting how offensive satirical expression is given greater freedom where the subject addresses legitimate public interests and contributes to a debate of general concern.[66]

Limiting hateful expression is important when promoting social cohesion but problematic when it clashes with the right to freedom of expression. Political groups, like those who support the far-right, are blaming limits on freedom of expression as part of dog whistle tactics to convince others that only political speech on the right is being repressed. In a democratic society it is agreed that freedom of expression is vital to expose the audience to 'a number of ideas, which … allows citizens to form their opinions (and cast their votes) on an informed basis'.[67] However, because unfettered freedom of expression is problematic there are several laws which curb hate speech within Europe,[68] but the legal definition of hate speech itself has proved elusive. The Council of Europe states that there is 'no particular definition of hate speech in international human rights; it is a term used to describe broad discourse which is extremely negative and constitutes a threat to social peace'. It includes but is not limited to; expression that spreads, incites, promotes or justifies racial hatred, xenophobia, antisemitism or forms of hatred based on intolerance.[69] It was not until the non-binding Council of Europe's Committee of Ministers Recommendation 97 (20) on Hate Speech that hate speech was defined as

> [A]ll forms of expression which spread, incite, promote or justify racial hatred, xenophobia, anti-Semitism or other forms of hatred based on intolerance, including intolerant expression by aggressive nationalism and ethnocentrism, discrimination and hostility against minorities, migrants and people of immigrant origin.[70, 71]

Manifestation of hatred through discriminatory speech should be regulated in a civilised society to ensure the equality and dignity of citizens irrespective of their race, sex, gender, sexuality, or religion. The need to restrict hate speech through legal means is for the good of social cohesion but must be balanced with the right

[65] *Perincek v Switzerland* App no 27510/08 (15 October 2015) from para 206.

[66] *Ziembińsk v Poland (no. 2)* App no 1799/07 (5 July 2016), *Eon v France* App no 26118/10 (14 March 2013) and *Alves da Silva v Portugal* App no 41665/07 (20 October 2009).

[67] J Mchangama and N Alkiviadou, 'Hate Speech and the European Court of Human Rights: Whatever Happened to the Right to Offend, Shock or Disturb?' (2021) 21 *Human Rights Law Review* 1008.

[68] The United States of America differs as hate speech is legally protected under the First Amendment, and the authorities may not discriminate against speakers because of their views.

[69] Council Of Europe online information page on hate speech, www.coe.int/en/web/freedom-expression/hate-speech.

[70] N Alkiviadou, 'Regulating Hatred: Of devils and demons?' (2018) 18(4) *International Journal of Discrimination and the Law* 218.

[71] Recommendation No R (97) 20 of the Committee of Ministers to member states on 'hate speech' (adopted 30 October 1997).

to freedom of expression. Therefore, when it comes to contentious humour, the Court needs to pick apart what is humour and if there is an implicit message or intent to cause societal or individual harm. The ECtHR acknowledged that hate speech is often 'disguised as a humorous appearance which, precisely for that reason, may prove to be as dangerous as direct speech'.[72]

There should be a distinction between deserving satirical targets, such as those who have power and authority, and attacking minorities and those with protected characteristics to entertain an audience, these types of 'jokes' are discriminatory. As the ECtHR noted, comedy can be used as a cover for direct attacks on vulnerable communities, or for hate speech, and it is here that judges need to be nuanced in their approach when applicants are claiming freedom of expression rights for discriminatory humour.[73]

B. The Strasbourg Court and Political Punchlines

Satire is 'essential for an engaged, sustainable, democratic public culture' and, as undemocratic state crackdowns show, it is a means of resistance, a way of confronting and deconstructing authoritarian discourse.[74] Democratic states should only restrict political speech as a last resort and the ECtHR has emphasised that any decision to do so should be made with particular care.

The following section will discuss court cases, Ofcom investigations, and Meta Oversight Board (MOB) decisions in which the use of humour or satire was given as a reason for protecting contentious expression. Examples are drawn from domestic case law and case law from the European Court of Human Rights. The examples will primarily focus on political entertainment or content which was considered harmful and/or teetering on the limits of offensive content. Just as broadcasting professionals assess the potential issues arising from contentious comedy or potentially harmful or offensive content when deciding what to broadcast, courts also determine what freedom of expression is worthy of protection.

As established, satire is a genre which has long been used to scrutinise and ridicule the powerful. The following case examples range across verbal and non-verbal expression, encompassing cartoons, caricatures and memes. The Court recognises that these forms of expression can play an important role in the discussion of matters of public concern and are an indispensable feature of a democratic society.

The following cases which went before the European Court of Human Rights reflect thematic issues raised in the empirical interviews which, in broadcasting terms, were deemed as problematic, or even taboo. The cases are grouped together under the themes of political satire, religious offence, and hate speech as humour.

[72] *Z.B. v France* App no 46883/15 (2 September 2021).

[73] See eg *M'Bala M'Bala v France* App no 25239/13 (20 October 2015).

[74] G Baym and JP Jones, 'News Parody in Global Perspective: Politics, Power, and Resistance' (2012) 10 (1–2) *Popular Communication* 2.

This presents the opportunity to compare the way in which the Court protects humorous expression to the way that broadcasters might defend writers' and/or performers' contentious creative works. Where there is some overlap the case has been grouped with the most appropriate theme.

Starting with political satire, the first case is *Eon v France*.[75] The applicant was arrested and charged after he had held a placard up to President Sarkozy reading, 'Casse toi pov'con' (trans 'Get lost, you sad prick'). His phrase was echoing the words that the President had said to a farmer who had refused to shake the President's hand at a public event. The president's comment had received wide media coverage. Eon was prosecuted by the national court for insulting the president under French law, this was punishable under section 26 of the Act of 29 July 1881. His appeal was rejected, and he was denied legal aid. He took his case to the ECtHR arguing that the state had interfered with his right to access to a fair trial and his right to freedom of expression. The Court decided that the phrase on his placard was satirical in nature and that the imposition of a criminal penalty was disproportionate and unnecessary in a democratic society. The Court believed it could have a chilling effect on freedom of expression and be detrimental to public debate if the national ruling was to stand. The ECtHR found the interference had breached Eon's Article 10 right.

Another case involving a satirical attack on a politician is that of *Alves da Silva v Portugal*.[76] Mr Alves da Silva was convicted on a charge of defamation after he drove around a puppet representation of Mortágua's mayor during a carnival whilst playing a disparaging satirical message about the mayor's political conduct. The applicant argued, given the defamatory expressions were used during carnival festivities, the context was clearly satirical.[77] This setting of a carnival context gave added protection to the applicant's defamatory statements. He argued that his words should be taken as satirical, rather than as a bone fide accusation, and the European Court agreed. The judgment reiterates the high protection the ECtHR gives to the importance of freedom of expression, even offensive expression which targets politicians, seeing it as essential to a functioning democracy.[78]

The ECtHR's case law repeatedly states that people in the public eye and political players must tolerate a greater degree of criticism, and this includes being the targets of insulting content in the form of satire.[79] Broadcasters and producers should bear this in mind when commissioning and complying programming.

The Court has expected even minor political figures to show a higher degree of tolerance when targeted by insulting and offensive satirical content. In the case of *Patrício Monteiro Telo de Abreu*, a female *assistente* who worked with the

[75] *Eon v France* App no 26118/10 (14 March 2013).
[76] *Alves da Silva v Portugal* App no 41665/07 (20 October 2009).
[77] ibid para 20.
[78] *Lingens v Austria* App no 9815/82 (8 July 1986) para 42.
[79] *Patrício Monteiro Telo de Abreu v Portugal* App no 42713/15 (7 June 2022), *Vereinigung Bildender Künstler v Austria* App no 68354/01 (25 January 2007), *Lingens v Austria* App no 9815/82 (8 July 1986).

mayor of Elvas was depicted in a series of caricatures as a blond-haired sow wearing lace stockings, a garter belt and high heels. Whilst there were other male political characters depicted as animals, none of them had been sexualised.

Judge Motoc in her concurring opinion took the opportunity to address the issue of semiotic violence against women in politics. Whilst she agreed with the finding of a violation of Article 10, she noted that there were 'regrettable stereotypes against women of power'.[80] She described how these acts were aimed at the purpose of excluding women from the political sphere. It is therefore odd that this was unanimously held as a violation of the applicant's Article 10 right when, as indicated in the concurring opinion, women are often not treated equally in the political sphere. Given the preamble in the Charter of Fundamental Rights of the European Union regarding equality there could have been more emphasis on the sexualisation of the only female political character depicted in a way in which woman as serious political participants are denigrated.[81] The judgments also reflect the importance of evaluating expression in context, something which courts, MOB members and the participants in the research often stress as being integral to deciding if offensive satirical content can be justified.

Strasbourg judgments are not always unanimous on where the line of acceptability can be drawn regarding humorous expression, or indeed necessarily agree on what satire is. This is especially true when the target or the message of the satire is not clear. This is illustrated in *Vereinigung Bildender Künstler v Austria*.[82] The case features high profile political and religious figures. It centres on the collage *Apocalypse* by Otto Mühl, which depicts various people, including the former head of the Austrian Freedom Party (FPÖ) Mr Jörg Haider, and Mr Meishchberger, a former general secretary of the FPÖ. They are painted in sexual positions with other public figures. These incorporate depictions of Mother Teresa and an Austrian cardinal as well as others. Mr Meischberger was depicted gripping the ejaculating penis of Mr Haider.

Mr Meischberger brought proceedings under section 78 of the Copyright Act seeking an injunction prohibiting the collage's further display and publication. He also requested financial compensation. This was granted on appeal with the Supreme Court, rejecting an appeal from the applicant association of artists Vereinigung Bildender Künstler (VBK). VBK brought the case to the ECtHR. The majority of the Strasbourg judges found that whilst the interference was prescribed by law and pursued the legitimate aim of the protection of the rights of others, the state interference was disproportionate to the aim pursued and therefore not necessary in a democratic society. The Court found a breach of Article 10 of the Convention. The Court echoed *Handyside* regarding content which might 'offend, shock or disturb the State or any sector of the population'.[83] The dissenting

[80] *Patrício Monteiro Telo de Abreu v Portugal* App no 42713/15 (7 June 2022) para 43.
[81] Charter of Fundamental Rights of the European Union [2012] OJ C 326/02.
[82] *Vereinigung Bildender Künstler v Austria* App no 68354/01 (25 January 2007).
[83] *Handyside* (n 64).

Judge Loucaides questioned if an offensive collage could be described as artistic and satirical. He found the collage 'a senseless, disgusting combination of lewd images whose only effect is to debase, insult and ridicule each and every person portrayed' with no 'criticism or satire'. He argued that, in the same way insults are not protected by Article 10, nor should 'insulting pictures that undermine the reputation or dignity of others' and reiterated that artists were not immune from the limitations provided in Article 10(2) as had been observed in the judgment.[84] This illustrates how judging humorous expression is not a straightforward process and contrasts with the unanimous judgment in *Telo de Abreu*.

Staying with religious figures, the next example is a further contrast and is considered by many as an example of where the ECtHR was overzealous in its application of the margin of appreciation doctrine.[85] The case of *Otto-Preminger-Institut v Austria*[86] concerns the film *Das Liebeskonzil*, a satirical portrayal of heaven. In the film key religious characters including God, Jesus and Mary, are depicted as wanton or idiotic. It was a live performance filmed in Rome for international distribution. The film was seized by the national court and destroyed on the grounds that it criticised religious doctrines. The ECtHR came up with the bizarre decision that:

> [T]he Austrian authorities acted to ensure religious peace in that region and to prevent that some people should feel the object of attacks on their religious beliefs in an unwarranted and offensive manner. It is in the first place for the national authorities, who are better placed than the international judge, to assess the need for such a measure in the light of the situation obtaining locally at a given time.[87]

Here the margin of appreciation was very much in the minds of the judges. The Court's argument that there was a 'pressing social need for the preservation of religious peace' and to protect public order seems rather extreme given the applicant had ensured that the audience would not be surprised by the film content. The film had an age restriction and information about the film had been widely circulated to warn potential customers about the contentious nature of the film. The judgment certainly did not consider the protections stated in *Handyside* should be afforded to this film regarding offending, shocking or disturbing the State or sectors of the population. The Court has since evolved from this attitude towards satire as can be seen in later judgments.[88]

Often with Article 10, claims are balanced against other Convention rights, this is especially so with offensive or disparaging remarks. The famous gay Portuguese

[84] *Vereinigung Bildender Künstler* (n 62) (Dissenting).

[85] The margin of appreciation doctrine in the European Court of Human Rights means that the Court must consider, amongst other things, the cultural and socio-political individuality of each member state as part of the three-part test.

[86] *Otto-Preminger-Institut v Austria* App no 13470/87 (20 September 1994).

[87] ibid para 56.

[88] See eg *Sekmadienis v Lithuania* App no 69317/14 (30 January 2018) and *Gachechiladze v Georgia* App no 2591/19 (22 July 2021).

television presenter Sousa Goucha brought a case to the ECtHR[89] stating that his Article 8 and 14 rights had been violated because the state had not protected his right to reputation and he had suffered discrimination because of his sexuality. A broadcaster had transmitted a joke on a late-night comedy show in which he was named as 'the best female Portuguese TV host'. The national court referred to his 'colourful [feminine] clothes', a stereotype which the Government described as being arguably unfortunate but not a violation of the Convention. The issue that the ECtHR decided on was the conflict between Mr Goucha's Article 8 right and the broadcaster's Article 10 right to freedom of expression. The Court decided that the broadcaster's right to freedom of expression outweighed Mr Goucha's right to reputation. The cases of *Patrício Monteiro Telo de Abreu* discussed above, and *Sousa Goucha v Portugal* illustrate how individuals who are the target of (arguably) humorous attacks using stereotypes are not always as well protected by the Court.

Stereotyping is problematic but is often relied on in comedy. There can be a fine line between stereotyping to find a common ground in recognising certain character types and using humour to try to disguise discrimination. 'It was just a joke' is a well-worn argument but sometimes it is not just a joke. Humour can be used to disguise harmful speech and unite people around extreme and racist ideologies.[90] The far-right have harnessed humour to spread racist viewpoints using the tools of satire and irony in the hope of radicalising and recruiting people to their cause.[91] Courts, regulators and online moderators are aware of the issues of stereotyping through humour and how this can lead to the normalisation of discriminatory language. This can be seen in our final ECtHR cases discussed here, *Bonnet v France*[92] and *Le Pen v France*.[93]

Bonnet was president of the far-right group Égalité et Réconciliation. He produced an online magazine which used antisemitic troupes to parody the front page of the French satirical magazine *Charlie Hebdo*. Following this, he was convicted of public insult of a racial nature and Holocaust denial by the national authorities, he brought his case to the ECtHR. As is usual for Holocaust denial, the ECtHR found his application inadmissible, applying Article 17 (the prohibition of abuse of rights).[94] The *Le Pen* case is similar, and in *Le Pen*, the Court specifically acknowledged that Le Pen applied the tools of humour when addressing his audience to blur the lines of interpretation. When talking about the habits of the Roma

[89] *Sousa Goucha v Portugal* App no 70434/12 (22 March 2016).

[90] R Pérez, 'Racism without Hatred? Racist Humor and the Myth of "Colorblindness"' (2017) 60(5) *Sociological Perspective* 956.

[91] VS Greene, '"Deplorable" Satire: Alt-Right Memes, White Genocide Tweets, and Redpilling Normies' (2019) 5(1) *Studies in American Humor* 31.

[92] *Bonnet v France* App no 35364/19 (25 January 2022).

[93] *Le Pen v France* App no 45416/16 (28 February 2017) para 6.

[94] A Godioli and J Young 'Special Collection of the Case Law on Freedom of Expression', (Columbia Global Freedom of Expression, 2023) 18, www.globalfreedomofexpression.columbia.edu/wp-content/uploads/2023/06/GFoE_HUMOR.pdf.

community he used the dual meaning of the French verb 'to fly' which can also mean 'to steal', in order to stigmatise them.[95] As with *Bonnet* the French domestic court convicted Le Pen of public insult of a racial nature and the ECtHR declared the case inadmissible, but this time on the grounds that the interference was necessary in a democratic society.

In dealing with such cases, just as production teams do with contentious scripts and programme material, the Court considers the context and meaning behind the words to decide if it is merely offensive or if it is harmful, and this becomes more difficult when the expression is labelled as humour.[96] It might be easier to dismiss hateful words as 'just a joke', or for speakers to accuse their audience of having 'no sense of humour' when they find 'jokes' offensive.[97]

C. Ofcom

Just as Article 10 of the European Convention on Human Rights does not protect hate speech, neither do the domestic English and Welsh courts nor the Ofcom Code. Judges, regulators and those in editorial roles need to differentiate between different types of speech acts when dealing with broadcast satire and to draw the contested 'line' of acceptability.

Ofcom is a state authority, and the Code is underpinned by the Communications Act of 2003, so should Ofcom consider it necessary to interfere with the freedom of expression right of the broadcaster it must take a measured approach. It must pass the three-part test under Article 10 ECHR. When an individual or a broadcaster considers that Ofcom breached its right to freedom of expression, it can go to the national court, and if the broadcaster fails there, it can then go to the supranational court to appeal against the interference.[98]

Writers, producers and broadcasters working on contentious programming need to ensure that their output will not breach the regulations or the law, and some broadcasters have additional editorial policies as another layer of concern. Editorial teams need to apply the same type of deliberations as judges around the contextual aspects and legal or regulatory limits of their programmes, with the added complication of trying to anticipate how the content might be (mis)interpreted by the audience. This is because they are dealing with contentious programming before it is broadcast, rather than the courts and regulators who judge content after it has been disseminated. They cannot see an audience reaction to the material, they can only imagine and anticipate one.

[95] *Bonnet v France* App no 35364/19 (25 January 2022) and *Le Pen v France* App no 45416/16 (28 February 2017) para 6.

[96] A Godioli, J Young and BM Fiori, 'Laughing Matters: Humor, Free Speech and Hate Speech at the European Court of Human Rights' (2022) 35 *International Journal Semiotics of Law* 2241.

[97] See eg *Egill Einarsson v Iceland (No.2)* App no 31221/15 (17 October 2018) para 6.

[98] See eg *R (Gaunt) v OFCOM* [2010] EWHC 1756 (QB) (13 July 2010) and *Jon Gaunt v the United Kingdom* App no 26448/12 (6 September 2016).

Potentially harmful and/or offensive language and humour must be contextualised and analysed to ensure that the satire of racism, for example, is not confused with racism per se. Broadcast comedy and drama which shocks and offends using, for example, racist protagonists can be a useful medium to challenge racism. They can highlight bigotry and discrimination by having bigoted and discriminatory characters, but this needs to hit the mark by ensuring those portrayals are both justified, to defend the use to the regulator, and repellent enough to the audience so they do not consider the characters to be aspirational or worthy of emulation. Such portrayals need to be carefully considered by the writer, performer and production team before they are broadcast. Stereotypical characters in programming can be harmful to a pluralist society by perpetuating racist and other discriminatory views.[99] It is important that satirical and socio-political comedy using discriminatory language about race, disability and sexuality does not lead to an acceptability by the audience of victimising those who do not conform to society's ideals of 'normal'. Rather they should help expose the prejudices of sections of society and enable an audience to challenge the concept of 'normality'.[100] If the theory holds this should promote social integration and a better understanding of different cultures and communities.

It is right that broadcasters should need to contextualise any strong or discriminatory language.[101] If one considers the racial element in the groundbreaking British situation comedy *Till Death Do Us Part*, creating bigoted characters who use 'offensive terminology' means that the audience can laugh at their prejudices and stupidity. 'In this regard, the terminology is certainly not retained for comedic purposes … it is retained to expose for serious analytic purposes the unfunny aspects of so called humour'.[102]

Subtleties might be lost on some viewers and instead reinforce their existing biases. Many viewers felt an affiliation with the programme's intentionally bigoted main character named Alf Garnett, and related to 'the humorous representation of threats to British livelihood, and thus identified with the anti-liberal messages the programme presented as laughable satire'.[103]

Yet offensive terms should be defendable when they are essential in the formation of critical thinking.[104] In a defamation case brought by the comedian Frankie Boyle, *The Mirror* newspaper had argued that the comedian used words in his

[99] M Billig, 'Comic Racism and Violence' in S Lockyer and M Pickering (eds), *Beyond a Joke* (London, Palgrave Macmillan, 2005) 27.

[100] M Pauwels, 'Anti-racist Critique Through Racial Stereotype Humour What Could Go Wrong?' (2021) 68(4) *Theoria* 169.

[101] Ofcom Broadcasting Code, The (with the Cross-promotion Code and the On Demand Programme Service Rules) December 2020 (last updated 12 June 2023) Section Two, Harm and Offence (this is covered in more detail in ch 5).

[102] M Billig, 'Comic Racism and Violence' in S Lockyer and M Pickering (eds), *Beyond a Joke* (London, Palgrave Macmillan, 2005) 27.

[103] B Bebber, 'Till Death Us Do Part: Political Satire and Social Realism in the 1960s and 1970s' (2014) 34(2) *Historical Journal of Film, Radio and Television* 253.

[104] See eg *M.T.C v Public Prosecutor* Cass Pen N320/2022 10 January 2022.

comedy programmes and stand-up shows which made clear that he was a racist, rather than considering the context of those words.[105] Boyle contended there was,

> a critical distinction between, on the one hand, a comic who satirises or makes fun of stereotypical or institutionally racist comments or whose comic character or stage persona tells jokes containing racial elements, and, on the other hand, a comic who personally holds racist beliefs or views. It is said that only the latter could sensibly be accused of being a racist.[106]

If the target of a joke is not clear this becomes problematic. This was certainly the case for Frankie Boyle's particularly unpleasant rape and incest joke about the British model and media personality Katie Price and her son Harvey (at the time, eight years old). Harvey has the medical condition septo-optic dysplasia and is autistic. Boyle made his joke on his Channel 4 television series, *Tramadol Nights*. This series covered contentious subjects like religion, sex, paedophilia, rape and incest as well as disability. Price complained to Ofcom that his comments were 'discriminatory, offensive, demeaning and humiliating'.[107] Whilst Boyle argued that his target was the media circus surrounding Price and her encouragement of it, the target of the joke is easily interpreted as being her son. If this was not what Boyle intended, then he is still responsible for the poor construction of an unpleasant joke.

In this case, Ofcom acknowledged that broadcasters should be able to explore controversial and challenging issues and ideas, and the public must be free to view and listen to those issues and ideas. However, Ofcom found the programme in breach of the rules on harmful and offensive material because of 'an erroneous decision on a matter of editorial judgement on the broadcaster's part'.[108]

The Ofcom Code requires editorial justification for discriminatory language and stereotyping, but Ofcom's approach is not always consistent. In some cases, it has not found programming in breach where there appears to be no justification beyond ridicule. In a 2020 episode of *Good Morning Britain*, 1,600 viewers complained about Piers Morgan's mimicry of a Chinese accent.[109] There had been a discussion in the programme about minor members of the British Royal family using their position for financial gain. An advertisement was shown in which Queen Elizabeth II's grandson, Peter Phillips was promoting Chinese State milk with a Chinese voiceover. Piers Morgan mimicked the voice using the words 'ching chang'. His co-host Susan Reid said, 'taking the mickey out of foreign languages is rather 1970' and Morgan repeated the words 'ching chang'. Reid then said, 'do you not realise the kind of woke times we're living in?'. This argument seems to blame 'woke times' for the audience taking offence rather than Morgan's actions

[105] See *Boyle v MGN Ltd* [2012] EWHC 2700 (QB).
[106] ibid para 13.
[107] Ofcom Broadcast Bulletin, Issue 179 *Tramadol Nights* (Ofcom, 4 April 2011).
[108] ibid.
[109] Ofcom Broadcast and On Demand Bulletin Issue 400 *Good Morning Britain*(Ofcom, 6 April 2020).

of mimicry as being offensive to minority viewers. Ofcom did not pursue the complaints, yet nor can such content be easily editorially justified.

In defence of Morgan's behaviour Ofcom cited *Redmond-Bate v DPP*[110] which includes the sentence:

> Free speech includes not only the inoffensive but the irritating, the contentious, the eccentric, the heretical, the unwelcome and the provocative provided it does not tend to provoke violence. Freedom only to speak inoffensively is not worth having.

Whilst it is unlikely that Morgan's words would have provoked physical attacks, this type of content can normalise discriminatory behaviour. If there is no justifiable context then it can cause harm to marginalised and vulnerable groups, it has a cumulative effect, and perpetuates stereotypes which contribute to societal harms by undermining social and political equality.[111]

Ofcom research shows audiences understand that programmes can use offensive content to educate and raise awareness of topics such as discrimination or the negative effects of stereotyping. Some felt such content was only acceptable in terms of education, others mentioned that satire too could use offensive words to make a point about social issues.[112] In the case of *Good Morning Britain* Ofcom seems to have been less concerned about contextual justification and negative stereotyping than the audience, who in 2021 research, described 'ching chong' as very offensive.[113]

D. The Meta Oversight Board

The very large social media platforms Facebook, Instagram and Threads, owned by the company Meta, have set up a body to ensure compliance with their own community standards. Meta established the Meta Oversight Board (MOB) in 2020. Under the European Union's Digital Services Act (DSA), platforms such as those controlled by Meta must remove illegal content and can remove content which does not comply with their own terms and conditions of service. Platforms are expected to remove legal but harmful content whilst being able to define what is harmful content themselves. The DSA gives no definition of the term 'harmful content' because of the problems this might cause in relation to free speech. The platforms have to inform their users when they have taken down their content and explain why they did so as part of their transparency agreement.

[110] [1999] 7 BHRC, 375, para 20, per Sedley LJ.

[111] A Matamoros-Fernández, L Bartolo and L Troynar, 'Humour as an online safety issue: Exploring solutions to help platforms better address this form of expression' (2023) 12(1) *Internet Policy Review*.

[112] Ipsos MORI research, 'Public attitudes towards offensive language on TV and Radio: Summary Report' (Ofcom, September 2021) 45 www.ofcom.org.uk/siteassets/resources/documents/research-and-data/tv-radio-and-on-demand-research/tv-research/offensive-language-summary-report.pdf?v=326909.

[113] ibid 26.

The MOB reviews content moderation decisions against Meta's own Community standards. Since its first cases, the MOB has received over a million appeals from users challenging decisions made by Meta's moderators. The MOB only selects those appeals which it considers will have an impact on Meta's policies. The MOB provides an 'independent check on Meta's content moderation' which 'protects freedom of expression and other global human rights standards'.[114]

The MOB is faced with similar issues to the courts and broadcasters' editorial teams when deliberating humorous content on Meta's platforms. Several content examples using satire have been referred to the MOB. Four of the most relevant humour cases are discussed next to see how the MOB implemented changes both to protect satire and to protect vulnerable groups from harmful content.

The first case is the 'Two Buttons Meme' brought to the attention of the MOB in 2020.[115] It was *The Daily Struggle* meme, depicting a sweating man trying to decide which one of two buttons to push. In this version the man's face was replaced with the Turkish flag with one button marked 'The Armenian Genocide is a lie' and the other marked 'The Armenians were terrorists that deserved it'. The meme was flagged by a user and removed according to Facebook's Cruel and Insensitive Community Standards, and later, after the original poster appealed, under the Hate Speech Community Standards. The original poster argued that the purpose of the meme was to highlight the conflicting arguments surrounding the genocide, that the genocide could not be both a lie and an event which was justified.

The MOB overturned Meta's decision and the meme was reinstated on the grounds that it was political speech which should be protected as artistic expression under international law. The MOB also suggested a version of the ECtHR's margin of appreciation, recommending that Facebook use local teams to make editorial decisions as they would have a better understanding of the cultural and geopolitical context.

Before this appeal, Facebook had a humour exemption for content which used hate speech to draw attention to and critique social issues, but a civil rights audit conducted at Facebook suggested that the subjective nature of humour meant it could not be 'well-defined'. Therefore, a narrower exception for satire was recommended. Satire was defined by Facebook as content that

> includes the use of irony, exaggeration, mockery and/or absurdity with the intent to expose or critique people, behaviors, or opinions, particularly in the context of political, religious, or social issues. Its purpose is to draw attention to and voice criticism about wider societal issues or trends.[116]

[114] 'Providing an independent check on Meta's content moderation', www.oversightboard.com.

[115] 'Two Buttons' Meme (Oversight Board, 20 May 2021) www.oversightboard.com/decision/fb-rzl57qhj/.

[116] LW Murphy, 'Facebook's Civil Rights Audit – Final Report' (8 July 2020) www.about.fb.com/wp-content/uploads/2020/07/Civil-Rights-Audit-Final-Report.pdf.

This was incorporated into both Meta's Hate Speech and Dangerous Organisations and Individuals Community Standards with the caveat that the intent of the humorous expression must be clear. The issue of intent was considered by some on the MOB as problematic, with the majority believing that if users had to be explicit in their satirical intent this would lessen the satirical effect. Humour is much like a rose and tends to lose its appeal when it is deconstructed.

Three later cases from 2024 indicate that whilst the MOB's recommendations on the satire exception were incorporated into Meta's community standards, they are not always incorporated into the moderation process.[117] The MOB states that Meta should put 'adequate procedures in place to assess satirical content and relevant context properly'. The MOB also suggests that Facebook's moderators escalate content if they are unsure if a meme is satirical.[118]

The following three cases were incorrectly assessed by moderators, these are, 'The Elon Musk Satire', the 'Cartoon Showing Taliban Oppression Against Women' and 'Polish Post Which Targeted Trans People'. The first two of these illustrate how moderators did not understand what or who was the target of the joke, whilst the final example indicates that the moderators did not recognise the implicit meaning within the post.

The 'Elon Musk Satire' was posted on Instagram and parodied an X thread, it contained a fictitious reply from Musk. Comments on the thread included, 'KKK never did anything wrong to black people,' 'Hitler didn't hate Jews,' and 'LGBT are all pedophiles.' The fictitious reply attributed to Elon Musk was 'Looking into this …'.

It was originally removed on the grounds that it violated Meta's policy on Dangerous Organisations and Individuals. This was because the post mentioned both the KKK and Hitler. As the user who posted the content pointed out, the aim was 'to call out and criticize one of the most influential men on the planet for engaging with extremists on his platform' rather than endorse the KKK and Hitler.

Satirical content which uses hate speech or refers to dangerous individuals and organisations to condemn, or raises awareness to condemn it, should be protected by Meta's Community Standards. Meta acknowledged that the content should not have been removed and reinstated it. Similarly with a cartoon which depicted male members of the Taliban crushing women using a button marked 'oppress-o-meter', the user had to explain the satirical nature of the cartoon. It was to highlight the increasing oppression of women in Afghanistan rather than calling for the oppression of women. Again, it had been initially removed under

[117] J Young, 'Meta, Moderation and the Satire Exception' (*Forhum*, 3 July 2024) www.forhum.org/blog/meta-moderation.
[118] 'Elon Musk Satire' (Meta Oversight Board, 7 March 2024) www.oversightboard.com/decision/IG-JLSBGADZ.

the Dangerous Organisations and Individuals policy. The MOB was concerned that the overreach by moderators could 'potentially lead […] to artistic expression linked to legitimate political discourse being removed'.[119]

In the final example, the MOB overturned Meta's decision to leave up a Facebook post which suggested transgender people should hang themselves.[120] The post was a picture of a curtain in the colours of the transgender flag alongside Polish text translated as 'New technology … Curtains that hang themselves, […] spring cleaning <3.' Even though the poster's bio stated 'I am a transphobe' the moderator did not consider the implicit message violated the Suicide and Self-Injury Standard. The MOB considered the implicit words and imagery was 'malign creativity.' This was explained as a 'novel means of targeting the LGBTQIA+ community through posts and memes they defend as "humorous or satirical, but are actually hate or harassment."'[121]

In all the cases discussed here, the contentious material had already been published, spoken or broadcast and brought to the attention of the MOB. The satire exception is only engaged when the content can be identified as being satirical and if it were not, then it would potentially breach community rules. The MOB must judge the content against Meta's policies and decide not only if the content is appropriate under the rules but also if the rules are too restrictive and impact on freedom of expression. They have the advantage of the material already being in the public domain and seeing users' reaction to the content. This contrasts with decisions made by those in editorial positions who work in broadcasting. They must decide if they should remove or retain content before the material is in the public sphere and consider the potential consequences of these decisions. The production teams do not have the power to override any of their broadcasters' policies or the advantage of seeing the reactions of their audience before transmission.

VII. Conclusion

There is a long tradition in political entertainment of holding the powerful to account. Satire itself is an integral part of political debate, a tool by which to strip away hypocrisy and scrutinise policy. As demonstrated the courts, regulators and some social media platforms have developed precedents and policies to give satire a high level of protection and people in public roles are expected to accept their position will open them up to attacks on their dignity.[122]

[119] 'Cartoon Showing Taliban Oppression Against Women' (Meta Oversight Board, 7 March 2024) www.oversightboard.com/decision/FB-L0XMZ0RP.

[120] 'Post in Polish Targeting Trans People' (Meta Oversight Board, 16 January 2024) www.oversightboard.com/decision/fb-uk2rus24.

[121] ibid.

[122] *Lingens v Austria* App no 9815/82 (8 July 1986) para 41.

These satirical attacks need to be limited. Gratuitously offensive treatment of politicians might lead to a greater disenchantment and disengagement with politics. This could make voters apathetic, believing that no politician will change anything, resulting in fewer people voting.[123] To put this simply, badly executed humour could be bad for democracy. And yet, as some of the cases indicate, the target is not always easy to judge, and content can be considered offensive where no offence was intended. Material created to highlight discriminatory treatment can be interpreted as discriminatory by missing the mark. Humour can be subjective, elusive and uncomfortable. Making judicial or editorial decisions about what is or is not acceptable is difficult especially when contentious content collides not only with the boundaries of the law but also when they go against societal norms or raise taboo subjects.

Satire has been established as a valuable means of expressing social and political critique. Therefore, like other political speech, there should be a higher threshold for any broadcasting restrictions.[124] Ofcom defends satirical commentary along similar lines to the courts. In reaction to audience complaints about the British actress Miriam Margolyes, who said she 'had difficulty not wanting Boris Johnson to die' of coronavirus, Ofcom stated,

> There is a long tradition in UK broadcasting of satirical programmes where comedy will be derived from contributors making provocative and challenging statements about people in the public eye, including elected politicians.[125]

The complaints were not upheld, and Ofcom published the reasons why the decision was reached. Such provocative and challenging content may offend an audience, wishing someone dead is offensive, and 'offence' comes in many guises. Given the context she was likely to be attacking Johnson's behaviour and policies rather than attacking him as an individual. It is these contextual factors that producers of political entertainment, broadcasters and regulators must consider before approving content for transmission. Unless the programme is live, they could choose to edit out anything that they find problematic before it goes to air. The broadcaster has the power to choose what type of political entertainment is broadcast to the public.

Ofcom has underlined the importance of reporting political speech and opinion,[126] and in rulings referred to 'the high level of protection that must be afforded to forms of political speech'.[127] Ofcom has acknowledged that Section Five of the Code, the due impartiality requirement, restricts the broadcasters' right to

[123] P Keighron, 'The Politics of Ridicule: Satire and Television' in M Wayne (ed), *Dissident Voices the Politics of Television and Cultural change* (London, Pluto Press, 1988) 141.

[124] E Polymenopoulou, 'Does One Swallow Make a Spring? Artistic and Literary Freedom at the European Court of Human Rights' (2016) 16(3) *Human Rights Law Review* 511.

[125] Ofcom's Broadcast and On Demand Bulletin Issue 404 (Ofcom, 8 June 2020) 3.

[126] Ofcom Broadcast Bulletin Issue 254 (Ofcom, 19 May 2014) 55.

[127] Ofcom Broadcast Bulletin Issue 290 (Ofcom, 12 October 2015) 40.

freedom of expression.[128] Section Two of the Code which covers harm and offence states that broadcasters must apply generally accepted standards to their output, so this too sets limits to freedom of expression.

Ofcom states that whilst protecting the audience from offensive content 'there should be significant room for creative freedom and challenging material in comedy programmes'.[129] If challenging material is considered important by the regulators, then a risk averse interpretation of the regulations by broadcasters is disproportionate. A chilling effect would mean that expression is curbed before it is broadcast, so it is never broadcast. As will be shown later, some writers experience a chilling effect and self-censor. They do not create content, because they assume it will not be broadcast. It is likely that this same chilling effect takes place in editorial teams because of the threat of financial sanctions, or removal of a licence to broadcast, under Ofcom powers to fine or take a broadcaster off air.

If a producer is concerned that any programme she or he is producing might be sanctioned by Ofcom, this will have a chilling effect. Where this chilling effect exists, there is no equality of speech, it narrows the diversity of voices. This has a negative consequence on tolerance, equality, plurality and so democracy.

Any chilling effect of political satire is problematic, regulations and rules, rather than black letter law, can create a censorious environment. This then restricts what ideas and information are broadcast to the audience. Whilst reasoning exists behind Ofcom's decisions and the courts' decisions not to find certain material in breach of the law or regulations, there is no reasoning available about how editorial decisions are made in broadcasters' production teams.

The argument for most media regulation is that it exists to protect the audience. This is not the case entirely, historically rules and regulations protected those in power. Those with editorial control could control the political message. They made a mockery of democracy by restricting political knowledge and understanding. Ric Bailey referred to the 'sub-conscious cultural media atmosphere' and this has developed over centuries of law and regulation.[130]

The following chapters trace the evolution of regulation from the early restrictions of British Parliamentary reporting to the contemporary landscape of the Communications Act 2003. Laws, rules and regulatory bodies were established and reworked to fit around changing institutions and technologies, and that process affected the production (or censorship) of creative content. Political information and entertainment, with a focus on political satire, was controlled through copyright, licensing, or through statutes.

These limitations caused a chilling effect as writers self-censored. This self-censorship meant that many important political and socio-political events were not covered in the form of accessible entertainment and narrowed public debate. Historically British writers were constricted by laws which lasted centuries and

[128] Ofcom Broadcast and On Demand Bulletin Issue 363 (Ofcom, 8 October 2018) 34.
[129] Ofcom Broadcast and On Demand Bulletin Issue 395 (Ofcom, 27 January 2020) 5.
[130] Bailey (n 52).

were unable to write freely about political issues of the day. As such work was never written, it never came to exist, so it never entered the public sphere. Works have gone unwritten, and characters never fully formed, the marketplace of ideas was strictly monitored and anything untoward was removed. Then, as now, writers and performers were concerned about how the audience would react to them and this then shaped their output. All this caused a different chilling effect, restricting political information, causing gaps in creative work, and stifling the expression of progressive ideas.

3

Regulating and Repressing Information, Ideas and Entertainment

> All censorships exist to prevent anyone from challenging current conceptions and existing institutions. All progress is initiated by challenging current conceptions, and executed by supplanting existing institutions. Consequently, the first condition of progress is the removal of censorship.[1]

I. Introduction

As George Bernard Shaw argues, progress is initiated by challenging current conceptions. If no one challenges the status quo then conceptions stagnate, new and radical ideas are not discussed, and society cannot progress. The censorship of works which have been considered offensive, immoral and satirical span back over millennia. Some Latin literature was restricted until the twentieth century because it was considered just too obscene.[2] In the last days of the Roman Republic the Romans were happy to indulge in such crudeness, but times changed along with the rulers. As he got older, Emperor Augustus took his title of *Pater Patriae*[3] very much to heart. In his later years he embraced a more paternalistic style of leadership passing laws to reflect this more sober approach to life.

Augustus brought in the *Lex Iulia de adulteriis coecendis*[4] (c18 BC.) to punish citizens who committed adultery. Augustus wanted to encourage citizens to uphold the sanctity of marriage by penalising those who indulged in nonmarital sexual relationships.[5] Unfortunately, some contemporary writers were too slow to reflect his moral shift. One was the poet Ovid, he published his *Ars Amatoria*, (*The Art of Love*), a collection of poetry which included tips for men and women on how

[1] George Bernard Shaw, 'Preface to Mrs. Warren's Profession' in *Plays Pleasant and Unpleasant* (first published 1946, Penguin, 2000).

[2] See eg Gaius Valerius Catullus, *Carmen 16*.

[3] Trans: Father of the Country (or Fatherland).

[4] *Lex Iulia de adulteriis coecendis*[4] (c.18 B.C.) Part of the Julian Laws legislating moral behaviour.

[5] TAJ McGinn, *Prostitution, Sexuality, and the Law in Ancient Rome* (New York, Oxford University Press, 2003).

to have affairs. It is widely thought that Augustus punished Ovid for undermining him and his new law. Ovid was exiled and he cited the reasons as 'carmen et error' (trans: a poem and a mistake). Whilst it is not generally agreed what his error was, the *carmen* is widely believed to be a poem from *Ars Amatoria*. Was Augustus concerned for the morals of the Roman people, did he believe they needed 'protection' from Ovid's poetry, or did he simply decide Ovid's poems might weaken his authority and undermine his position as a powerful ruler?

Ovid was not alone in this punishment; it was likely the satirist Juvenal was also exiled because of his work. His exile came after he wrote *Satires* in around the first century AD and mocked a popular actor who was influential in the court.[6] Exile is a very effective form of cancellation and would certainly have created a chilling effect amongst his contemporaries. Juvenal wrote the evergreen line 'quis custodiet ipsos custodes' (trans: who watches the watchmen?). This question has echoed through the centuries, people still ask it today when new laws are brought in, existing laws broadened, or restrictions placed on developing technology.

For centuries legal restrictions on writers and performers constrain art and halt entertainment's ability to challenge the powerful, stopping artists from using provocative and radical ideas. Throughout the years the same taboos recur, sexual themes, religion and morality, and socio-political entertainment. Rules are put in place to guard against material which could offend people's taste and decency, they evolve with technology. In the case of broadcast media, these are the rules on Harm and Offence put in place by the Office of Communication (Ofcom).

Other restrictions on political entertainment are applied to protect against bias reporting, such as the due impartiality regulations. Reasons that are given for restricting content include the age-old claims about the importance of protecting the audience from shocking subject matter, that might be offensive or dangerous to society. Of course, sometimes there is offensive and dangerous expression, but at other times these restrictions give greater protection to those who implement and enforce them than they give to the average citizen.

This chapter discusses the evolution of regulation, how in the light of technological advances it develops from black letter law and the whims of those in power hoping to preserve their gravitas and authority. Just as later chapters discuss the interactions between producers of political entertainment and the modern broadcasting law, this chapter considers what laws and rules influenced what could or could not be published or performed historically.

The regulations on political content developed from checks on the written word through to socio-political works in theatre, and the political and social news and entertainment shown in cinemas. Chapter four is dedicated specifically to broadcasting, and the evolution from black letter law to the soft law of modern broadcast regulation. This chapter is a starting point to that evolution and

[6] EG Hardy, *The Satires of Juvenal*, 2nd edn (London, Macmillan, 1970) xxvi.

discusses what led to the establishment of one of Britain's most powerful censors, the Lord Chamberlain.

His office, as the Lord Chamberlain's role was filled by a succession of men down the centuries, influenced the rules developed at the British Board of Film Censors and from there to the Independent Broadcast Authority and then, through various regulatory bodies, to the 'super-regulator' today, Ofcom. This chapter exemplifies the influences which encouraged innovation or caused writers or performers to self-censor political entertainment. It discusses why some work was never performed publicly, and the effects censorship had on writers. It also explains how members of the public stepped into the limelight as unofficial censors when they believed that entertainment had overstepped that fragile line of taste and decency.

For centuries in Britain, the Crown, the Church and the Government believed that attending the theatre or reading pamphlets or other printed media could lead to insurrection and incitement. To counter this fear, powerful people censored political news and artistic content. They gave themselves remarkable powers which caused British writers to self-censor or create more conformist work than much of the rest of the free world at the time. Historical events, political turmoil, sexuality and morality were excluded from playwrights' work because they believed the Lord Chamberlain's office would refuse to grant them a licence to stage their plays. The historical and legal perimeters of political entertainment provide insights into how and why regulatory frameworks governing satire evolved and how they impact on democratic debate.

Whilst the framework of many of the regulatory rules has not dramatically changed, the current institution Ofcom is very different from the Church or the State. Whilst the institution describes itself as an independent regulator, the regulations are still underpinned by statute decided by the Government. Some of the current regulations have been built upon the foundations laid in the eighteenth century created to protect those in power from ridicule in print or the theatre. Understanding the effect that historical restrictions had on creativity, and examining the chilling effect on writers and producers of political satire, can offer solutions for the future.

II. Regulating the Printed Word

Catullus', Ovid's and Juvenal's publications would have been restricted to a few readers and small audiences. It would have been costly, and time consuming, to replicate and circulate their poetry. Nothing changed dramatically in Europe until the mid-fifteenth century and Gutenberg's printing press. Its arrival meant information could be spread more quickly and cheaply in Europe. Mass reproduction of documents offered the public an opportunity to discuss the same issues across the country at roughly the same time. Rather than celebrating an invention which raised citizens' knowledge of the world around them, those in power were concerned. There were anxieties that this new media, out of the control of the ruling classes, could incite people to commit heresy or whip up dissent against the Crown and Government. They needed to take back control.

Early attempts to regulate the press were ineffective because they were based on a framework established some 50 years earlier to deal with manuscripts and ill-equipped to control the new technology.[7] Established treason laws could not be used easily, and so an Act was passed in 1534 to make it possible to commit treason by words in writing.[8] Printed content could be controlled by The *Bull Exurge Domine* used by Pope Leo X in 1520 to condemn the Lutheran scripts and order their confiscation and burning.

Initially the Church was given control over printed material, as the overriding reason for regulating it was to stop the spread of Lutheran works and 'vernacular Bibles'. This restricted access to a Bible which the average person might more easily read. This remit was then extended to cover all books. Books had to be submitted to the office of the Lord Legate, the Archbishop of Canterbury or the Bishop of London to be approved for publication. The work could then be printed, but only if it was approved. If a work was imported, or had no licence, then publishers could be physically punished for producing and circulating it. In April of 1551 this was expanded to include the spoken word. A royal proclamation stated that 'vagabondes, tellers of newes, sowers of seditious rumours, players and printers without licence' could be fined or imprisoned for spreading news or performing publicly without the privy council's or the king's permission. This is thought to be the first formal attempt to censor material in theatres.[9]

In 1574 The Master of the Revels, originally Henry VIII's producer of theatrical productions, was given the power to license and censor plays. By 1589 The Master of the Revels was well established as a censor because of his role in trying to stop the distribution of the satirical pamphlets the *Martin Marprelate tracts*. These anonymous pamphlets satirised individual bishops and attacked the hierarchy of the Church of England. Satirising the Church was most unwelcome, after all this could lead to people questioning its power and authority. It might lead to critical thinking and the public to reject the status quo.

To add further protection to the powerful, the Star Chamber established the common law of seditious libel in the *De Libellis Famosis Case* of 1606. It stated that one could libel the dead, and that it was 'not material, whether the libel be true or false' and that the libeller 'may be punished by fine, imprisonment, and by pillory and loss of ears'.[10] This meant any criticism of the Government or the

[7] D Harvey, 'Law and the Regulation of Communications Technologies: The Printing Press and the Law 1475–1641' [2005] *Australian and New Zealand Law & History Society E Journal* 160.

[8] ibid.

[9] R Dutton, *Mastering the Revels: The Regulation and Censorship of English Renaissance Drama* (London, Macmillan, 1991) 19.

[10] *De Libellis Famosis* (1606) 5 Co Rep 125a, 77 ER 250.

Crown could be seditious even when it was based in fact. This law suppressed political pamphlets and criminalised written libels.[11] It arose from the *Scandalum Magnatum*, enacted during political unrest to suppress 'false news' and the defaming of noblemen, in other words it was established to put an end to criticism of the ruling classes.[12]

During the early reign of King Charles II, both Houses had concluded that public reporting of proceedings was a breach of privileges. At this time the press was owned by monopolies. As the law limited what people could read about parliamentary proceedings, the fear of losing their monopolies chilled the expression of press owners ensuring there was no official media criticism of those in power. The press owners preferred to keep their monopolies rather than aggravate politicians.

This suppression of political speech stretched beyond the printed word into theatrical productions, further suppressing political criticism. By 1663 King Charles II brought in laws for regulating both the theatre and the press. Reasons given for regulating the press were that;

> … by the general licentiousnes of the late times many evil disposed persons have been encouraged to print and sell heretical schismatical blasphemous seditious and treasonable Bookes Pamphlets and Papers and still doe continue such theire unlawfull and exorbitant practice to the high dishonour of Almighty God endangering the peace of these Kingdomes and raising a disaffection to His most Excellent Majesty and His Government.[13]

Licensing publications discouraged writers from questioning the authority of the church and the behaviour and policies of those in power. This curbed writers' output, making it conformist. A writer or publisher would think twice about challenging authority if it could lead to a sanction. These sanctions included being unable to trade for three years. Repeat offenders could be fined, imprisoned or subject to corporal punishment. Church and political leaders also had issues with theatre productions, the 'audio-visual media' of the day. This was exacerbated by the fact that the theatre was rife with satirical content and so in 1663 a patent called for censorship to ensure,

> all prophanenes, oathes, ribaldry, and matters reflecting vpon piety, and the present governement may bee obliterated, before there bee any action [vpon] in a publique Theatre.[14]

[11] L McNamara, *Reputation and Defamation* (Oxford, Oxford University Press, 2007) 89.

[12] JC Lassiter, 'Defamation of Peers: The Rise and Decline of the Action for Scandalum Magnatum, 1497–1773' (1978) 22(3) *The American Journal of Legal History* 216, 217.

[13] 'Charles II, 1662: An Act for preventing the frequent Abuses in printing seditious treasonable and unlicensed Bookes and Pamphlets and for regulating of Printing and Printing Presses' in J Raithby (ed), *Statutes of the Realm: Volume 5, 1625–80 (s.l, 1819)* (British History Online) www.british-history.ac.uk/statutes-realm/vol5/pp428-435.

[14] KW Scheil, 'Sir William Davenant's use of Shakespeare in The Law Against Lovers (1662)' (1997) 4 *Philological Quarterly* 369.

Those who sought to restrict content could claim it was done to protect people against the licentious times, wicked individuals and protect the peace. The statement that anything which concerned the 'present Government may bee obliterated' underlines that the patent was there to protect those in power from being targeted by satirists or playwrights challenging the status quo. This was not a new idea, even the Roman poet Horace (65 BCE–8 BCE) wrote of how a law was put in place to forbid attacking living people on stage.[15] It protected those in power by restricting criticism in the form of socio-political entertainment and doubtless caused a chilling effect on the writers of ancient Rome.

There were no protections for audience interests and contemporary creative writers recognised the stymying effect on the public. In 1644, the poet John Milton wrote *Areopagitica: A Speech for the Liberty of Unlicensed Printing to the Parliament of England*, protesting censorship prior to publication. Milton was not against regulation on the grounds of defamation, or blasphemy but argued that censorship had a negative effect on the population,

> primely to the discouragement of all learning, and the stop of truth, not only by disexercising and blunting our abilities in what we know already, but by hindering and cropping the discovery that might be yet further made both in religious and civil wisdom.[16]

III. The Stage Licensing Act 1737

Robert Walpole, the first de facto Prime Minister of Great Britain, was not keen on encouraging an informed electorate either. He was much more concerned about protecting himself and his Government from criticism and ridicule. He perceived satirical plays to be a risk not only to his position and his Government but also to the established order of society. Political plays in the theatre were becoming increasingly popular, and Walpole and his Government's corruption provided a rich source of material for satire. In response to this he passed an incredibly influential act of Parliament.

At this time of increasing political volatility, the Stage Licensing Act 1737[17] was introduced to try to stifle anti-Government feeling. Apparently upset by Henry Fielding's satirical play, *The Historical Register*,[18] Walpole passed the Act, giving his Lord Chamberlain extraordinary powers to censor the theatre. The Lord

[15] D Shuger, *Censorship and Cultural Sensibility: The Regulation of Language in Tudor-Stuart England* (Philadelphia, University of Pennsylvania Press, 2006) 84.

[16] J Milton, *Areopagitica; A Speech For the Liberty of Unlicens'd Printing, to the Parliament of England* (London, 1644).

[17] The Licensing Act 1737 (10 Geo 2 c28), s IV.

[18] Some attribute this to Fielding's 'lost' play *The Golden Rump* see eg SD Burch, 'When Satire More Than Closed on Saturday Night: Henry Fielding and the licensing act of 1737' (2008) 16(75) *Theatre Symposium* 135.

Chamberlain was appointed by the monarch on the advice of the Government, and given the authority

> as often as he shall think fit, to prohibit the acting, performing, or representing, any interlude, tragedy, comedy, opera, play, farce, or other entertainment of the stage, or any act, scene, or part thereof, or any prologue, or epilogue.[19]

This Act secured state control by underpinning it with statute law, so plays could only be performed in theatres which were licensed. Scripts were submitted to the Lord Chamberlain who could impose both financial and penal sentences to theatres and works which did not comply with the Act. This was in stark contrast to the press where the state's pre-publication control had been repealed in 1694.

Now the theatre found itself in a situation where every play had to be approved pre-performance or it could not be legally performed to an audience. If any part of the work, or the complete work, was found unacceptable by the Lord Chamberlain it could be censored. The Act lasted for an extraordinarily long time, meaning plays could neither reflect nor challenge any of the political upheavals during two centuries of English Theatre. The Act

> would effectively muzzle the English stage for the next 200 years and prevent it from expressing any controversial views on politics, religion, morality, or sexuality.[20]

The 1737 Act hindered the production and performance of any plays with socio-political themes until the 1960s. The penalties for not complying with the Lord Chamberlain's office discouraged writers from exploring new boundaries and instead theatre managers turned more regularly to the tried and tested safe plays such as those by Shakespeare and his contemporaries. This may be one reason why Shakespeare and his peers are still going strong today. In modern broadcast terms, they started to show repeats.

No contemporary playwrights could represent crucial political events from the late eighteenth century until the twentieth century. Huge political turmoil, from the 'loss of the American colonies; the threatened abdication of George III; and the French Revolution',[21] to all the political and royal scandals had to be ignored by playwrights. Anything damaging to the reputation of the British Government or royal institutions could be legitimately censored by the Lord Chamberlain. This one Act prevented the creation of a body of work which could have explored religious and sexual attitudes, and the contemporary socio-political landscape over two centuries of British history. One law from 1737 caused an enormous gap in British creative output.

[19] The Licensing Act 1737, s.IV.

[20] D Thomas, 'The 1737 Licensing Act and Its Impact' in J Swindells and D Francis Taylor (eds), *The Oxford Handbook of the Georgian Theatre, 1737–1832* (Oxford, Oxford University Press, 2014) 96.

[21] ibid 105.

IV. Press Freedom and Theatre Censorship

It was not just the 1737 Act which stopped people's access to political information and entertainment. Other legal factors such as the Stamp Act 1712 limited the circulation of current political affairs. This Act was described as a 'tax on knowledge'.[22] It drove up costs, so that only the wealthy could afford to buy print publications. It was another form of control, higher pricing meant that only those with a disposable income had access to information about current affairs. Costs limited the participation in political debate to the privileged few.

As the Age of Enlightenment swept into Britain, people became more aware of the constraints on freedom of expression. By the 1770s arguments against restricting press freedom by using established seditious libel laws – where even truth was no defence – had reached Parliament. At this point the political times were turbulent and there was a steady movement across Europe to reject the absolute authority of the Church and the State. Following the Peterloo Massacre in 1819, the 'Six Acts' were passed to try to curtail future political radicalism in the general population. Two of these Six Acts were the Blasphemous and Seditious Libels Act[23] and the Newspapers Stamp Duty Act 1819.[24] These Acts increased penalties for libel and widened the remit of The Stamp Act to include political periodicals with the aim of deterring further political protest. Now all publishers had to place a financial bond with the authorities. This guaranteed that only the wealthy could own political publications. In this way the Government could keep media power confined to those in

> possession of capital … [being] in general a guarantee for the possession of respectability. Men of property had generally a regard to their character, and to the peace of society in which they had so deep an interest.[25]

If those who owned the newspapers were wealthy men with connections to Government, there should be no need to regulate the content of the newspapers. After all, when governments and press barons are on friendly terms it is unlikely a government needs to be concerned about negative press. Not much has changed over the centuries with successive British Governments installing people sympathetic to the Government in key roles within the BBC and Ofcom and cosying up to newspaper owners.

Luckily for the general population, the Stamp Duty Act proved difficult to enforce. Evasion of the law by unlicensed newspaper publishing led to a repeal of the law. This created more competition between the press owners and so lowered the price of legitimate newspapers. The unlicensed press became less appealing as there was little price difference between legal and illegal newspapers. Sales

[22] M Hewitt, *The Dawn of the Cheap Press in Victorian Britain: The End of the 'Taxes on Knowledge,' 1849–1869* (London, Bloomsbury, 2014).
[23] Also known as the Criminal Libel Act (60 Geo III & 1 Geo IV c 8).
[24] The Newspaper Stamp Duties Act (60 Geo III cap 9).
[25] The Blasphemous Libel Bill HC Deb 23 December 1819 Volume 41 col 1543.

floundered and the abolishing of taxes enabled the licensed press to grow in number and increase their sales.

The licensed newspaper industry had relied financially on political subsidies, making them indebted to the Government for survival, but from 1840 the newspaper industry began to fund themselves through advertising revenue. This meant greater resources for news gathering and lessened their dependency on official Government sources for news content. Whilst it focussed the owners on being more profit orientated it also gave politically motivated journalists the freedom to write opinionated pieces. This might be the most important part of press history as newspapers were able to move out of the Government's pocket.[26] On the flip side, this change in revenue generation meant there was a chance that advertisers could exert control over the press.[27] However, the newspapers were finally free of Government control and could exercise political independence. Stamp Duty was abolished in 1855, the same year as the *Daily Telegraph* launched. By 1869 proprietors no longer needed to pay a financial bond and this opened the newspaper market further. *The Daily Mail, Daily Express* and *Daily Mirror* were all established between 1869 and 1903 and are still very much a part of the British press scene.

Whilst there had been major changes in freedoms for the press there was none in the theatre, although there were attempts to change this. A House of Commons Select Committee was established in 1832 to examine the laws on theatre licensing and censorship. Edward Bulwer-Lytton MP, who oversaw the committee, recommended the abolition of censorship believing that plays should be judged by public taste rather than 'any ignorant and bungling Censor'.[28] Unfortunately for playwrights, this was not to be, instead of ending censorship, the committee's report was ignored by Parliament. This Act remained in place making it 'a uniquely repressive mechanism during a period of growing political enfranchisement and liberalisation'.[29]

There were some changes in the regulation of political entertainment. The Theatre Regulation Act 1843[30] discontinued the Lord Chamberlain's ability to stop performances through restricting patents to only a few theatres, giving magistrates the power to grant licences for entertainment performed in saloons and pubs. This developed into music hall which reached its commercial peak between 1889 and 1919.[31] Musical productions, such as *A Gaiety Girl* could be more outspoken, and able to make jokes at the expense of powerful institutions.[32]

[26] I Asquith, 'The structure, ownership and control of the press 1780–1855' in G Boyce, J Curran and P Wingate (eds), *Newspaper History From the Seventeenth Century to the Present Day* (Constable, Sage Publications, 1978) 111.

[27] ibid 113.

[28] *Hansard*, HC Vol 13, col 245 (31 May 1832).

[29] D Thomas, D Carlton and A Etienne, *Theatre Censorship: From Walpole to Wilson* (Oxford, Oxford University Press, 2007) 2.

[30] The Theatres Act 1843 (6 & 7 Vict c 68).

[31] BJ Faulk, *Music Hall and Modernity: The Late-Victorian Discovery of Popular* Culture, 1st edn (Athens, Ohio University Press, 2004) 10.

[32] L Platt, *Musical Comedy on the West End Stage, 1890–1939* (London, Palgrave Macmillan, 2004).

Still, the Lord Chamberlain continued to censor plays in theatres, and could revoke licences for anything that he or his office considered to be inappropriate. Inappropriate is very difficult to define and open to a great deal of subjectivity. The Lord Chamberlain could ban a performance to preserve 'Good Manners, Decorum or … the Public Peace'.[33] All new plays had to be submitted to his office at least seven days before the first performance to be approved.[34]

The work of the Lord Chamberlain and his office continued, with no external checks or transparency. There were no grounds for appealing a decision, and he was under no obligation to explain the decisions he took. The portrayal of notable people on the stage was still forbidden, the argument being that such people should not be represented in plays to protect them from impropriety, rather than for political reasons. This rule had the result of ensuring that no person involved in political life could be lampooned or satirised in a play. These included British and foreign members of the royal family, Government, and 'anyone whose name was a topic of public interest'.[35] This was a direct consequence of Walpole's law, introduced over a century earlier, which he had established to protect himself and his Government from scrutiny and ridicule.

To bypass the restrictive nature of stage censorship, private theatre clubs began to appear. It was here that unlicensed plays could be performed as long as no money changed hands. This ensured that the requirement for a play to be 'for hire' was not met and a performance would not breach section 15 of the Theatres Act 1843. The audience had to be members of a theatre club or society rather than a public audience paying to see the staging of a play. Whilst this loophole brought otherwise banned plays to the stage, the productions were rarely well-funded and were generally restricted to a Sunday performance. They were unlikely to satisfy an established playwright as a remedy to the issue of censorship. They were also unlikely to create much profit for those involved in the writing, producing or performing of a play.

Further parliamentary inquiries came and went in attempts to loosen the Lord Chamberlain's extraordinary grip. Conversely, some attempts appeared to reinforce his powers rather than relax them.[36] During a parliamentary debate about how the Lord Chamberlain had refused to grant a licence for George Bernard Shaw's play *Mrs. Warren's Profession*, members of the House of Commons acknowledged that the responsibility

> of allowing or disallowing plays or parts of plays submitted to him is placed exclusively upon him by section 12 of the Theatres Act, 1843[37]

[33] The Theatres Act 1843, s XIV.
[34] ibid s XII.
[35] JR Stephens, *The Censorship of English Drama 1824–1901* (Cambridge, Cambridge University Press, 1980) 116.
[36] N de Jongh, *Politics, Prudery and Perversions: The Censoring of the English Stage 1901–1968* (London, Methuen, 2000) x.
[37] Mr. Bernard Shaw's Play (Licence Refused) HC Vol 5, col 1477 (27 May 1909).

'him' being, of course, the Lord Chamberlain. This statement confirmed that there could be no avenue of appeal against the Lord Chamberlain's decisions.

George Bernard Shaw submitted *Mrs. Warren's Profession* to the Lord Chamberlain in 1894. The Lord Chamberlain's office deemed the play immoral, because the title character was a prostitute. It is unsurprising at a time of Victorian puritanism that the Lord Chamberlain would reject it. To be able to publish this play and still protect his performance rights, Bernard Shaw heavily censored *Mrs. Warren's Profession* changing her profession to thief rather than prostitute. Once he was granted a licence for this version of his play it was given a single public reading in 1898. This enabled Bernard Shaw to publish the unexpurgated version of *Mrs. Warren's Profession* in the same year.[38] Published plays did not fall under the control of the Lord Chamberlain. This double standard in censorship is seen regularly and continues into the age of television and radio broadcasts and now the internet. It begs the question why it was deemed inappropriate to see a performance when it was acceptable to read it? The subject matter of prostitution remains the same whether the play was read or performed.

To evade breaching the law, the play was first performed in a private club in 1905. Bernard Shaw continued submitting *Mrs Warren's Profession* to a succession of Lord Chamberlains, all of whom rejected it until finally it was granted a licence in 1924 on the grounds that public opinion had changed over time.[39] It was first publicly performed in 1925, 31 years after Bernard Shaw had first submitted it to the Lord Chamberlain's office.

But who was the Lord Chamberlain? He was a senior courtier appointed by the monarch and who in turn appointed the Examiners of Plays, 'Comptrollers' and 'Readers'. The theatre's version of our modern-day compliance teams and editorial teams who check content for broadcast television, radio – streamed content, and sometimes websites. The Examiners of Plays were often retired senior officers from the armed services.[40] They may not have been particularly open-minded or motivated by a love of the arts. Often, as reflected in their approach to *Mrs Warren's Profession*, they would take a patriarchal approach to their work, assuming the role of protectors of morals and standards for the theatre goers.

Unsurprisingly, Bernard Shaw was a vocal opponent of the Lord Chamberlain's editorial powers. He wrote a letter to the effect which was published in *The Times* in 1907 and co-signed by famous authors such as Thomas Hardy, W.B. Yeats and Henry James. They were all campaigning for a change in the law. The authors raised the objection that the office of Lord Chamberlain had been introduced for political rather than for 'the so-called moral ends to which it is perverted'.[41] They complained of the lack of appeals process against the Lord Chamberlain's

[38] LW Conolly, 'Mrs. Warren's Profession and The Lord Chamberlain' (2004) 24(1) *The Annual of Bernard Shaw Studies* 46.

[39] de Jongh (n 36) 51.

[40] ibid.

[41] Letter to The Editor, *The Times* Issue 38476 (London, England, 29 October 1907) p 15.

decisions, referring to his office as 'autocratic', 'opposed to the spirit of the constitution, contrary to common justice and common sense' and 'neither responsible to Parliament nor amenable to the law'.[42]

In the 1909 Joint Select Committee on Stage Plays (Censorship) Bernard Shaw led playwrights as witnesses before the committee to argue for a change in the law. During one of these sessions, the playwright and novelist J.M. Barrie described censorship as making 'drama a more puerile thing in the life of a nation and is a stigma on all who write plays'.[43] Thus, encapsulating how restrictive theatre regulation was, how damaging censorship was to the writers, and how regulation effectively narrowed the opportunities for an audience to experience radical and innovate work. With playwrights being unable to push against the social and cultural norms of the times, there was still no real exploration of progressive ideas and socio-political and ethical issues, or any critique of social mores. This was especially problematic for exposing political misconduct or hypocrisy, given that '…the representation on the stage of political personages is distinctly forbidden by the endorsement on every licence'.[44]

There still could not be theatrical plays performed about contemporary politics. Nothing changed significantly, and the 1909 select committee failed to bring any real reform. Perhaps surprisingly, theatre managers did not support any type of change. They were concerned about losing their licences if plays were not pre-approved by an external body. They would rather the external body took the responsibility of making an editorial judgment of the content of the plays, relieving them of any fears of being found in breach of the law. This was even though theatre managers had acknowledged that this external body stifled challenging and creative work and they put on private performances to evade censorship. They did not want to take risks which might have repercussions on their careers and income. This type of risk aversion can be seen today; it came up during the interviews for this book where those in production were aware careers could be affected when people in editorial control made the wrong decision and allowed the broadcast of contentious content which might then result in a sanction from Ofcom.

One outcome of the 1909 Joint Select Committee was a list of recommendations to guide the Lord Chamberlain's decisions. This stipulated that licences should be granted to any play unless he considered it:

- To be indecent
- To contain offensive personalities
- To represent on the stage in an invidious manner a living person, or any person recently dead

[42] ibid.

[43] UK Parliament, Joint Select Committee on Stage Plays (Censorship) *Report from the Joint Select Committee of the House of Lords and the House of Commons on the stage Plays (Censorship)* (London: Printed for H.M.S.O. by Wyman and Sons, 1909).

[44] *Hansard*, HC Vol 44, col 1490 (28th November 1912).

- To do violence to the sentiment of religious reverence
- To be calculated to conduce to crime or vice
- To be calculated to impair friendly relations with a Foreign Power: or
- Be calculated to cause a breach of the peace.[45]

Even after these recommendations one MP recognised in Parliament that such restrictions meant an

> alleged tendency to the encouragement of plays of a low intellectual and moral character at the expense of drama opening up new vistas of thought in social, political, and ethical matters.[46]

Nothing had really improved; playwrights still could not write radical and progressive content. These regulations would still create gaps of writing, with no one being able to kick against the orthodox.

Reformers' failure to get the Act repealed meant that two layers of censorship still existed. The first layer, the Lord Chamberlain's office, could ban new, challenging material, and the second layer was self-censorship because of the chilling effect the Act had on writers. Writers, fearing the Lord Chamberlain's 'blue pencil', did not write plays in the way that they otherwise would have done. Radical characters were diluted down, and playwrights produced work with the restrictions in mind, only writing material that they knew the censors would approve. Rather than creating thought-provoking, innovative plays, they self-censored to ensure their work would be licensed for public performance. This gap, a missing body of work through self-censorship, still happens. This will be further explored in the interviews later in the book. They reflect on what influence someone in an editorial position might have over socio-political media content and the chilling effect it can have on creative output.

A second change brought by the Committee was the introduction of an advisory board to assist the Lord Chamberlain, his Comptroller, and Examiner of Plays in decisions regarding 'doubtful or difficult plays.' As always, the final decision of the play's fate lay with the Lord Chamberlain.[47] The members of the Advisory Board were also selected by the Lord Chamberlain and his Comptroller. It was rare for there to be a female Board member, and all the members' views would reflect their upper and middle class, mainly male, status. Ultimately very little changed, it was still impossible to be granted a licence for any play which questioned the politics of the day or the morality of the time. Anything which dealt openly with sexual themes, representations of figures from Christianity or the royal family was censored. Plays with any kind of political content were considered very problematic and heavily censored.[48]

[45] Report of the 1909 Joint Select Committee on Stage Plays (n 43).
[46] *Hansard*, HC Vol 32, col 582 (30 November 1911).
[47] J Johnson, *The Lord Chamberlain's Blue Pencil* (London, Hodder and Stoughton, 1990) 66.
[48] S Nicholson, *The Censorship of British Drama, 1900–1968 (Vol. I:1900– 1932)* (Exeter, University of Exeter Press 2003).

Politicians were protected from the playwright's pen by the censor's blue pencil. The paternalist belief that the audience needed protection from anything unseemly influenced editorial decisions. The Lord Chamberlain wished to ensure each play would not offend a family audience and apparently did not trust families to be able to make an informed choice by themselves. The Lord Chamberlain based the audience's sensitivities on his own views, and his belief of what content might cause offence or embarrass the audience was far reaching.[49]

V. The Arrival of Moving Pictures and World War I

In 1896, whilst the select committees were still debating theatre regulation, films arrived in England. This was followed by the Cinematograph Act 1909 which required that all cinemas held a licence granted by local authorities. Initially the Act was to ensure adequate safety to cinema goers because of the flammable property of film; however, it soon became apparent that the local authorities were also using the Act to exercise power over editorial content.

An early example of editorial influence concerned a film about the murderer Charles Peace. The film led to criticism from the public and the press, whilst the Metropolitan Chief Commissioner raised concerns that such films were glorifying crime. I do wonder what they would make of the proliferation of true crime programming as popular entertainment now. The Commissioner's concerns led to the involvement of the Home Office which was urged to bring film content under its control. This did not sit well with members of the film industry, they in turn suggested they establish the British Board of Film Censors (BBFC) to carry out self-regulation. Mr G.A. Redford was appointed as 'censor of cinematograph performances', his suitability for the post being that he was 'at one time Examiner of Plays under the Lord Chamberlain'. Home Secretary Mr. McKenna stated that the arrangement was 'entirely unofficial' and would 'protect the public from any risk of the production of objectionable pictures'.[50]

The BBFC advocated that film should be more tightly controlled than theatre as it would appeal to families and young people.[51] This was the same argument used almost a decade before by the Lord Chamberlain for censoring theatre content, to ensure plays were suitable for family attendance.[52] The structure of the BBFC was copied from the Lord Chamberlain's office with the President's role

[49] ibid.

[50] *Hansard*, HC Vol 43, col 1612 (8 November 1912), *NB* in *Hansard* 'Redford' is incorrectly referred to as 'Bedford'.

[51] JC Robertson, *The British Board of Film Censors: Film Censorship in Britain, 1896–1950* (London, Routledge, 2016) 20.

[52] Nicholson (n 48).

being akin to that of Lord Chamberlain and the full-time secretary fulfilling that of Comptroller.[53]

This moral and political stance is reflected in the BBFC's 1914 Annual Report, in which it stated that

> [T]here is every reason to believe that its [The BBFC's] influence is having the desired effect of eliminating certain subjects which are altogether unsuitable for British audiences.

These unsuitable subjects included, but were not restricted to

- Unnecessary exhibitions of feminine underclothing.
- Scenes tending to disparage public characters.
- Incidents injurious to the reputation of Governmental Departments.
- Gruesome murders, suicides, strangulation scenes and massacres.
- Scenes suggestive of immorality.[54]

Many of these echo the theatre restrictions which progressive playwrights and parliamentarians had criticised. This similarity is unsurprising given the appointment of Redford who appears to have transposed a version of the rules for the stage over to the cinema.

In 1913 the BBFC reported that it had received a communication from the Home Office about censoring South African films on the Rand Riots; in which 20 white mine workers were killed and 150 injured when two squadrons of the Royal Dragoons and police were dispatched to quell the strikers.[55] There was a concern that showing these films publicly 'might lead to trouble' and so the films were given to the Home Office and to the War Office 'prior to publication'.[56] The BBFC then censored the films, 'to the apparent satisfaction of the authorities'.[57] Clearly, the BBFC was not always a self-regulatory body on political topics.

In the 1914 Annual Report, the BBFC refers to 'a report' which suggested 'any film subject dealing with the War would be prohibited'.[58] In contradiction to the 1913 report, this report indicated that the BBFC had banned certain films, possibly due to Governmental pressure. These films had included scenes which contained 'incidents calculated to afford information to the enemy'.[59] There was little concern about affording information to the audience. A threat to national security is often used as a reason for State censorship.

[53] A Aldgate and JC Robertson, *Censorship in Theatre and Cinema* (Edinburgh, Edinburgh University Press, 2005) 2.

[54] The BBFC Annual Report 1914.

[55] Staff Reporter, 'The Riots. Rand Death Roll' *The Sydney Morning Herald* NSW 1842–1954 (8 July 1913) 9.

[56] The BBFC Annual Report 1913.

[57] ibid.

[58] The BBFC Annual Report 1914.

[59] Robertson (n 51) 10.

Local authorities were now ruling that only films passed by the BBFC could be shown and added this clause into licences issued under the Cinematograph Act 1912. Whilst there was no statutory regulation, the Government appears to have had considerable editorial control over films with political, 'topical' in BBFC terminology, content.

VI. Progression on the Stage and Post-War Booms

With the onset of war theatres were briefly shut down but soon reopened when the Government realised productions could be used for propaganda and political purposes. Theatre productions were still very much under the control of the Lord Chamberlain, and the war had brought an end to ongoing parliamentary considerations of reforming stage censorship. There was no more parliamentary debate on the subject again until 1944.

This debate was prompted by the Lord Chamberlain's refusal to license the play *Mr. Lincoln meets a Lady*. The play was about a fictional meeting between Queen Victoria and the American President. It had previously been performed on the radio in the UK but did not meet with the approval of King George VI. On application the theatre licence was refused for the play's stage performance.[60] The protection of royal reputation, albeit a fictional reputation, still had the power to curb stage performances. Given that the radio production would have had many more listeners than the stage production might have audience members, it seems an odd decision for both King George VI and the Lord Chamberlain to make. It also illustrates the extraordinary powers that the Theatres Act 1843 still had to be able to influence the suppression of a stage play, and another example of different rules and regulations for different types of performances.

Following a vote at the British Theatre Conference in 1948, a Private Member's Bill was raised calling for an end to stage censorship.

> Political allusions, political satires, lampoons against the Court and the aristocracy, as well as matters susceptible of the widest and freest opinion, all came under the savage veto of the then Lord Chamberlain; and I would remind the House that that is a veto against which there is no appeal. It is almost shocking to say this, but it is a veto which is above Parliament and, by an incredible anomaly, it is a veto which is above the Law. The Lord Chamberlain was confirmed in his position as Dramatic Censor by Sir Robert Walpole in his Licensing Act of 1737, which is the evil parent of the Act of 1843, is still in force today.[61]

Unfortunately, recognition that the Lord Chamberlain could veto content and was above the law, whilst debated in Parliament as outrageous, made no advances in changing legislation.

[60] Thomas, Carlton and Etienne (n 29) 2.
[61] *Hansard*, HC Vol 463, col 715 (25 March 1949).

Lord Scarborough became the penultimate Lord Chamberlain. He was considered the most liberal of all his predecessors. He preferred to negotiate licences with playwrights rather than ban them absolutely, even so he came under heavy press criticism. The absurdity of complying with an act from 1843 and the growing popularity of theatre clubs performing unlicensed plays, made it increasingly difficult to justify the process of licensing plays. The anomalies between what was permitted on television and radio but not in the theatre were increasingly apparent. These included many instances of plays which had popular runs abroad but could not be produced uncut in England because of the Theatres Act.

Moves were made by Lord Scarborough's office to align with public feeling; this was especially apparent in the licensing of plays dealing with homosexuality. There had been an absolute ban on the theme of homosexuality by the Lord Chamberlain until 1958. One of the reasons given was young people might be 'introduced' to homosexuality by seeing it represented in a play.[62] The ban led to self-censoring, Terence Rattigan had self-censored his play *Separate Tables*, knowing that if he were to include a reference to a male character 'importuning' another, it would not be licensed.[63] The theatre critic Kenneth Tynan, who campaigned against theatre censorship, believed that Philip King's play, *Serious Charge*, would have been much better had it not been written in the shadow of the Lord Chamberlain's standpoint on homosexual themes.

> Perhaps the idea [of giving the hero suppressed homosexual tendencies] occurred to him; and with it the certain knowledge that the Lord Chamberlain would have crushed it on sight. One cannot blame him for playing safe.[64]

This is another example of self-censorship. Playing safe or erring on the side of caution to get work performed in the public sphere means a certain weakening of themes which may be innovative, shocking or provocative for an audience. This tendency continues today as we will see in the interviews with contemporary writers and producers in later chapters.

The Lord Chamberlain reconsidered his position on homosexual themes after recommendations were put forward in the Report of the Committee on Homosexual Offences and Prostitution[65] (the Wolfenden Report commissioned in 1954). This was, in part, to consider 'The law and practice relating to homosexual offences and the treatment of persons convicted of such offences by the courts'.[66] One reason the report had been commissioned was the increase in, and

[62] Johnson (n 47) 172.

[63] D Pattie, *Modern British Playwriting: the 1950s* (London, Methuen Drama, 2012) 40.

[64] As quoted in D Shellard, S Nicholson and M Handley, *The Lord Chamberlain Regrets … A History of British Theatre Censorship* (London, The British Library, 2004) 146.

[65] Report of the Committee on Homosexual Offences and Prostitution (London, Her Majesty's Stationery Office, 1968).

[66] ibid 4.

the media coverage of, prosecutions of prominent people for homosexual acts, these included the actor Sir John Gielgud and Lord Montagu of Beaulieu.[67]

After the publication of the report, the Lord Chamberlain spoke with the Home Secretary about plays which included themes around homosexuality. He concluded that given the publicity there was 'no point in continuing to debar it from the stage'.[68] One of the first plays to test public opinion on homosexual themes was Shelagh Delaney's *A Taste of Honey*. It was favourably received by the audience and cited as a reason for the Lord Chamberlain lifting the ban.[69] It was a ground-breaking production, given that one of the characters was openly gay, and the play discussed, rather than implied, his homosexuality.

The Chief Play Reader, CD Heriot, of the Lord Chamberlain's office recommended the play for licence and suggested two cuts but referred the play on to the Lord Chamberlain and the Comptroller, so cannot have felt comfortable taking responsibility for licensing what would have been a cutting-edge play. He described it as being 'balanced on a knife-edge' and a 'perfect border-line case' as it was 'concerned with the forbidden subject'. Not all in the Lord Chamberlain's office agreed with his recommendation for approval. Underneath the typed report about the play was a handwritten comment from the Lord Chamberlain's Assistant Comptroller, Brigadier Sir Norman Gwatkin, which stated,

> I think it's revolting, quite apart from the homosexual bits … To me it has no saving grace whatsoever. If we pass muck like this, it does give our critics something to go on.

But Scarborough did not agree with Gwatkin. He requested some cuts as per Heriot's notes, and the play was approved.[70]

A few months later Lord Scarborough wrote a letter to the Chairman of the Theatres National Committee explaining he was going to relax the rules on themes of homosexuality. This was followed by him laying down guidelines with caveats that plays which were 'violently homosexual' would not be granted a licence, homosexual characters had to be intrinsic to the play and 'embraces between homosexuals' were not allowed.[71] It was a move away from the strictures of previous Lord Chamberlains and set the scenes for more radical playwrights.

Economic growth at the end of World War II brought stability and security to Britain. It also brought a new breed of young people who rebelled against the 'Establishment', did not engage politically and felt markedly different to their

[67] CJ Summers, 'Wolfenden Report' (2015) www.glbtq.com.

[68] Johnson (n 47) 172.

[69] N de Jongh, 'Taste of Honey led to end of gay ban' *The Guardian* Letters (25 November 2011) www.theguardian.com/stage/2011/nov/25/taste-of-honey-gay-ban.

[70] *Lord Chamberlain's report and correspondence Lord Chamberlain's Office*: © Crown Copyright. Gerry Raffles: © Gerry Raffles Estate. Held by British Library British Library Collection Items, www.bl.uk/collection-items/lord-chamberlains-report-and-correspondence-about-a-taste-ofhoney#footnote1.

[71] Johnson (n 47) 172.

parents' generation. They had an 'often delirious addiction to rock-and-roll'.[72] In the theatre, such radicals were led by writers whom the press termed as *Angry Young Men*. They produced work based around a grittier, grimmer Britain. One might wonder why there were no angry young women given Shelagh Delaney's ground-breaking work.

Unfortunately, no matter how much the angry youth railed against the Establishment, compared to their counterparts in the rest of Western Europe and America, English theatre's movement towards a truer reflection of modern society was still massively restricted. This was especially true for political entertainment. It was specifically stated in the 1909 recommendations that the Lord Chamberlain was able to withhold a licence if a play were

> To represent on the stage in an invidious manner a living person, or any person recently dead.

As the decade progressed the Lord Chamberlain became more liberal. His office's interpretation of 'an invidious manner' became less restrictive. By the 1960s, public figures, including politicians, became 'fair game in sketches and reviews'.[73] In a production of *Beyond the Fringe*, Peter Cook impersonated Harold MacMillan, and it is likely that this was the first time in the twentieth century that a politician was parodied on a West End stage.[74] Surprisingly the Lord Chamberlain did not request a script change even though he had attended a performance of the show with Queen Elizabeth II.

The 1950s had started something akin to a new Age of Enlightenment. This was not welcomed by everyone; there were many who considered it was the birth of a more permissive society.[75] The 1950s and 1960s upset the traditionalists as more rights were given to women and minority groups. There were new laws which appalled them, abortion law reform in 1967, divorce law reform and the decriminalisation of homosexuality.

VII. The Permissive Age

These new Acts all had repercussions on society. More legal protections came into force for writers and publishers, allowing more permissive literature with sexual content and contemporary themes to be published. The Obscene Publications Act 1959 amended '… the law relating to the publication of obscene matter; to

[72] J Mays, 'Teen-Age Culture in Contemporary Britain and Europe' (1961) 338 *The Annals of the American Academy of Political and Social Science* 22.

[73] Johnson (n 47) 110.

[74] de Jongh (n 36) 12, de Jongh puts the date at 1960, but Johnson (above) puts it at 1961.

[75] G Saunders 'A Last Hurrah? Joe Orton's Until She "Screams", Oh Calcutta and the permissive 1960s' (2017) 37(2) *Studies in Theatre and Performance* 221 and Hansard, HC Vol 801, col 95 (4 May 1970).

provide for the protection of literature …'. The test for obscenity changed to be based on the complete work, rather than just one section, which might

> tend to deprave and corrupt persons who are likely, having regard to all relevant circumstances, to read, see or hear the matter contained or embodied in it.[76]

The defence was if the publication could be

> justified as being for the public good on the ground that it is in the interests of science, literature, art or learning, or of other objects of general concern.[77]

Now the context of the contentious material could be taken into account, and the justification considered the merits of the work for the benefit of the reader or audience. These defences parallel the justification requirement in Ofcom's restrictions on harmful or offensive programme material.

As if to test this new Act, Penguin books published an unedited version of DH Lawrence's scandalous novel *Lady Chatterley's Lover*. More scandalous in some eyes was that the low cost of the book at 3'/6 created the opportunity for both 'women and the working classes' to purchase the novel and read detailed descriptions of sexual intercourse. A criminal case was brought against the publishers Penguin Books.[78,79] Expert witnesses were invited to speak on behalf of the defence, including the famous female author Enid Blyton who, whilst supporting the cause, was unable to appear as her husband forbade it.[80] Not all aspects of the sixties were progressive.

The first run of *Lady Chatterley's Lover* sold out with 200,000 copies bought on the first day of publication and two million in the first year, outselling the Bible. This was a clear indication that the public had an appetite for more shocking content. Penguin Books won their court case, and this too had repercussions in the Lord Chamberlain's Office with the Assistant Comptroller questioning 'Since the evidence at the trial of Lady Chatterley I am beginning to wonder who one is trying to protect'.[81]

Now the Lord Chamberlain had to consider the Sexual Offences Act 1956 and the Obscene Publication's Act when balancing his decisions on plays, and the concept of protecting the audience by restricting challenging and provocative content was thrown into question.

Joe Orton's arrival on the scene was perfect timing. He was a new playwright, rebellious, homosexual, and to many people quite obscene. Moreover, he was a 'radical [who] refused to accept that gay desire was inherently problematic or dangerous'.[82] His 1964 play *Entertaining Mr. Sloane* did not shy away from

[76] The Obscene Publications Act 1959, s 1(1).
[77] ibid s 4(1).
[78] *Regina v Penguin Books, LTD* [1960] [1961] 1 WLUK 17; [1961] Crim LR 176.
[79] G Robertson, 'Trial of the Century: Lady Chatterley' (2010) 60(11) *History Today* 41–44.
[80] ibid.
[81] Johnson (n 47) 165.
[82] de Jongh (n 36) 119.

homosexuality, in fact it was central to the storyline. First opening at a private theatre, its popularity led to the script being submitted to the Lord Chamberlain's office for a licence. The Reader of Plays suggested many cuts, passing it with the caveat, 'if you are prepared to accept the thread of homosexuality which runs strongly through the play'.[83] These cuts surprised Orton, insomuch as the references to homosexuality could stand but the Lord Chamberlain's office requested the heterosexual ones be removed.[84]

Orton enjoyed creating mischief and did not restrict himself solely to the theatre. He liked to bait the newspapers and moral crusaders. He created a fictional character in the form of a white, conservative, judgemental woman named Mrs Edna Welthorpe. He shaped her in the form of a self-proclaimed protector of public morals.[85] Orton would write letters to newspapers expressing shock and outrage, both in Edna's name and using other pseudonyms to generate publicity for himself. Had he decided that no publicity was bad publicity? Was he creating a fictional façade of cancel culture to whip up outrage and by doing so sell more tickets, an early version of clickbait?

This character of Edna has a more serious side too; she is significant insomuch as she embodied the chill that many playwrights felt at the time. The character was inspired by the playwright Terence Rattigan who said he wrote for the 'symbolic playgoer, "Aunt Edna" – a nice respectable, middle-class, middle-aged, maiden lady, with time on her hands and the money to help her pass it'.[86]

The influence that the fictitious Edna held over playwrights even reached the echelons of Parliament when she was discussed in the House of Lords during yet another debate on Theatre Censorship.

> Mr. Terence Rattigan has said that every time he writes a play he has in mind a mythical figure called 'Aunt Edna', and he asks himself, 'Would Aunt Edna like that? Would she understand it?'. … but most serious dramatists cannot write with 'Aunt Edna' looking over their shoulders.[87]

Similarities have been drawn between the fictitious Mrs Edna Welthorpe and the very real moral crusader Mrs Mary Whitehouse. Johnny Speight, the writer of the popular British situation comedy *Till Death Do Us Part*, a sometimes-controversial social satire first broadcast in the mid-1960s, had complained that he would stop writing scripts for the programme 'if it meant Mrs. Whitehouse was looking over his shoulder'.[88] Mrs Whitehouse will be discussed in detail later in this chapter.

[83] Lord Chamberlain's Plays Correspondence Files, *Entertaining Mr Sloane* 1964/4267 Play reader's report, 2 June 1964 as cited in Aldgate and Robertson (n 53) 120.

[84] Joe Orton Online, *The Plays*, www.joeorton.org/Pages/Joe_Orton_Plays3.html.

[85] ibid *Mrs Welthorpe Letters*, www.joeorton.org/Pages/Joe_Orton_Life9.html.

[86] M Franks, 'From Public Library Prankster to Playwright: Joe Orton and Postwar Britain's Nanny State' (2017) 20 *Book History* 394.

[87] Lord Anan in *Hansard*, HL Vol 272, col 1162 (17 February 1966).

[88] A Briggs, *The History of Broadcasting in the United Kingdom Volume V: Competition* (Oxford, Oxford University Press, 1995) 948.

Orton was not only affected by the Ednas of the world but also felt obliged to tiptoe around the Lord Chamberlain's office. In his diary he refers to the Lord Chamberlain, and how he attempted to 'second guess' what changes the Lord Chamberlain's office might suggest for his plays. This second guessing potentially influenced some of the decisions about what he wrote. Orton recalled a conversation with his agent, Peggy Ramsay, who suggested that Orton's fourth play should 'perhaps be a little more conventional' so that they would not 'always be associated with subjects of scandal and concern'.[89] Stage directions were removed from scripts 'In order not to annoy the Lord Chamberlain too much' and when it was suggested that *What the Butler Saw* might not trouble the Lord Chamberlain, Orton admits that the very idea made him tremble and said, 'It probably means the play will be banned outright'.[90]

Whilst Orton was negotiating with the Lord Chamberlain there were attacks against propriety coming from many other directions with the explosion of satire in theatres, magazines, and television. The comedian Peter Cook who wrote and starred in *Beyond the Fringe* set up 'The Establishment Club' with a nightly satirical show. As a private club it was beyond the reach of the Lord Chamberlain's blue pencil. Next *Private Eye*, the satirical news magazine, first published on 25 October 1961, and then television followed suit to take a dig at the Establishment.

At the same time as the rise of television satire, private theatre club performances were increasing and were forcing the issue of further reviewing the law on Theatre censorship. By 1965 the Lord Chamberlain pressed the Director of Public Prosecutions to bring actions against various club performances of unlicensed plays. It eventually became a parliamentary issue and in November a formal meeting took place between the Home Secretary, Lord Chancellor and Solicitor General. They decided that the current form of theatre censorship was not viable. The Director of Public Prosecutions (DPP), in a letter to the Home Secretary of 22 October 1965 encapsulates the Government's position,

> … the law is being systematically evaded and thereby brought into disrepute. On the other hand a prosecution under Section 15 of the Theatres Act 1843 would spotlight the manifest absurdities of the present system.[91]

The DPP was aware of the 'manifest absurdities' of the Act and that the situation was becoming unenforceable. It was much like that of the 'underground' press where the systematic evasion of the law led finally to a repeal of the law. It was agreed that there should be an inquiry into censorship. The Lord Chamberlain hoped that films and television broadcasting might be included in the inquiry, as he was keen that his role might be taken by a board similar to the BBFC.[92] The

[89] J Lahr (ed), *The Orton Diaries* (London, Methuen, 1986) 250.
[90] ibid 252.
[91] Thomas, Carlton and Etienne (n 60) 189.
[92] ibid 191.

Lord Chamberlain's office was trying to align itself more with the decisions that the BBFC was taking[93] but that was possibly because of the inconsistencies of some productions being cut for the stage whilst radio, film or television productions ran uncut. It was impossible for the Lord Chamberlain to license plays which were against the law and meant that theatre performances were under greater restrictions than any other medium.

The practice of censoring one medium strictly but not others, began to make the regulation of the stage appear ridiculous. Much like today, with the variations between regulation of audio-visual media content on the internet and on broadcast media, the arrival of film and television had made theatre regulation seem heavy handed and archaic. Debates in the House of Lords referred to the censorship exercised by the Lord Chamberlain as producing 'anomalies and embarrassments'.[94] Plays which had been banned by the Lord Chamberlain could be filmed and shown in cinemas or on television. Sketches mocking living people and improvisation were performed on television regularly but not strictly permitted in the theatre. Any deviation from a pre-approved script in a licensed play could be punishable in law.[95] The Joint Committee on the Censorship of the Theatre set up in 1966 proved to be more successful in finally overturning the power of the Lord Chamberlain.

Whilst the Joint Committee concluded that the Theatres Act 1843 should be abolished, it wanted to ensure some level of audience protection by amending various Acts to include stage plays, these included the Public Order Act, Race Relations Act and Obscene Publications Act.[96] Not everyone was in favour of a sweeping abolition of the Theatres Act and unsurprisingly this included politicians who did not want to be the subject of plays. This very issue reflected Walpole's driving force to establish the Stage Licensing Act 1737 in the first place, to ban the depiction of living persons on stage. The Act protected those in power against theatrical performances which might satirise or ridicule them.

The Prime Minister, Harold Wilson, was one of those politicians not keen for playwrights to portray living people on the stage. Like the Crown and other politicians before him, he believed the theatrical productions could be unpredictable and dangerous.[97] Wilson was sensitive to parody and had discussed his concern of politicians being satirised with Lord Hill, the new Chairman of the BBC.[98] Unfortunately for Wilson, he and his wife were to be the target of a new satirical play.

[93] Nicholson (n 48) 179.

[94] Lord Annan, *Hansard* HL Vol 272, col 1151 (17 February 1966).

[95] The innovative Theatre producer Joan Littlewood had been twice fined for allowing improvisation on stage.

[96] Johnson (n 47) 233.

[97] de Jongh (n 36) 3.

[98] ibid 13.

In 1967 the script for *Mrs. Wilson's Diary* was sent to several public figures, all of whom appeared as characters within it. The play was written by Richard Ingrams and John Wells, and it had been initially published as a *Private Eye* column. Two years previously a book of the same name had been withdrawn following 'friendly conversations' between Mrs. Wilson's solicitors and the publishers.[99] According to *The Times* the complaint was about transparency of the book's authorship and not the content. Rather than making the authorship clearer, the book had been shelved but this play was not.

The characters in the play included the Wilsons, various members of his cabinet and the Prime Minister's Security Adviser.[100] The Chief examiner, Heriot, had recommended that the play be banned. The Foreign Secretary and Mrs. Wilson requested edits to the script.[101] It was passed with 'savage cuts', 'three pages of disallowances and five of substitutions'[102] after six months of discussions with the Lord Chamberlain.[103] It was ground-breaking for the stage, given that many of the characters portrayed were living persons in positions of power.[104]

VIII. Abolition of Lord Chamberlain as Censor

Harold Wilson's concerns about living persons on the stage may have been exacerbated by those of Queen Elizabeth II. She was not keen that the royal family be depicted on stage. She discussed the subject with Lord Cobbold, the last Lord Chamberlain to act as censor.[105] Wilson had received representations from Buckingham Palace to clarify how this matter might be dealt with if there were no form of censorship. But ultimately it was concluded that there was no solution to this issue. It would be impossible to remove the Act but retain a restriction on living persons. Although Lord Cobbold did try to persuade members of Parliament to do otherwise.

Seeking to protect the 'special position of the Sovereign and the Royal Family', Lord Cobbold argued that there were parallels to be drawn between the depiction of living people on the stage and on the screen. He suggested that living persons should be afforded protection by wording as per the Television Act 1954. It should be noted that by 1964 the reference to 'any offensive representation of or reference to a living person' had been dropped from the Act. Lord Cobbold instead had to satisfy himself with referring to the ban on content

[99] '"Mrs. Wilson's Diary" Withdrawn.' *The Times*, *The Times Digital Archive* (26 November 1965) 5.
[100] A Travis, 'How Harold censored diary spoof' *The Guardian* (17 September 2000).
[101] de Jongh (n 36) 10.
[102] Johnson (n 47) 117.
[103] 'Wilson Satire Planned' *The Times*, *The Times Digital Archive* (23 June 1967) 12.
[104] I Wardle, 'Precedent set in censorship' *The Times*, *The Times Digital Archive* (22 September 1967) 7.
[105] de Jongh (n 36) 4.

> which offends against good taste or decency or is likely to encourage or incite to crime or to lead to disorder or to be offensive to public feeling.

Lord Cobbold argued, without noting the omission to living people in the new Act,

> that at least so far as representation of and reference to living people is concerned, the theatre is far more akin to television than to the written word and that it would be eminently reasonable for a similar degree of protection to be afforded in both media, stage and television. No one would wish to restrict genuine political satire, and indeed it could never be held to be offensive to public feeling. But a clause making it an offence to represent or refer to living persons and those recently dead in a way calculated to offend public feeling would bring the standard that applies on the stage into line with that for plays on television and would afford, in my judgment, much needed protection to certain categories of people.[106]

By certain categories of people, Lord Cobbold meant the British Royal Family. Of course, it is very difficult to make genuine political satire without potentially offending some members of the public. The House did not agree with him, and it was concluded that those in the public eye should have the same form of redress as the public themselves, relying on the libel laws or an injunction for protection. Plays would therefore be subject to criminal law in line with newspapers and printed literature. It was considered, 'impossible to draft an Amendment to the Bill which would protect living individuals from presentation on the stage without at the same time banning justifiable satire'.[107]

On 26 July The Theatres Act 1968 was enacted, ending centuries of the Lord Chamberlain's power to refuse to license a play and this aspect of his role became defunct.

IX. The Arbiters of Taste and Decency

Whilst the abolition of stage censorship reflected the more progressive and liberal attitudes attributed to the 1960s, there were other unofficial censors waiting in the wings. During the Debate on the Theatres Bill in the House of Lords, Lord Stow Hill[108] had pondered who could be the arbiter of taste if not the Lord Chamberlain. He need not have concerned himself, there were plenty happy to fill the Lord Chamberlain's shoes. The Court of Public Opinion is seldom adjourned.

Loudly declaring herself the voice of the 'silent majority', Mrs Mary Whitehouse stepped into the limelight.[109] Mrs Whitehouse did not limit herself to only one

[106] *Hansard*, HL Vol 292, cols 1059–1060 (28 May 1968).
[107] *Hansard*, HC Vol 759, col 831 (23 February 1968).
[108] *Hansard*, HL Vol 257, col 1326 (7 May 1964).
[109] J Prestidge, 'Housewives having a go: Margaret Thatcher, Mary Whitehouse and the appeal of the Right Wing Woman in late twentieth-century Britain' (2019) 28(2) *Women's History Review* 277.

medium, she brought complaints and court actions to plays, publications and television. She sent her first letter of complaint about programme content to the BBC in 1963.[110] Whilst broadcasting and its regulatory evolution is going to be covered in greater detail in chapter four, it is worth noting here how much it was shaking up the traditionalists in the country, epitomised by Mrs. Whitehouse. The BBC under new, liberal Director General Hugh Greene,[111] was one of her main targets. She protested vociferously about the 'blasphemy, bad language, violence and indecency' which she saw on television.[112]

An art teacher from a Shropshire School, Whitehouse was a formidable force. A search for her name in *Hansard* between 1963 and January 2019 returns 99 results. She was concerned about protecting her pupils from exposure to what she saw as inappropriate content on television.[113] She co-founded the Clean Up TV campaign coming from a

> 'Christian' perspective, troubled at how topics such as sex and sexuality had become regular subjects for teatime television.[114]

She then went on to establish the National Viewers' and Listeners' Association (NVLA) which she presided over for 30 years, campaigning for higher moral standards in programming.

Sir Hugh Greene did not suffer self-appointed campaigners such as Whitehouse gladly. In a speech delivered to the International Catholic Association for Radio and Television in 1965 Greene talked of resisting censorship which came from those who 'claim to speak for "ordinary decent people"' and considered them both 'anti-intellectual and unimaginative'. This type of censorship was considered dangerous by Greene as it caused

> artists and writers not to take risks, not to undertake those adventures of the spirit which must be at the heart of every truly new creative work.[115]

Greene believed that it was a major broadcaster's responsibility to 'cultivate young writers who may be considered "too advanced" by many, even "shocking"'.[116] This issue is still alive and well today and, as we will see, some of the writers discuss a chilling effect on shocking content that has dulled their own 'adventures of the spirit'.

[110] Briggs (n 88) 332.
[111] L Black, 'Whose finger is on the button? British Television and the politics of cultural Control' (2005) 25(4) *Historical Journal of Film, Radio and Television* 547.
[112] Staff Reporter, 'Mary Whitehouse: Moral Crusader or spoilsport?' (*BBC News Online Obituary*, 23 November 2001) news.bbc.co.uk/1/hi/uk/763998.stm.
[113] Prestidge (n 109).
[114] T O'Mally, 'The Response to Television in the UK 1947–77' in S Nicholas and T O'Malley (eds), *Moral Panics, Social Fears, and the Media: Historical Perspectives* (New York, Routledge, Taylor & Francis Group, 2013) 118.
[115] Sir Hugh Greene, *The Third Floor Front: A View of Broadcasting in the Sixties* (London, The Bodley Head, 1969) 100–101.
[116] ibid 101.

Whitehouse was not alone in her concerns about television having a negative impact on young people. By 1963 the Home Secretary had set up a Television Research Committee to 'initiate and co-ordinate research into the influence of television and the other media on the attitudes, values and behaviour of young people.'[117] The third working paper published in 1976 carried out research on 'the television viewing habits of certain categories of delinquent' but could draw no substantive conclusion that television caused delinquency, arguing that if that were the case then everyone who watched television would become delinquent.[118]

The social satire *Till Death Do Us Part* was a particular irritant to Whitehouse. In 1967 she was so incensed by an episode entitled *Sex Before Marriage*, that she sent a telegram to the then Prime Minister Harold Wilson. After the telegram was published in the newspapers, the viewing figures for the show were boosted from 8.5 million viewers to 16.3 million, this was unlikely to be the desired outcome.[119] It does indicate that, much like the conclusion that the Lord Chanceller drew after the publication of *Lady Chatterley's Lover*, not all audience members wish to be protected from the outrageous and the shocking, some actively seek it out.

In the same year Whitehouse and the NVLA brought a successful libel action against the BBC and *Till Death Us Do Part* writer Johnny Speight. In a BBC radio interview Speight had referred to Whitehouse and NVLA members as fascists 'hypocritically concealing their fascism under the cloak of a moral campaign'.[120] Whitehouse also took out a successful private prosecution against the editor of Gay News Magazine for blasphemous libel.[121] The magazine had published a poem and illustration depicting Christ as a homosexual and sexual acts being performed on his body following his death. The words of the poem were not read out during the trial, but two other publications reproduced the poem.[122,123] Whitehouse did not pursue these other publications in the courts.

Whitehouse took another private prosecution out against National Theatre Director Michael Bogdanov over the staging of *The Romans in Britain* for a scene in which three Roman soldiers rape three male Britons. Whitehouse had not seen the play, so it is impossible to judge how she might have found it to be obscene. The Theatres Act 1968, section 8 had stipulated proceedings against a play for obscenity, incitement to hatred, breach of the peace, or defamation during its

[117] JD Halloran, RL Brown and DC Chaney, *Television and Delinquency* (Leicester, Leicester University Press, 1976) 7.

[118] ibid 179. In interview Lord Grade recalled how he had raised a similar argument during a public debate with Mary Whitehouse.

[119] Briggs (n 88) 529.

[120] 'Damages for radio statement' *The Guardian* (28 July 1967) p.4.

[121] *Whitehouse v Gay News and Lemon* [1979] AC 617; [1979] 2 WLR 281; [1979] 1 All ER 898.

[122] LJ Moran, 'Dangerous Words and Dead Letters: Encounters with Law and The Love that Dares to Speak its Name' (2001) 23(2) *Liverpool Law Review* 153.

[123] 'Profane poem is republished in newspapers' *The Times* Issue 60055 (14 July 1977) p 4.

performance could not be brought without the consent of the Attorney General and the Attorney General did not consent to Whitehouse.[124] Whitehouse then took Bogdanov to court for procuring an act of gross indecency under the Sexual Offences Act 1956. It was the first time a law relating to criminal action in real life was applied to a dramatic representation in a theatre production.

Surprisingly the judge, Mr Justice Staughton, made three rulings:

- the Sexual Offences Act could be applied to events on the stage
- a simulated sexual act could still amount to gross indecency
- the motive of 'sexual gratification' did not have to be proved for the offence to stand.[125]

It was reported that following this Whitehouse withdrew her action but in a letter to *The Times*, Whitehouse insists that it was the Attorney General who made the decision that the case be withdrawn.[126] Whilst most of Whitehouse's costs of £20,000 were paid by an anonymous donor, the subsidies for the National Theatre were cut.[127] The ruling did not lead to the scene being censored but there was a belief that Sir Horace Cutler, leader of the Greater London Council, who had walked out of the play, subsequently cut subsidies to the theatre's annual grant.[128] If this is the reason, then it is another way in which indirect censorship leads to a chilling effect on the type of productions which might be written, or that theatres would consider staging. If theatre companies are concerned about a cut in subsidies they might be deterred from producing content which will offend, shock or disturb. More gaps in creative content are caused.

X. Conclusion

Often the population can be more progressive than those rules which restrict innovative and challenging creative content. These rules cause censorship by omission. Regulation trails both progressive audiences and advances in technology. The regulation of the printing press was based upon that established for manuscripts. Laws on treason were extended to control the press by including 'words in writing', and at an early stage the Church's ability to control the publication of religious writings was extended to capture pre-publication approval for all books. This need for pre-publication approval spread to performance in the

[124] A Travis, *Bound and Gagged: A Secret History of Obscenity in Britain* (London, Profile Books, 2000) 267.

[125] '1982: Judge halts "obscenity" trial' (BBC online, n.d.) news.bbc.co.uk/onthisday/hi/dates/stories/march/18/newsid_2524000/2524269.stm.

[126] 'The Romans in Britain' Letters *The Times* Issue 61195 (30 March 1982) p 13.

[127] 'Trial Cash for Mrs Whitehouse' *The Daily Telegraph* Issue 39436 (29 March 1982) p 3.

[128] D Webb, 'Romans Won Whitehouse Nil' (The NCROPA Virtual Archive *n.d.)* www.infotextmanuscripts.org/ncropa/ncropa-free-1.pdf.

theatres. There were various ways in which those in power sought to protect their reputation and to escape scrutiny impacting on journalists, writers, playwrights and performers. It was nigh on impossible for them to produce socio-political content and take risks.

The dissemination of newspapers was restricted by a 'tax on knowledge', there were libel prosecutions where truth itself was not a defence. Those who owned newspapers had subsidies and connections with Government and so were less likely to challenge those in power. Whilst the press was freed from Government influences in 1855, the theatre had to wait over a century longer for restrictions to be lifted and for playwrights to be able to create content that could mock those in powerful positions or introduce unorthodox characters and storylines.

Again, with the arrival of the cinema, regulations were based on those in the theatre and the Lord Chancellor's examiner of plays moved from the theatre to run the BBFC. Broadcasting too fell foul to rules deemed restrictive in the theatre, which meant that satires could not be made on the commercial channels without interference from Government in the form of the Television Act 1954. Broadcasts, like books and plays before them, had to go through a process where they were approved before being transmitted. Themes which were progressive and could have benefitted society and social cohesion were restricted on the stage. Political events were censored; this had a negative effect on the free flow of information and radical ideas impacting democratic debate and engagement.

Protection of the audience was not always the reason for censoring content, as has been shown protection of the powerful played an important part. There was always someone, somewhere, put in place by the Government, deciding on what was appropriate for the British audience. Outside the Government was Mary Whitehouse whose focus was mainly on broadcasting, and chapter four now considers the legal regulation of broadcasting content and how politicians react to media scrutiny.

4

Politicians as Entertainment and Entertainers

Those in favour of televising the House will only get sufficient support for this if we make clear that control of television will be firmly in our hands.[1]

I. Introduction

There is an uneasy relationship between the media and those in power. They feed off each other; it is like a toxic relationship. Politicians want media coverage but not coverage of their idiotic or hypocritical behaviour. They do not want to be challenged or ridiculed by the media; this would undermine their power. This conundrum that politicians face is perfectly illustrated by the British situation comedy *The Thick of It*. This BBC satire is set in a fictitious Government department and revolves around the concept that politicians waste time desperate to get media attention for their campaigns whilst simultaneously firefighting the media to ensure they are not made to look ridiculous. The politicians and their advisers spend so much energy worrying about media attention that they never actually achieve anything of any worth.[2]

Before the arrival of television, politicians generally enjoyed a much cosier relationship with the media, after all, in general newspapers had been under the control of their peers, and possibly friends. Now politicians' relationship with radio and public service television has become increasingly fraught. As this chapter goes through the birth of broadcasting, we will also look at the broadcasting of Parliament. The endless debates about allowing cameras into the House, and the arguments against it, meant this process took several decades and the British Parliament was one of the last in Europe to allow cameras into the debating chambers.[3] The chapter will also examine the role of Government in regulating broadcasting and how this evolved into the rules that stand today.

The British Broadcasting Company began daily radio transmissions in 1922. Then there was no concern over due impartiality, as it was restricted by the

[1] Mr Paul Bryan (Conservative) *Hansard*, HC Vol 713, col 1119 (28 May 1965).

[2] S Fielding, *A State of Play: British Politics on Screen, Stage and Page, from Anthony Trollope to The Thick of It* (London, Bloomsbury, 2014).

[3] B Franklin, *Televising Democracies* (London, Routledge, 1992) 5.

Government from exercising editorial control over its own news output. Unless the Post Master General (a politician) granted special permission, the BBC could only broadcast news which had already appeared in print.[4] This was because of concerns that broadcast news would be in direct competition with traditional newspapers and would impact the Post Office's income from both newspapers and news agencies. Newspapers were free to editorialise and be as partial as their editor wished, just as they are now.

The Government sought changes to this new media and the following year the Sykes Broadcasting Committee concluded the company should become a corporation, funded by a licence fee, the British Broadcasting Corporation (BBC). A draft from the committee's working paper considered if the BBC should be under a Government Department or under a licence, and to what extent it should be censored.[5]

The BBC's Royal Charter was established in 1927, and this is still renewable every ten years by the Government. The Charter was intended to give the BBC greater legal autonomy, separating it from Government and symbolising its political independence.[6] The Post Master-General thought the Charter would make the public less likely to think the BBC 'a creature of Parliament and connected with political activity'.[7] One might conclude from this that the appearance of independence was more important than guaranteeing actual independence. Its political independence seems likely to be more in principle rather than in practice because the Charter comes up for renewal around every ten years, and the Government must agree to renew it, and controls the BBC's income by setting the licence fee. If the BBC is too negative in its coverage of Government policy, the Government could refuse to renew the charter or to restrict its income, or as happened in the past, require the BBC to fund free licence fees for older people and by doing so, slash its income for programme making.[8]

In 1928 the Prime Minister allowed the BBC to start broadcasting 'political, religious or industrial controversy' but editorial pronouncements were still banned.[9] In itself this was a form of impartiality set through the Charter. This striving for impartiality is believed by some practitioners to have a detrimental effect on certain genres of programming, especially news and socio-political entertainment.

The potential of broadcasting to inform and possibly influence its audience, and that the Government could control it through the Charter, did not go unnoticed.

[4] A Briggs, *The History of Broadcasting in the United Kingdom Volume 1: The Birth of Broadcasting* (Oxford, Oxford University Press, 1961) 96–97.

[5] ibid 10.

[6] T Gibbons, *Media Law in the United Kingdom* (Alphen aan den Rijn, Kluwer Law International, 2012) 82.

[7] Briggs (n 4) 353.

[8] J Woodhouse, 'TV licences for the over-75s', House of Commons Library, research briefing (21 October 2024) commonslibrary.parliament.uk/research-briefings/sn04955/.

[9] *Hansard*, HC Vol 214, cols 811-2 (5 March 1928).

Sir Arthur Willert, both a journalist and a diplomat who held the position of Head of the Ministry of Information, wrote in 1939 that radio was an

> immensely important instrument for the formation of opinion [...] The B.B.C. functions under a parliamentary charter which gives the Government considerable authority over it. The Postmaster-General can require the Corporation to refrain from sending any broadcast matter[.][10]

That control which the Government had over the corporation was put into force in the lead up to World War II. Censorship decisions were made 'in liaison' with the Press Division of the Ministry of Information and was 'indirect, informal, and voluntary'.[11] Television broadcasts ceased two days before the war, and services reduced to avoid radio signals and weather forecasts helping enemy aircraft. The National Union of Journalists accused Whitehall of having 'the censorship mind',[12] so it is questionable how indirect, informal and voluntary wartime censorship truly was. As seen in chapter three, cinematic films too were 'vetoed for political reasons [...] the "Government propaganda organization" has been exercising something tantamount to a political censorship over the cinema'.[13]

After the war there was a push from advertisers to open television to commercial providers. The Labour Party was concerned about commercial television and its influence on young minds, but the BBC's monopoly was also seen as a potential threat to Government authority. A 1949 broadcasting committee report considered television to be

> the most persuasive, and therefore one of the most powerful of agents for influencing men's thoughts and actions, for giving them a picture, true or false, of their fellows and of the world in which they live.[14]

Some parliamentarians were concerned that the BBC might become an 'uncontrolled bureaucracy' given it was not under 'full parliamentary control'.[15] This was not true as the Postmaster General had the power both to censor programmes and to prevent the BBC from publicising that any censorship had occurred.[16] In addition the Government could appoint and dismiss the BBC Governors, the board which oversaw editorial policy and complaints, and, of course, had financial control through setting the licence revenue the BBC received annually. There was also less formal control; most of the BBC's chairmen have been from the same political party as the Government which appointed them, giving them additional backroom power over editorial decisions. This all makes the BBC's objective

[10] Sir A Willert, 'British News Controls: Foreign Affairs' (1939) 17(4) *Council on Foreign Relations* 712.

[11] A Briggs, *The History of Broadcasting in the United Kingdom Vol II, The Golden Age of Wireless* (Oxford, Oxford University Press, 1965) 650.

[12] Willert (n 10).

[13] ibid.

[14] Report of the Broadcasting Committee 1949 (His Majesty's Stationery Office, 1951) 163.

[15] R Nottage, 'Report of the Broadcasting Committee 1949: Some of its Administrative Aspects' (1951) 29(2) *Public Administration* 173.

[16] Report of the Broadcasting Committee 1949 (n 14) 7.

of political impartiality seem impossible. In the 1950 general election the BBC excelled itself in its impartiality by not making any reference to the election whatsoever until the polls had closed.[17]

With the arrival of commercial channels came further regulation and a new regulatory body. The Television Act 1954 led to the creation of the Independent Television Authority (ITA). Whilst the BBC was mainly self-regulating, the commercial channels were to be regulated by the ITA. It had strict rules for programming, and much like Ofcom today, laid down quotas for news, children's programming, educational and religious programmes. Unlike Ofcom today, it also had the authority to check and ban programming pre-transmission. A synopsis of every programme, episode and serial had to be submitted to the ITA pre-transmission.[18] The ITA was like the Lord Chamberlain's office, prechecking content before allowing (or not) the audience to see it. News was to be presented 'with due accuracy and impartiality'. Like the BBC Charter, and the Ofcom Code today, it stipulated that due impartiality had to be preserved on subjects which concerned 'matters of political or industrial controversy or relating to current public policy'.[19] Commentators at the time found some of the Act problematic. One queried the idea that news need only be presented with 'due' accuracy, asking 'What degree of inaccuracy is permissible before it becomes "undue"?'[20]

The Act imposed certain additional obligations upon the ITA, which included ensuring a programme would not offend against taste or decency or contain offensive representations of living people. Parts of the Act appear similar to the Lord Chamberlain's rules, whilst some – such as proscribing content which might cause incitement to violence – are in the public interest, the issues of offensiveness are subjective. This included a ban on offensive references or representations of living people, which protects those in the public eye, including politicians.

Seeing the success of the political satire revolution on the stage, television producers also wanted to put on their own satirical programming. As with the early attempts of performing satirical content on the stage, television too ran into issues with the regulators. When ITV launched their satirical show *What the Public Wants* in October 1962, it was short-lived. This was because, unlike the BBC, the Independent Television (ITV) channels were statutorily obliged to comply with the Television Act 1954, and this stated:

> (a) that nothing is included in the programmes which offends against good taste or decency [...] or to be offensive to public feeling or which contains any offensive representation of, or reference to, a living person;

[17] M Cockerell, *Live from Number 10* (London, Faber and Faber, 1988) 9.

[18] J Potter, *Independent Television in Britain Volume 3 Politics and Control, 1968-1980* (London, MacMillan Press, 1989) 104.

[19] The Television Act 1954, s 3.

[20] D Lloyd, 'Some Comments on the British Television Act, 1954' (1958) 23(1) *Law & Contemp Probs* 165.

The Television Act worked in much the same way for ITV political entertainment as the Theatres Act worked for the stage.[21] It protected those in power from ridicule, ensuring that commercial television satire could have no real bite. Production teams would have to submit a programme synopsis to the Independent Television Authority (ITA) rather than a script to the Lord Chamberlain but 'Self-censorship was practised by writers, directors and producers', although the ITA rarely viewed the full programmes.[22] The ITA was created to supervise commercial television, and writers described how political and sexual content was censored, and a cast member said that they 'were scarcely allowed to mention anyone in public life who was actually alive'.[23] Clearly this is a major stumbling block when attempting to write a satirical show. According to a report in the *Sunday Telegraph*, Granada TV also piloted a satire but concluded that 'it couldn't get away with it in terms of the Act'.[24] Therefore, once more the law created a gap in satirical output and those in power were able to escape satirical scrutiny.

It was in this satirical space that the BBC had a major advantage over its commercial rivals. It was not governed by the Television Act 1954, it only had to comply with the BBC Charter and its own editorial policy. The BBC was self-regulating and created its own editorial policy – originally compiled from a series of memos. These memos then formed the 1948 *BBC Variety Programmes Policy Guide For Writers and Producers*,[25] known as *The Green Book*. This laid down guidance for writers and producers of light entertainment programmes, these were programmes which contained songs, jokes or sketches. The book was a guide to the handling of taboo subjects and language deemed inappropriate to broadcast on the BBC. It stated that programme makers must, 'keep programmes free from vulgarity, political bias, and matter in questionable taste'.[26] The guide covered 17 areas, many which are relevant in terms of the history of the rules, including those which evolved into 'Harm and Offence' and 'Impartiality'.

A general section of *The Green Book* prompted programme makers to consider their diverse audience. It reminded producers that programmes should be entertaining without 'giving reasonable offence'.

There was an absolute ban on jokes about:

- Lavatories
- Effeminacy in men
- Immorality of any kind

[21] Report of the 1909 Joint Select Committee on Stage Plays (Censorship) Q897 licence for a play could be restricted if it represented 'on the stage in an invidious manner a living person, or any person recently dead'.

[22] Potter (n 18) 104.

[23] H Carpenter, *That Was Satire That Was: The Satire Boom of the 1960s* (London, Victor Gollanez, 2000) 227.

[24] ibid.

[25] *BBC Variety Programmes Policy Guide for Writers and Producers* (1949) 2 www.g4dmp.co.uk/bbc-guide.pdf.

[26] ibid.

Suggestive references to:

- Honeymoon couples
- Chambermaids
- Fig leaves
- Prostitution
- Ladies' underwear, eg winter draws on
- Animal habits, eg rabbits
- Lodgers
- Commercial travellers[27]

Taste should be measured by what would 'be accepted by most rational people', which is the same concept of Ofcom's 'generally accepted standards' today. The guide also specified that producers had to refer to management regarding any impersonations of leading public and political figures (which were actively discouraged but not forbidden) and gain the consent of those figures before transmitting any derogatory impersonations of them. One might assume particularly derogatory impersonations would not get any consent. The guidance advised producers to avoid impersonations of those who had 'died within living memory or whose relations may still be alive', which effectively rules out most people.

Regarding political references, there is the first indication that editorial decisions could be taken on a case-by-case basis with 'humour' being a key factor. The policy guide quotes directly from a BBC directive:

> We therefore reserve the right for Variety programmes in moderation to take a crack at the Government of the day and the Opposition so long as they do so sensibly, without undue acidity, and above all funnily.[28]

'In moderation' and 'funnily' are open to interpretation, yet as the interviews will show later in the book, funny is still an element which will drive more contentious comedy to air today.

All swearing, including religious words, was banned for light entertainment programming. Even at this time the BBC highlighted to producers the importance of considering cultural differences, reminding them that other countries had different social, political and religious taboos which may make certain comedy unacceptable. Much of this guidance is still reflected to some degree in the current BBC and Ofcom codes and guidance.

It was under these rules that the BBC first transmitted *That Was The Week That Was* (*TW3*) in November 1962. Unusually for an entertainment programme,

[27] ibid.
[28] ibid 11.

it was not produced under the Light Entertainment programming team but by Television Talks and Current Affairs which gave it greater freedom.[29] The editorial team took their lead from satirical stage productions such as *Beyond the Fringe* and began to challenge the traditional way politicians had been presented on television, ridiculing the ruling classes. Many of the writers and performers claimed to have no political allegiance. *The Goon Show* written by and starring the anarchic Spike Milligan was very influential at the time, and scornful of authority figures. Wagg argues that such comedy illustrated a huge shift in societal values, moving decision making away from the party political and towards the individual.[30] This may have had the effect of turning the viewers away from parliamentary politics. *TW3* also impacted the BBC as it was 'to rock the BBC and raise, abrasively, the relationship between the BBC and the leaders of the political parties'.[31]

The reasons that the BBC could produce such a radically different programme was not only because it sat outside the oversight of the Television Act but also because there was a change in the BBC's senior management. The liberally minded Hugh Carlton Greene became Director General at the end of 1959. He was a fan of political satire and gave *TW3* his patronage.[32] With the backing of such a powerful patron *TW3* would have felt able to push harder at the boundaries.

The show only ran for 37 episodes, from 24 November 1962 to December 1963. Whilst ground-breaking, *TW3* was problematic from the outset because it polarised the audience.[33] At its peak, the programme attracted twelve million viewers, and generated hundreds of letters of complaints because it targeted the powerful and challenged the orthodox view that such people should be treated with respect. It shocked some of the Governors and the public because of its biting satirical nature and was constantly on the Governors' agenda.[34] On the other hand, it also was ground-breaking by highlighting racism as worthy of contempt and did not shy away from previously taboo themes such as homosexuality, which is another reason why it was so controversial at the time.[35] A champion for the programme came from an unexpected quarter, MacMillian liked Willie Rushton's impersonation of him. Unfortunately, some backbenchers felt differently and ensured that the BBC was aware of their dislike of the programme.[36] There were also complaints

[29] Carpenter (n 23) 212.

[30] S Wagg 'You've never had it so silly: The politics of British Satirical Comedy from Beyond the Fringe To Spitting Image' in D Strinati and S Wagg (eds), *Come On Down?: Popular media culture in post-war Britain*, 1st edn (London, Routledge, 1992) 167.

[31] G Wyndham, *Facing the Nation: Television and Politics 1936–1976* (London, Bodley Head, 1977) 220.

[32] ibid 221.

[33] S Hood and T Thabary-Peterssen, *On Television*, 6th edn (London, Pluto Press, 1997) 54.

[34] A Briggs, *The History of Broadcasting in the United Kingdom Volume V: Competition* (Oxford, Oxford University Press, 1995) 350.

[35] Wagg (n 30).

[36] ibid 360.

from those in management about lapses of taste.[37] However, the programme-makers believed that it fulfilled the requirement of 'political balance'.[38]

TW3 finished its run in 1963 and was scheduled to come back in the autumn after a careful review. The Charter was due to expire in 1964, and the Governors and Greene must have been sensitive to this. The review suggested fewer, better directed personal attacks and less 'smut'. The review also requested that nothing should be ad-libbed.[39] Later that year Greene announced that *TW3* would be taken off air due to 'political considerations' because of the General Election.[40] The Governors were becoming 'uneasy about some of the more free-spoken, politically critical, and sexually explicit programmes' and this show fell into all of those categories.[41] Whilst there are theories that Government intervention caused the removal of the show, it is possible that trying to balance the aim of the show with the BBC's obligations to maintain impartiality was one of the main considerations for its cancellation.[42,43] It was difficult for a programme to kick against the Establishment when 'an anti-Establishment programme tends to be anti-Government' and an obligation to be impartial does not allow for continual attack on one political party.[44] This is an ongoing problem with marrying political entertainment, especially political satire, with a requirement for due impartiality.

Whilst the permissive age brought about huge change in political entertainment, the greater freedoms that television had initially experienced over those of the theatre were slowly rolled back. The writers of Monty Python's Flying Circus, another hugely popular programme influenced by Spike Milligan, found themselves subject to censorship, to the point that the writer and performer Michael Palin complained that they could 'no longer surprise and shock'.[45]

II. Politicians as Entertainment

> Every Tuesday and Thursday we shall have 'The Maggie [Thatcher] and Neil [Kinnock] Show' – an everyday story of people having a bash at each other.[46]

As the power of television became obvious, Minsters were becoming keener to appear on it. Unfortunately for them, getting on air was difficult; they needed

[37] D Attenborough, *Life On Air: Memoirs of a Broadcaster* (London, BBC Books, 2002) 200.
[38] ibid 173.
[39] ibid 366.
[40] ibid 372.
[41] ibid 200.
[42] Wyndham (n 31) 231.
[43] Hood and Thabary-Peterssen (n 33) 54 and Wyndham (n 31).
[44] Wyndham (n 31) 225.
[45] M Palin, *Diaries 1969–1979: The Python Years* (London, Macmillan, 2007) 215, 222 as quoted in P Bramham and S Wagg (eds), *The New Politics of Leisure and Pleasure* (London, Palgrave Macmillan, 2010) 175.
[46] Mr Joseph Ashton (Labour), *Hansard*, HC Vol 87, col 305 (20 November 1985).

permission from both the Prime Minister and the BBC's Director of the Spoken Word. The Director had to clear appearances with Government officials, and the Director could decide who to clear. The BBC would not give MPs permission to appear in programmes if the BBC thought it would be unsuitable or undignified for them to do so. How times have changed.

Television executives held a lot of power. They could decide which politicians could speak to the nation; the politicians wanted to take back some kind of control over broadcasting their work. It was not a new idea, as early as 1926 politicians were considering broadcasting parliamentary proceedings, but it had proved a thorny issue. Yet, there were many politicians who considered that broadcasting from Parliament was preferable to allowing those with contacts in the media industry to push their own political agenda by using their 'old-boy network' to get on screen.[47] A type of Parliament TV would stop television executives being able to select speakers who fitted with their own ideology, and the argument was that this would give some control over impartiality. Two decades earlier, one MP had envisaged 'an authorised film version of [the radio programme] *Today in Parliament* which would be edited, issued and copyrighted by the House itself, very much under the control of the House'.[48] Televising the House was considered a way of taking back control of political debate from television studios and placing it firmly within the democratic heart of the United Kingdom.[49] Nye Bevan had judged it shameful that high ranking MPs were 'selected by unrepresentative persons' and considered MPs taking appearance fees from the BBC and ITV 'essentially squalid' and 'inconsistent with the dignity of a democratic procedure'. It is unlikely he would have enjoyed watching Nadine Dorries or Matt Hancock in *I'm a Celebrity Get Me Out of Here* or politicians putting in paid appearances on *Russia Today* or *GB News*.

The argument to televise Parliament did not persuade many MPs; radio broadcasts of proceedings came first. It might seem surprising that sound recording was more palatable to Members, but their reasons are clear in the debates. One MP suggested that listeners would pay more attention to what politicians said if they were on the radio, rather than 'wondering why so-and-so is showing his braces and why somebody else appears to be nodding off'.[50] There were concerns that the electorate, easily distracted by pictures, might focus on the trivial, such as ladies' ankles, rather than important political points.[51] Ten years later another male MP suggested that it might not just be the audience focusing on the trivial but also the female members of Parliament, who may be more likely to wear pretty hats for the cameras.[52] Another, recurring claim, which has been borne out, was

[47] Mr Andrew Faulds (Labour), *Hansard*, HC Vol 87, col 289 (20 November 1985).
[48] Mr Thomas Iremonger (Conservative), *Hansard*, HC Vol 713, col 1038 (28 May 1965).
[49] Mr Charles Pannell (Labour) *Hansard*, HC Vol 736, col 1638 (24 November 1966).
[50] Mr Joseph Ashton (Labour) *Hansard*, HC Vol 887, col 148–149 (24 February 1975).
[51] Mr Joseph Ashton *Hansard*, HC Vol 887, col 143 (24 February 1975).
[52] Mr John Stokes (Conservative) *Hansard*, HC Vol 87, col 301 (20 November 1985).

that Members of a more theatrical nature might try to seek out greater attention from the public by playing to the cameras and not just the gallery. There was a concern that 'some Members would tend to address listeners and viewers direct, in prepared statements of a demagogic nature, instead of debating in the traditional Parliamentary manner'.[53] An apt description of much of contemporary Prime Minister's Questions.

Worries were raised about the potential for personality cult politics, where the media built up political players, and that this personality cult politics might play well to the electorate.[54] It was deemed unfair to some that those who were more charismatic than others might use it to their electoral advantage. Again, this fear is being played out considering the rise in populism.

Whilst broadcasting proceedings might give the opportunity to play to the electorate, it could also bring opportunities for humour to prick a politician's pomposity, and the Members of Parliament were very aware of this. There was a fear that broadcasters would 'misuse' parliamentary footage.[55] There were concerns about 'editorialising and the smart-Alicking of commentators' whilst, at the same time, they claimed not to be worried about being seen 'warts and all'. One was concerned about 'some clever dick from the BBC adding joke shop warts to the ones that I already possess'.[56]

In 1976 Philip Whitehead MP, a former television producer and vociferous advocate for the televising of proceedings, argued that exhibitionism would irritate the public. He also pointed out that the precedent of televising parliaments had been set by other major democracies, none of which had experienced any 'catastrophic or comical consequences' at the hands of broadcasters.[57] Others, who also argued in favour of television, believed that a misinterpretation or adverse report would be 'a small price to pay for informing people of what is happening, if they wish to learn it'.[58] But this argument of misuse did not convince everyone. References were made to the House being satirised but that it should not be a reason to refuse the cameras.[59] In an article written in *The Sunday Times* Robert Harris concluded that 'It is the Commons which has decided that it wants protection from the prying eyes of the public. Thus is democracy … stood on its head'.[60]

A fear of ridicule was mentioned or intimated during many of the parliamentary debates. Politicians on both sides of the House were worried about their reputation. This mistrust was nothing new, as far back as 1738, Walpole, never

[53] Broadcasting, &c., of proceedings in the House of Commons Select Committee, in the minutes of evidence taken before the committee HC 146, para 51 (Her Majesty's Stationery Office, 1966).

[54] Mr Joseph Ashton (Labour) *Hansard*, HC Vol 87, col 298 (20 November 1985).

[55] Mr Jack Ashley (Labour) *Hansard*, HC Vol 15, col 166 (15 December 1981).

[56] Mr. Frank Dobson (Labour) *Hansard*, HC Vol 154, col 622 (12 June 1989).

[57] Mr. Jack Ashley (Labour) *Hansard*, HC Vol 15, cols 166-7 (15 December 1981).

[58] Miss Janet Fookes (Conservative) *Hansard*, HC Vol 87, col 282 (20 November 1985).

[59] Mr. Jack Ashley (Labour) *Hansard*, HC Vol 736, col 1706 (24 November 1966).

[60] As quoted by Mrs. Edwina Currie (Conservative) *Hansard*, HC Vol 154, col 644 (12 June 1989).

keen on his Parliament undergoing any form of scrutiny, passed a resolution claiming that the House would 'proceed with the utmost severity' against news writers who gave accounts of the House or Committee proceedings.[61] He claimed he was misrepresented by reporters, and made to look ridiculous.[62] Like Walpole, some members were concerned that their words might be twisted, and they might be satirised. This is likely due to the long history of satirical cartoons and parliamentary sketch writers that already existed. There was concern that television would be 'used by the establishment' who had the ability to 'manipulate modern media dangerously' and would do so for their own interest. However, the conclusion was that Parliament would set the terms for Parliament TV.[63]

Whilst the State Opening of Parliament was broadcast first in 1958, radio broadcasts of parliamentary proceedings did not begin until April 1978, and cameras were not permitted to televise Parliamentary proceedings until 1989. Parliament did not give approval for permanent arrangements for television broadcasting of the House of Commons until 1 May 1991. The MPs drew up tight rules of coverage to allay any reputational and party-political concerns, ensuring that the House was represented with impartiality. They stipulated specific rules about footage being used in satirical programming, as can be seen in the Parliamentary Recordings Unit Licence Agreement still used today.[64]

III. Keeping Control – Editorial Ownership

> It would be quite interesting for the public to see all sorts of things we do, but what lessons they would learn I hesitate to lay down.[65]

Losing editorial control over the material was a key argument against televising Parliament. Someone else having editorial control over the footage was 'one of the greatest dangers in the whole project. ... it is impossible to find the perfect editor who will make it absolutely right'.[66] There was concern that editing could not produce a true representation of the work of Parliament, that it might not be impartial. It is odd that there was such a concern about broadcast journalists editing, given that press journalists in the gallery already had carte blanche to select and edit members' speeches. Further, unlike broadcasters, the press had no obligation to be impartial in their reporting and therefore

[61] J Vice and S Farrell *The History of Hansard* (House of Lords Hansard and the House of Lords Library, *n.d.*) www.parliament.uk/documents/lords-library/History-of-Hansard.pdf 7.

[62] ibid.

[63] Mr Eric Heffer (Labour) *Hansard*, HC Vol 87, col 333 (20 November 1985).

[64] *Licence to use Parliamentary proceedings from the House of Commons for Broadcast* (Parliamentary Recording Unit, May 2016 Amendment) www.parliament.uk/documents/PRU/Commons%20Broadcast%20Licence%20May%202016%20with%20Annexes.pdf.

[65] Mr Harold MacMillan (Conservative) *Hansard*, HC Vol 615 col 741 (10 December 1959).

[66] Mr Neil Marten (Conservative) *Hansard*, HC Vol 843, col 576 (19 October 1972).

could be as biased as their editor wished. It was raised on several occasions that the broadcasters had to be impartial either through the charter or statutory requirements.[67]

Impartiality concerns was a somewhat contrived reason against televising Parliament. During debates members had not raised significant complaints about the way that the broadcasters reported proceedings in existing political programming. Yet it seemed important to members that there should be more restrictions on broadcasters than on the press. One of the reasons was their recurring notion of potential misrepresentation. It was considered that whilst summaries of proceedings were problematic already, television would cause 'far more difficult problems of editorial balance'.[68] Why editorial balance might be harder to achieve across television than radio, or more needed in television than in the press, was never explained. It could just be that in the 1960s especially, attitudes towards politicians were changing. Many felt the need to be protected from misrepresentation and from ridicule in the form of the rising popularity of satire.[69] The media had also covered a string of political scandals throughout the 1960s and 1970s. Politicians were being revealed as human, carnal, and flawed. They were exposed as not being worthy of the respect which their esteemed position in the political arena would usually give them. They realised this and did not wish Parliament TV to become 'a sort of alternative programme to *That Was The Week That Was* or *Steptoe and Son*, or *Coronation Street*'.[70]

As the debate ran into the 1980s, a new ITV comedy programme was broadcast, mercilessly satirising politicians. *Spitting Image* was a puppet show and caricatures of politicians routinely ridiculed their real-life counterparts. It hit a nerve with some and was used to illustrate how television might insult the reputation of Members to attract viewers, with politicians ultimately ending up as the 'nation's clowns'.[71]

Although not all politicians were concerned by their portrayal in *Spitting Image*; as a junior minister, Edwina Currie was pleased with the exposure. Currie suggested the then Prime Minister Margaret Thatcher so liked her masculine image as portrayed on the programme, she began to behave more like her puppet in terms of voice and clothing.[72] The MP Tony Benn also referenced *Spitting Image* when the rules of coverage were being finalised. He felt Members should be able to handle the criticism satire might bring, 'We cannot stand on our dignity if people

[67] See eg *Hansard*, HC Vol 791, col 1694 (21 November 1969) and *Hansard*, HC Vol 87, cols 298–299 (20 November 1985).

[68] Mr. Edward Short (Labour) *Hansard*, HC Vol 887, cols 51–52 (24 February 1975).

[69] Lord Rea (Liberal) *Hansard*, HL Vol 275, col 72 (15 June 1966).

[70] Mr Herbert Bowden (Labour) *Hansard*, HC Vol 673, col 1749 (15 March 1963).

[71] Mr Joe Ashton (Labour) *Hansard*, HC Vol 87, col 305 (20 November 1985).

[72] E Addley, '"Thatcher loved it": Spitting Image victims on being lampooned' *The Guardian* (28 September 2019) www.theguardian.com/tv-and-radio/2019/sep/28/spitting-image-victims-on-being-lampooned-livingstone-currie-kinnock.

want to see our proceedings and nothing could be more amusing or damaging than "Spitting Image" is'.[73]

This was not to be, the Committee decided satire should be off limits when allowing broadcasters use of parliamentary footage. To this end they wrote a restriction of use into the footage licensing agreement. This still stipulates that '6 (a) no extracts of Parliamentary proceedings may be used in any light entertainment programme or in a programme of political satire'.[74]

To ensure that the rules were followed by broadcasters, a Supervisor of Broadcasting was appointed by Parliament to 'protect the interests both of the House generally and of individual members'.[75] Additionally a director was to 'have regard to the dignity of the House and to its function as a working body rather than a place of entertainment'.[76] MPs were media trained by the Commons TV Unit.[77] One assumes the training was to give them the wherewithal to protect their dignity from potential media shenanigans.

It is claimed that The Select Committee on Televising of Proceedings of the House first introduced rules of coverage in 1989.[78] This is not strictly correct, one can see the way in which the rules, especially those on impartiality and re-use of material for satire and light entertainment, were drawn from the various Select Committees which discussed the sound recording of proceedings during the 1960s.

During April and May 1968 MPs had permitted a closed-circuit radio experiment which came to nothing. This experiment was revived nine years later but rather than closed-circuit, it was broadcast to the public, leading to radio broadcasting on a permanent basis. During the public experiment, an incident occurred in a Granada Television drama, *The Nearly Man*. The play was about a fictional Labour MP. The producers used a snippet of recorded parliamentary proceedings during the programme and on hearing it the fictional MP remarked, 'We are not exactly *Hancock's Half-Hour*, are we?'.[79] This is both a slight on the engaging quality of parliamentary debate and on the agreement between parliamentarians and the broadcasters that they would not use parliamentary recordings in entertainment programming. This caused outrage in the House as they considered boundaries agreed with broadcasters had been breached, 'twisted and used in some kind of gimmick'.[80]

[73] Mr Tony Benn (Labour) *Hansard*, HC Vol 176 col 1263 (19 July 1990).

[74] *Licence to use Parliamentary proceedings from the House of Commons for Broadcast*, An amendment from May 2016 covers internet usage too.

[75] Franklin (n 3) xiv.

[76] Parliamentary Proceedings Licence (n 74).

[77] Austen Mitchell MP (Labour) in Franklin (n 3) 88.

[78] *House of Commons Broadcasting Committee The Rules of Coverage First Report of Session 2002–03* HC 786 published on authority of the House of Commons London (The Stationery Office Limited, 18 June 2003).

[79] Mr Phillip Whitehead (Labour) *Hansard*, HC Vol 907, col 151 (8 March 1976).

[80] Mr Bernard Floud (Labour) in *Broadcasting, &c., of proceedings in the House of Commons Select Committee*, in the minutes of evidence taken before the committee HC 146, para 246.

After transmission of *The Nearly Man*, the MP Phillip Whitehead explained to the House that the BBC and the IBA had assured him that extracts of parliamentary proceedings would be restricted to news, current affairs and educational programmes. The broadcasters did not want to agree to this, with the broadcaster ITN stating that they intended to use recordings outside these restrictions. It took quite a lot to persuade ITN that it would be ill-advised to do so.[81]

One wonders what techniques were used to persuade ITN that its actions were ill advised or unwise. Might it have been reminding broadcasters that without co-operation from politicians, political journalism cannot exist?[82] Broadcasters knew they had to keep politicians on side for them to agree to appear in their television interviews, but such interventions would cause a chilling effect.

To ensure that there should not be a recurrence of *The Nearly Man* incident, a Resolution of the House was passed before the radio broadcasting of proceedings was made permanent. This stipulated that no footage could be used 'in light entertainment programmes or programmes designed as political satire'.[83] Even after this resolution MPs' concerns regarding proceedings being used outside news and current affairs programming were still mooted as arguments against televising the House. In the light of these concerns, it appears surprising that radio broadcasts were approved as early as the 1970s.

Not all MPs wanted the electorate to observe them at work. It appeared not so much a concern about what they were saying but rather what the public might see (or not see if the MP was not present in the chamber). This was somewhat more serious than arguments of distraction by female MPs' ankles and their concern for hats. One MP, who was also a member of the General Advisory Council of the Independent Broadcast Authority, the regulator at the time for commercial television, addressed the 'genuine anxiety' of some members about televising the house. He believed that this was based on the fear 'that television does something more than merely record events. It can shape them as well'.[84] Television might shape them in the form of MPs being voted out if constituents did not feel their representative was representing them with their presence in the Chamber, but rather beavering away at a second job. However, in a democracy this transparency should be a tool to help inform the electorate. This may be one of the reasons that the unelected House of Lords was more eager to open their doors to cameras, they did not have to concern themselves with voters.[85]

Part of these fears were how the electorate might misconstrue the behaviour of their representatives in Parliament. Some Members liked to put their feet up on the benches or 'loll' about, it was deemed part of the character of parliamentary behaviour, and members felt that this character of the House would

[81] Mr Robert Cooke (Conservative) *Hansard*, HC Vol 907, col 1183 (16 March 1976).
[82] Franklin (n 3) 18.
[83] *Hansard*, HC Vol 936, col 539 (26 July 1977).
[84] Sir Geoffrey Johnson-Smith (Conservative) *Hansard*, HC Vol 887, col 106 (24 February 1975).
[85] *Hansard*, HL Vol 275, col 94 (15 June 1966).

change if they had to sit up straight and pay attention,[86] like ordinary people at work.

Such parliamentary behaviour included MPs sometimes laying their heads back and closing their eyes better to hear the debates through speakers in the head rests of the benches, but viewers might think them asleep. Of course, they argued, they might actually be sleeping on the benches because they had been up all night working or debating on behalf of their constituents. Or they might just have fallen asleep or be away from the chamber.[87] Or maybe they were in the British Virgin Islands or working as a broadcaster.[88] Without the television cameras we would not be treated to seeing MPs such as Jacob Rees Mogg lying on the benches and enjoying all the memes that his conduct inspired.[89]

Radio listeners cannot see if Honourable Members are snoozing on the benches. It was thought best to steer the directors away from such shots.

> There would be certain basic rules, such as that Members who were asleep would not be included in the picture. … There must be a degree of editorial control, otherwise Parliament could be brought into disrespect.[90]

If the cameras are filming members asleep during debates surely it is sleeping members bringing Parliament into disrespect? Whilst this was never formulised within the Select Committee's Rules of Coverage, an Assistant Editor of ITN recalled a Memorandum from 11 December 1984 stating, 'it would be unwise to use shots of peers asleep' during the televising of the Lords.[91] However one Member concluded that, 'When they are asleep, it should be explained that they are asleep, or they should go and sleep somewhere else'.[92]

There were concerns that the empty benches might make the electorate think their MPs were lazy, not understanding that they might be away working on select committees.[93] It may be for this reason that under the rules of coverage panning shots along the benches 'should not normally be used'.[94] It was suggested that before any television experiment would take place broadcasters should be told that this was 'to educate and to inform, not to provide entertainment or titillation or to ridicule.'[95]

[86] Mr. Herbert Bowden (Labour) *Hansard*, HC Vol 713, col 1072 (28 May 1965).
[87] See eg Mr Edward Heath (Conservative) *Hansard*, HC Vol 87, col 289 (20 November 1985).
[88] R Mason, D Sabbagh, H Stewart, A Allegretti and P Walker, 'Geoffrey Cox accrued at least £6m from second job while a parliamentarian' *The Guardian* (10 November 2021) www.theguardian.com/politics/2021/nov/10/geoffrey-cox-accrued-at-least-6m-from-second-job-while-a-parliamentarian. Whilst writing this book Reform UK MPs Nigel Farage and Lee Anderson present programmes on GB News.
[89] See Jack Peat 'Jacob Rees-Mogg gets meme treatment after Commons lie-down goes viral' (*The London Economic*, 4 September 2019) www.thelondoneconomic.com/politics/jacob-rees-mogg-gets-meme-treatment-after-commons-lie-down-goes-viral-159034/.
[90] Mr George Reid (SNP) *Hansard*, HC Vol 887, col 129 (24 February 1975).
[91] Glyn Mathias 'Putting the House on Television' in Franklin (n 3) 42.
[92] Mr. Edward Heath (Conservative) *Hansard*, HC Vol 87, col 289 (20 November 1985).
[93] Mr William Price (Labour) *Hansard*, HC Vol 887, col 163 (24 February 1975).
[94] *Parliamentary Recording Unit Rules of Coverage* (June 2003) Annex 1 {note}.
[95] Mr Willie Hamilton (Labour) *Hansard*, HC Vol 87, col 337 (20 November 1985).

It was proposed that there should be some kind of 'parliamentary television unit' which would be staffed by broadcasting professionals 'whose loyalty was to the House, who were officials of the House and under the control of the House.' According to the member, this would not be censorship as the material would have to be edited, however the editor would have to be one 'whose loyalty was to transmitting faithfully to the public what went on in the debate.'[96]

Two years later it was suggested that the Select Committee should have ultimate control over any broadcast output with broadcasters requesting permission to use the content before any transmission and in cases of repeat or re-use in a context which differed from the original output.[97] It was acknowledged that there were limitations already on using recordings of proceedings in political satire, and further suggested that '[I]f a programme of political satire is to be constructed, reference must be made to the Select Committee to ascertain whether permission will be given.'[98] Given the resolution of the house in 1977[99] that no content could be used in light entertainment or satirical programming it seems highly unlikely that the Select Committee would give permission. Additionally political satire is very much of the moment, and the Committee might be somewhat tardy in offering approval until that moment had passed.

The journalist and broadcaster Bernard Levin, an influential member of the popular satirical programme *That Was The Week That Was*, wrote that Parliament was attempting to control broadcasting to make themselves appear 'like plaster saints.' Plaster saints or not, many Members wanted to ensure that they had control over how the footage of them would be used and wished to be seen in a favourable light.

The experimental broadcasting of Parliamentary Proceedings finally made it to air on 21 November 1989, 30 years after Gaitskell originally suggested setting up a select committee on the televising of Parliament in 1959. In July 1990, following the success of the experiment, the House agreed to make it permanent on condition that the broadcasters follow the rules of coverage as laid down by the Select Committee.

IV. Rules of Coverage

> The person whom television appeared to affect most in the early stages was the Prime Minister. For the first three months she was almost unrecognisable to my hon. friends and me. She stopped sneering and started smiling at us. She looked up and appeared to enjoy life for a change. Thankfully, she has reverted to type and the snarls have returned. I am glad that television is consistently showing people as they are.[100]

[96] Mr. Alex Lyon (Labour) *Hansard*, HC Vol 843, col 557 (19 October 1972).

[97] Mr Wyn Roberts (Conservative) *Hansard*, HC Vol 943, col 1105 (6 February 1978).

[98] Mr David Crouch (Conservative) *Hansard*, HC Vol 943, col 1135 (6 February 1978).

[99] See eg *Hansard*, HC Vol 791, col 1694 (21 November 1969) and *Hansard*, HC Vol 87, cols 298–299 (20 November 1985).

[100] Mr Bruce Grocott (Labour) talking about Margaret Thatcher *Hansard*, HC Vol 176, col 1234 (19 July 1990).

The Select Committee of 1989 decided the rules of coverage, these were based on those for sound broadcasting established over ten years earlier.[101] Objectives included that the 'dignity of the House was to be protected at all times.'[102] This is a broad objective, open to subjective interpretation. The Select Committee, with the Leader of the House of Commons as chair, concluded that the House would have the final say in matters regarding televising, giving Members that all important editorial control over the output. Now, as then, a select committee and a supervisor of broadcasting (now renamed as Director of Parliamentary Audio/Video) enforce the rules of coverage. The Speaker owns the copyright on behalf of the House, under Chapter X of Part I of the Copyright, Designs and Patents Act.[103] The Speaker grants a sub-licence to broadcasters subject to compliance with the terms of the Licence to use Parliamentary proceedings for Broadcast. Part of the terms of licence are that the licensee complies with the rules of coverage.

When the rules of coverage were published in May 1989 Parliament was accused of censorship.[104] *The Guardian* argued that Opposition Members who sat on the Select Committee 'should hang their heads in shame' as, having previously been defenders of freedom of speech, they should not have agreed to the rules of coverage.[105] Channel Four so objected to the rules of coverage that its original plans for broadcasting footage live from the chamber were dropped.[106]

Following on from initial objections, in its First Report, Session 1989–90, the Select Committee on the Televising of Proceedings of the House noted that broadcasters were, in general, content with the rules of coverage except the ban on reaction shots.[107] They were last amended in May 2016 and there are similar additional rules for embedding Parliamentary material on websites. The first condition for internet usage is that the user must not use the material for 'satire, ridicule, or denigration' or 'in entertainment content or productions'.[108] Parliament may have lost control there. Baym and Jones believe that these reinforce the argument that politicians are afraid of being ridiculed.

[101] *House of Commons Broadcasting Committee The Rules of Coverage First Report of Session 2002–03* HC 786 141–1 (published by authority of the House of Commons London: The Stationery Office Limited, 18 June 2003).

[102] ibid para 37.

[103] The Copyright, Designs and Patents Act 1988, Chapter X, s 167(2).

[104] J Grist, '"As long as a piece of string": the role of the Supervisor of Broadcasting' in Franklin (n 3) 32.

[105] 'The TV club' *The Guardian* (18 May 1989) 22.

[106] Franklin (n 3) 56.

[107] *House of Commons Broadcasting Committee The Rules of Coverage First Report of Session 2002–03* HC 786 (Published by authority of the House of Commons London: The Stationery Office Limited, 18 June 2003).

[108] *Parliamentary Recording Unit licence agreements* 'Downloading and Sharing Terms and Conditions', www.parliament.uk/site-information/copyright-parliament/pru-licence-agreements/downloading-sharing-terms--conditions/.

> [T]he British rules of coverage implicitly recognize the power of the popular and the underlying danger that parody can pose for the status quo.[109]

The rules prohibit shots, including: the press and public galleries, officials' and visitors' boxes and behind the Speaker's chair. Broadcasters can only show shots of the Speaker receiving advice from a Clerk, Officers of the House and Doorkeepers when they are actively taking part in proceedings. The member who has the floor should not be shown in close-up and should remain in shot until she or he has finished speaking, one assumes this would avoid reaction shots of the opposition benches, although these are now permitted. Split-screen shots are banned and 'panning shots along the benches should not normally be used.'[110] This would appease those MPs' fears about cameras highlighting the empty benches which might alarm their constituents.

There was an argument to facilitate a way for the Speaker to take the feed off air if there were incidents 'such as the chanting of obscenities or the hurling of objects from the galleries' but this was considered unnecessary as a Resolution of the House ensured such footage was already prohibited given it was not part of the proceedings. As a last resort the Speaker had the ability to turn off the microphones thus ensuring ultimate control over what speech could be broadcast and thus protect 'the dignity of the House'.[111] During the debate on the rules of coverage Mr. Dennis Skinner (Labour) commented, 'That sounds a bit like state censorship to me'.[112] But the rules stood.

Since the rules first prohibited the use of footage for satire or light entertainment the UK introduced a new parody exception to copyright.[113] This allows limited use of copyright works without the permission of the copyright owner for the purpose of parody, caricature, or pastiche.[114] Parliament's own website used to describe political satire as using 'ridicule and irony to criticise politics and politicians in an entertaining way through caricature' but unfortunately that page no longer exists. I wonder if any of the recent Prime Minsters did not find ridicule and irony entertaining and instead thought it was undermining. One could argue that such a definition would make it acceptable to use parliamentary footage through the parody exception for satirical and light entertainment programming.[115] However,

[109] G Baym and JP Jones, 'News Parody in Global Perspective: Politics, Power, and Resistance' (2012) 10 (1–2) *Popular Communication*.

[110] *Parliamentary Recording Unit Rules of Coverage* s 2(c)ii.

[111] First Report from the Select Committee on Televising of Proceedings of the House Together with the Proceedings of the Committee, Minutes of Evidence taken in Sessions 1987–88 and 1988–89, and Memoranda Volume I Report and Proceedings of the Committee HC 141–11 (London, HMSO, 1989) para 47.

[112] *Hansard*, HC Vol 154, col 609 (12 June 1989).

[113] The Copyright, Designs and Patents Act 1988, s 30(a).

[114] Guidance, Exceptions to copyright (updated 4 January 2021) www.gov.uk/guidance/exceptions-to-copyright.

[115] T Hickman, 'Contempt of Parliament, Political Satire and the Case of the Rt Hon Rees-Mogg MP' (*U.K. Constitutional Law Blog*, 12 September 2019) ukconstitutionallaw.org/2019/09/12/tom-hickman-contempt-of-parliament-political-satire-and-the-case-of-the-rt-hon-rees-mogg-mp/.

Dr Rupa Huq (Lab) requested a statement on the uses of broadcast footage of the House of Commons on behalf of the satirist and broadcaster Charlie Brooker. According to Dr Huq, he was told he could not use parliamentary footage in his satirical programme *Screenwipe*. The MP Chris Grayling (Conservative) confirmed that coverage of the House was not available for satirical programming.[116] Yet that should not be the case because of the Parody Exception. In October 2019, the BBC updated their Editorial Guidelines and the restriction on using Parliamentary Footage in light entertainment programming and satire was a little relaxed. The rules were originally:

> We can only use parliamentary material in news and factual content or for educational purposes.
>
> We must not use any parliamentary material in light entertainment, fictional or drama content or political satire.[117]

And in the latest incarnation of the Guidelines are:

> Any proposal to use material from the chambers or committees of Parliaments or Assemblies – including Westminster – outside respective rules of coverage must be referred to Chief Adviser Politics. This includes any proposal to use material from the Parliaments or Assemblies outside news, factual programmes or content for educational purposes, which will also require relevant Intellectual Property Legal advice.[118]

As discussed earlier, satire and parody are different things and so the parody exception might not cover political satire under the Parody Exception in all circumstances. Additionally, there is a layer of self-censorship by broadcasters, they sometimes do not claim the Parody Exception to argue for the opportunity to use footage. This is because of a fear of losing access to members of Parliament (and similarly the Royal Family by using Crown footage).[119]

With editing and manipulation, the ability to take screen grabs and upload these to the internet, these rules now seem obsolete. Whilst the House has laid out the terms and conditions of downloading and sharing footage this is not always complied with, as exemplified by the Rees-Mogg memes. The onus of protecting the dignity of the House should be on the Members themselves.

Whilst the European Court of Human Rights has stated that politicians must 'display a greater degree of tolerance',[120] it is reasonable that politicians would not want their actions or appearance to be manipulated or taken out of context. However, memes, gifs and clips used satirically on the internet do not seem to have made a great deal of difference to politicians' standing with the electorate. If it is politicians' bad behaviour which attracts ridicule, then surely it is right that this should be exposed through satire. Political satire holds politicians to account. The

[116] *Hansard*, HC Vol 606, cols 1120–21 (3 Mar 2016).
[117] *BBC Editorial Guidelines* (BBC, 2019) 10.4.10.
[118] *BBC Editorial Guidelines* (BBC, 2025) 10.3.4.
[119] Richard Wilson (Executive Producer) *Have I Got News for You* (via email 3 July 2019).
[120] *Lingens v Austria* App no 9815/82 (8 July 1986) para 41.

audience has the right to see how their representatives in Parliament behave to help inform their choice when voting in an election.

The parliamentary Rules of Coverage protect Parliament's dignity and by extension, politicians. It shields MPs from political entertainment programmes ridiculing their bad behaviour. Humour is a useful political tool, as one MP realised:

> Use humour ruthlessly. Getting the nation to laugh at your opponents is more devastating than a hundred political debating points. Every politician claims to be able to take a joke but in truth we are the most sensitive creatures, desperate to be popular and loved, and to be laughed at, especially by our own supporters, is deeply wounding.[121]

V. One Step Further, Politicians as 'Entertainers'

> When they first started putting Ministers on television, broadcasters were very deferential to them. In 1951 or so, they used to go on their knees to get Ministers on television. It was a case of 'Yes sir, no sir, three bags full sir.'[122]

Outside of Parliament (and sometimes in the House) politicians have tried their hand at comedy to humanise themselves. Most are media savvy and have learned to use comedy to their benefit. Political leaders, such as former UK Prime Minister Tony Blair, have appeared on television in comedy sketches to raise money for good causes. They understand the importance of being considered good sports who have a sense of humour and can take a joke at their own expense, this could win more votes than simply appearing on a news programme.[123] The comedian Jeremy Hardy noted that some politicians were obsessed with the idea that comedy was the future of politics and wanted to be seen as funny people.[124] Jon Plowman, a former Head of Comedy at the BBC, described how some politicians realised that appearing in comedy programmes could give them an electoral boost. Armando Iannucci commented that 'We've all moved around one, journalists have become politicians, politicians have become comedians and comedians have become journalists'.[125] The former UK Prime Minister Boris Johnson created a comedy character for himself, a blustering buffoon. Yet it was sophisticated and played

[121] Mr Robert Key (Salisbury) quoting from a speech to the Nigerian Institute of International Affairs '*How to Survive Opposition in Democratic Politics: the Role of a Loyal Opposition*', *Hansard* HC Vol 355, col 801 (1 November 2000).

[122] *Hansard*, HC Vol 127, col 200 (9 February 1988).

[123] Jeremy Hardy quote from Peter Keighron's 'Interviews' in M Wayne (ed), *Dissident Voices: The Politics of Television and Cultural Change*, (London, Pluto Press, 1998) 138.

[124] ibid 137.

[125] Podcast 'Armando Iannucci on politics and satire' (*The Guardian* 28 January 2020) www.theguardian.com/news/audio/2020/jan/28/armando-iannucci-on-politics-and-satire-podcast?CMP=share_btn_link.

to his popularity, this persona was 'not simply clownish humour, but is a highly professional performance'.[126]

The Right Honourable Members are drawn to appearing on the media now, to such an extent that some of them are trying their hand at being radio and television presenters. Miraculously many of them have managed to do this at the same time as sitting as Members of Parliament. It is, for some, a very lucrative pastime, much more so than simply being a Member of Parliament.

At the time of writing there are two sitting politicians who are regularly presenting shows on *GB News*, Nigel Farage and Lee Anderson, both from the right-wing party Reform UK. Now those with contacts in the media industry who may wish to push their own political agenda are happy to use a version of the old-boy network. Owners of the channel include the Dubai based firm, Legatum Ventures and the hedge funder Sir Paul Marshall, who also owns *Unherd* and *The Spectator*. The Channel is right-leaning and has regularly been investigated by Ofcom for issues arising under the due impartiality requirements.

On GB News, in the programme *Peoples' Forum: The Prime Minister* broadcast on 12 February 2024, the then Prime Minister Rishi Sunak was questioned for an hour on the Government's policies and performance. Ofcom found that the programme did not uphold the due impartiality requirements and fined the channel £100,000. In other programmes on GB News, Conservative MPs were interviewing other Conservative MPs. These all came under investigation by Ofcom under the due impartiality requirements.[127] Some of the sanctions imposed were challenged by GB News who took their case to judicial review and won.[128] Whoever has editorial control can control the message, and this control comes in many forms, not only through editorial policy but also through media ownership, media laws and broadcasting regulations.

VI. Regulating Current Broadcast Media

Compared to the press, the theatre, the cinema and the internet, traditional media broadcasters are the most heavily regulated media bodies in the United Kingdom. The Ofcom requirements of due impartiality and harm and offence have the greatest impact on political entertainment content. Many of the current regulations were formed decades ago with the last major overhaul under the Communications Act 2003.

[126] D Beck, 'Humorous parodies of popular culture as strategy in Boris Johnson's populist communication' (2023) 26(3) *The British Journal of Politics and International Relations* 830.

[127] Ofcom Broadcast and On Demand Bulletin Issue 494 *Politicians acting as newsreaders, news interviewers or news reporters* (Ofcom, 18 March 2024) www.ofcom.org.uk/siteassets/resources/documents/about-ofcom/bulletins/broadcast-bulletins/2024/issue-494/gb-news-decisions-five-broadcast-standards-decisions.pdf?v=392718.

[128] *GB News v Ofcom* [2025] EWHC 460 (Admin).

Looking at the history of regulation prior to the Act, the first broadcasting content regulatory body arrived with commercial television, in the form of the Independent Television Authority. Since then, various institutions and Broadcasting Acts have been replaced or built upon to create today's super-regulatory body Ofcom. These first regulators were merged into different authorities to accommodate changing technologies in cable television and the telecoms industries. As can be seen in the flowchart in Figure 1 below, the Independent Television Authority became the Independent Television Commission, before it and the Radio Authority, Oftel and the Broadcasting Standards Commission was brought into Ofcom along with the Radiocommunications Agency under the Communications Act 2003.

Figure 1 Legacy Regulators flowchart

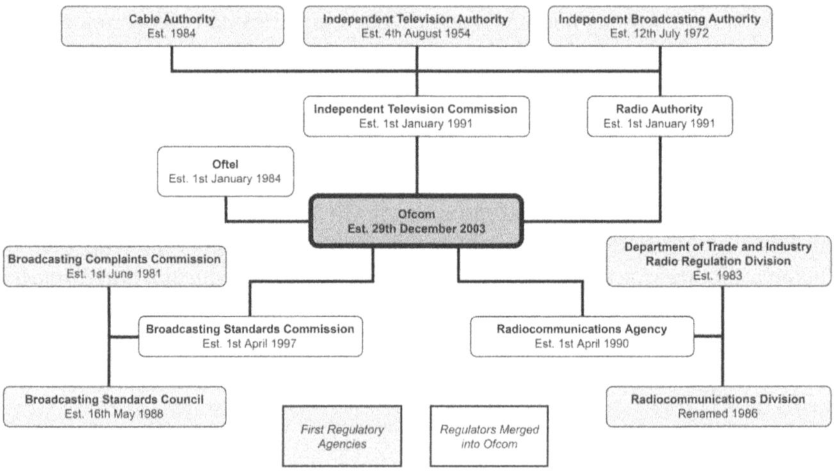

Source: Ofcom. See www.ofcom.org.uk/about-ofcom/our-website/regulator-archives for Ofcom's predecessor organisations. The table is correct as of 29 December 2003 and does not include Postcomm.

Ofcom is a public authority which regulates video on demand, fixed line telecoms, mobiles, postal services, and the airwaves over which wireless devices operate. Since 2025 with the introduction of the Online Safety Act, Ofcom has been given the responsibility of enforcing the Act and implementing new rules for strengthening the initial Codes of Illegal Harms and Protection of Children.[129] Ofcom regulates television and radio and has drawn up the Broadcasting Code that all licensed broadcasters must follow. The Code was last updated in 2020.

Ofcom became the BBC's first independent regulator in 2017.[130] This means that the Ofcom regulations are now incorporated into the BBC's Editorial Policy

[129] Ofcom 'Guide for services: complying with the Online Safety Act' (Ofcom, 21 May 2025) www.ofcom.org.uk/online-safety/illegal-and-harmful-content/guide-for-services.

[130] 'How Ofcom regulates the BBC' (Ofcom, 22 June 2022) www.ofcom.org.uk/siteassets/resources/documents/consultations/category-2-6-weeks/222191-how-ofcom-regulates-the-bbc/associated-documents/how-ofcom-regulates-the-bbc.pdf?v=328093.

Guidelines. Ofcom does not view any programming pre-broadcast. Ofcom will give programme makers general guidance on the interpretation of the Code before it is transmitted. The guidance is 'informal' and 'Ofcom will not be liable for any loss or damage arising from reliance on informal guidance.'[131] In other words this may not protect a broadcaster from being found in breach of the Code.

Whilst there are no pre-programme checks by external regulators there are instead often pre-programme checks from teams within, or contracted to, the broadcasters. These are in the form of the production teams and the compliance and legal teams who usually check contentious content and advise those responsible, normally the producers or executive producers. With no external regulators deciding if programming complies with the legal requirements of the Communications Act, the programme makers are left with the responsibility to ensure their programming will not breach the Act and the Ofcom Code, as doing so could lead to financial sanctions, possibly the broadcaster being taken off air and subsequent professional ramifications for those responsible.

The Code is written in the light of Article 10 of the European Convention on Human Rights (ECHR) and Ofcom must balance restricting broadcasters under the Code requirements with its obligation as a public authority under the ECHR to protect freedom of expression. Article 10 is not just concerned with freedom of expression for speakers but the right also includes the freedom for the audience 'to receive and impart information and ideas without interference by public authority and regardless of frontiers'.

Whilst writing this book the world has slipped further into the so-called culture wars. Freedom of expression is being used by various politicians and political players as an excuse to use contentious and malicious rhetoric and by doing so, to incite sections of the population to discrimination or hostility. Rather than being able to rely on the initial, positive rationales for freedom of expression, it is being weaponised by the far right. These arguments are constructed normally around online speech, misogyny, the manosphere and the alt-right.[132] They are interwoven with ideas around cancel culture and used to promote the idea that the liberal left is trying to close down debate because of their 'woke' ideology.

Freedom of expression is a valuable commodity for both the speaker in potentially influencing political opinion, and for the audience – to better inform their political decision making. The importance of protecting freedom of expression relies very much on the speaker speaking the truth. If the speaker is spreading misinformation, disinformation or discriminatory expression then should they be

[131] 'General Guidance' (Ofcom, 16 March 2023) www.ofcom.org.uk/tv-radio-and-on-demand/broadcast-standards/general-guidance?SQ_VARIATION_98746=0.

[132] S Judge and J Steel, 'Online misogyny and the manosphere: Defending discourses of "free speech" within the alt-right and beyond' (2025) *Ethical Space: International Journal of Communication Ethics* [Preprint].

worthy of speech protection? Speech should not be used to stir up hostility or incite violence. It is because of this that many democratic states limit these freedoms in the name of public good but these limits still need to be legitimate, necessary in a democratic society and proportionate.[133]

Entertainers, satirists and political players are now turning to the internet to escape the stricter rules of traditional broadcasting, and this brings problems of its own in terms of protecting legitimate democratic debate. Rather than a public authority being the regulator – or protector – of speech, now it is private bodies in the form of internet platforms who have no requirement to protect freedom of expression.

VII. Digital Democracy

A report by Ofcom illustrated that YouTube overtook ITV to be Britain's second favourite channel after the BBC.[134] Those born between 2012 and 2025 were most likely to watch YouTube on their home television before turning to any other channel and those over 55 had doubled their viewing time on YouTube. Contrary to many people's expectations, this does not sound the death toll for television, as the report shows much of the content popular on YouTube is now being produced in formats which resemble traditional TV. Whilst this shift puts YouTube in direct competition with commercial broadcast channels it also gives the traditional broadcasters the opportunity to reach a wider audience by using the platform service to stream their programming.

It does mean that now politicians and entertainers can get their message across without having to concern themselves with the worries of impartiality or traditional broadcasters' editorial policies, or even the Ofcom Broadcasting Code. They can retain absolute control over content and do not need to trouble themselves about an independent media filming them at public events, very different from *The Thick of It*. They can simply film themselves and set up their own channel on YouTube and broadcast straight to the nation, should the nation choose to watch. They do not need to worry about tricky questions from clever journalists or a slip up being recorded by a broadcaster and then transmitted to the nation. With their own camera crew and producers and editors they have ultimate control over the message and how it is conveyed. I interviewed a news producer in 2018 who was concerned about this practice even then. He said how the (then Conservative) government was not granting access to journalists but rather producing the content themselves and then handing out the footage to broadcasters. The producer had

[133] G Gunatilleke, 'Justifying Limitations on the Freedom of Expression' (2021) 22(91) *Human Rights Review* 108.

[134] 'Tuning into YouTube: UK's media habits revealed' (Ofcom, 30 July 2025) www.ofcom.org.uk/media-use-and-attitudes/media-habits-adults/tuning-into-youtube-uks-media-habits-revealed.

worked within a Government communications department and explained the rationale as the politicians being able to control the message so nothing negative was broadcast. He thought that this practice was a threat to democracy which both journalists and Ofcom should challenge.

Now the footage no longer needs to be picked up by a news outlet to be broadcast, as the internet is their news outlet and broadcasts globally. Other social media platforms are used too, such as Facebook, X and Tik Tok, and because there are no traditional media editors, politicians can control the narrative. By using these alternative outlets, they can influence public debate and shape society and, if their content is provocative, this is then reported by traditional media and given a level of gravitas through that. There are no calls for impartiality online, and no one needs to stick to any generally accepted standards to push a political message. As we have seen in the rise of populism and the right, online semiotic violence can lead to real world rioting, offline violence. If political players stay on the right side of applicable law, then they can spread hateful messages with impunity. If they make it more entertaining or mix it in with some humour, then their message goes further.[135] The freedom of the internet brings other concerns of audience protection, where politicians and activists may use their own platforms to evade journalistic scrutiny, spread misinformation and manipulate people.

The following chapters lead on from the historical to explore what contemporary regulatory considerations might affect the creation of contentious socio-political entertainment. This is carried out through interviews with broadcast practitioners. These examine how contemporary writers and broadcast teams decide what political and satirical content can be shared with an audience and how they make those decisions. The interviews establish that, like a Lord Chamberlain, sometimes one person can restrict content beyond statutory regulation and, by doing so, create gaps in socio-political entertainment and political satire. First, in chapter five this interview groundwork will be explained.

[135] J Young, 'Dogwhistles, Discrimination, Humour and the Law: Regulating Implicit Messaging' (2025) 11(2) *Open Library of Humanities*.

5

The Groundwork for the Interviews

I. Introduction

Earlier chapters of this book examined the roots and definition of satire and the important role that it can play in political discourse. They explored debates on satire and how political satire can inform debate, engage with audiences, and stimulate critical thinking. These earlier chapters also traced the evolution of regulating media content. Laws were established by Governments to give courts the power to judge the legal limits of political speech, which restricted socio-political content before it reached the audience, protecting the powerful and creating a gap in public debate. These gaps in creative works were not just created by censorship but also through writers self-censoring. These laws and restrictions then evolved to culminate in the creation of Ofcom, the body which currently regulates broadcast audio-visual media in the United Kingdom, described as Ofcom's former CEO as the 'soft touch' regulator.[1]

The previous chapters illustrate decisions in the areas of impartiality and harm and offence which affected what media content reached an audience. For example, newspaper reports, Orton's diaries, and the books of Grace Wyndham Goldie at the BBC and John Johnston in the Lord Chamberlain's office; these give some account of historical editorial choices, self-censorship and censorship. The next chapters address contemporary content creation and editorial decision making in the same areas of impartiality and harm and offence.

We have no Lord Chamberlain now, but who decides what person or people have the right to determine what an audience can – or should – be able to see or hear on broadcast television or radio? How transparent is the process? In the case of court judgments, we have an indication of what judicial decisions are based on, but these judgments are made after the publication of the content. This is how Ofcom decides which programmes breach (or do not breach) the Code. The way these decisions are made are published and are transparent. This is useful for the public in understanding where the legitimate limits of comedy and freedom of expression lie – should they choose to read the publications – and for practitioners to consider when they make their own decisions about what programme content

[1] Sharon White, Ofcom Chief Executive, in her speech *The consumer and citizen at the heart* at the *Which?* Conference (11 June 2015).

might go beyond the limits of the Code. These decisions are all made on a case-by-case basis. There is no one-size-fits-all rule for satire or comedy, there is nuance in tone of delivery and language used. Perhaps a wink or a knowing nod to the audience could change the whole meaning of a joke. These techniques make it impossible for practitioners, and for Ofcom, to take a formulaic approach when they are considering programme content.

This becomes more problematic when complying socio-political comedy and satire to Ofcom rules on due impartiality and harm and offence. Contrary to popular opinion there are no words or legitimate subjects that are banned outright on the broadcast media. Nor is there a set limit to the amount of swear words which can be used in one programme. It is all down to justification and context.

Whilst Ofcom has stated it holds comedy and satire as an important contribution to British entertainment, producers might be timid in their approach to allowing provocative content to be broadcast. It should be remembered that, as seen with the courts, Ofcom considers satire is in the public interest and has acknowledged that the broadcast landscape would be poorer if fewer satirical programmes are produced. Ofcom has defended offensive satirical commentary along similar lines as in the example in chapter two when audience members complained about Miriam Margolyes commenting that she was having difficulty in not wanting Boris Johnson to die of coronavirus.

Such provocative and challenging content may offend an audience, and offence comes in many guises. Within The Code, rules on Harm and Offence not only consider the use of swear words but also cover the use of discriminatory language. Ofcom research indicates that audiences find discriminatory language the most offensive type of language[2] but is that a reason to censor it?

It is often claimed in the courts that freedom of expression promotes a more pluralist and tolerant society, essential in a democratic society, and this is needed for progress and development.[3] On the other hand, the use of discriminatory language can minimise or normalise offensive terminology and create further societal tensions. It is all dependent on the context. At a time when far-right and extremist voices are more prevalent, it seems apt to explore the decision making around limiting freedom of expression within the broadcast environment.[4] Why is it deemed appropriate that there should be regulations on speech which might cause harm or offence? Why legislate so that only broadcast content must adhere to due impartiality rules when this might narrow the amount of information

[2] Ofcom, Ipsos MORI research, 'Public attitudes towards offensive language on TV and Radio: Summary Report' (Ofcom, September 2021) www.ofcom.org.uk/siteassets/resources/documents/research-and-data/tv-radio-and-on-demand-research/tv-research/offensive-language-summary-report.pdf?v=326909.

[3] *Handyside v United Kingdom* App no 5493/72 (7 December 1976) para 49.

[4] S Winlow, S Hall and J Treadwell, *The rise of the Right: English nationalism and the transformation of working-class politics* (Bristol, Bristol University Press, 2016).

available to a broadcast audience?[5] Regulating traditional broadcasting for harmful and offensive content seems to be just a drop in the ocean if completely different rules are applied in the press and online.

As explained earlier, the broadcasters have the right to freedom of expression, and the Ofcom Code was drafted in the light of the Human Rights Act 1998 and the European Convention on Human Rights. These incorporate the audience's right to receive creative material, information and ideas without interference but subject to restrictions prescribed by law and necessary in a democratic society.[6] Ofcom has underlined the importance of reporting political speech and opinion,[7] and referred to 'the high level of protection that must be afforded to forms of political speech',[8] yet licensees have complained that Section Five of the Code restricts their right to freedom of expression.[9] Additionally Section Two of the Code states that broadcasters must apply generally accepted standards to their output and this also sets limits to broadcasters' freedom of expression. There are legal limits to expression and Ofcom seeks an appropriate balance between ensuring members of the public are adequately protected from material which may be considered unjustifiably offensive on one hand, and the broadcaster's and audience's right to freedom of expression on the other.[10] Ofcom states that whilst protecting the audience from offensive content 'there should be significant room for creative freedom and challenging material in comedy programmes'.[11]

If challenging material is considered important by the regulator, might a risk averse interpretation of the regulations by broadcasters be applied disproportionately? Historically the curbing of expression extends beyond regulatory requirements. Those in editorial control do not allow media to be published or performed because they are worried about a breach of regulations and that they might be held responsible for any repercussions, or the writer not write challenging content, nervous about over-stepping boundaries. This leads to a (self) censorship of expression through omission, the juice not being worth the squeeze.[12]

Today might there be a fallibility in the regulations or of those in editorial control, leading to an 'over regulation' of content that might be legally acceptable? To explore this, discussions (the interviews) were had with broadcast practitioners about the production of political entertainment.

In the field of political comedy there is mainly American research which explores how satirical comedy and 'fake news' might affect viewers' political

[5] An interviewee who was a producer on *Have I Got News for You* talks about the difficulties of booking politicians from the (then Labour) opposition benches if members of the Conservative party refused to go on the show.

[6] The Ofcom Broadcasting Code (with the Cross-promotion Code and the On Demand Programme Service Rules) The legislative background (last updated 12 June 2023).

[7] Ofcom Broadcast Bulletin 254 (Ofcom, 19 May 2014) 55.

[8] Ofcom Broadcast Bulletin 290 (Ofcom, 12 October 2015) 40.

[9] Ofcom Broadcast and On Demand Bulletin 363 (Ofcom, 8 October 2018) 34.

[10] Ofcom Broadcast Bulletin 290 (n 8) 40.

[11] Ofcom's Broadcast and On Demand Bulletin 395 (Ofcom, 27 January 2020) 5.

[12] Writer Charlie Skelton in interview.

engagement.[13] There is also much academic work on how satire has been used in authoritarian states as a form of political protest and/or dissent, and how censorship is used to protect the Government from criticism.[14] The next chapters explore how an interpretation of the Ofcom Code and any additional broadcaster editorial guidelines might affect topical comedy output and what effects this might have on producers, writers, the audience and also the Government.

Producers must comply with the Code and may need to remove provocative or contentious humorous political expression from a programme before it is broadcast. Writers or performers may consider if they should self-censor to get their work broadcast. The reasons for this can be complex and chapters six to eight are given over to examining the thought processes of those who consider the suitability of a script or a rough cut for broadcast, and how the law might impact on that (or not) before the work is transmitted (or not).[15] Whilst the rule of law might cause a chilling effect after the material has been made public, the decisions and actions of practitioners mean that some work is never performed or made public at all. This also has chilling consequences for those within the industry and means, much like the impact on writers that the Stage Licensing Act had, sometimes work goes unwritten, or never performed, writers self-censor, and the audience misses out on new and innovative ideas. Of course, sometimes this is not a bad thing, and there are legal limitations to freedom of expression to protect, for example, vulnerable and minority groups. Rightly there should not be absolute freedom of expression, but the argument is much more nuanced than a black and white judgement of good or bad speech.

II. Aims and Questions

The interviews sought to understand broadcast professionals' approaches to making writing or editorial decisions in the production of British socio-political satire. They provided information about the 'human' side of the issue – the often-contradictory behaviours, beliefs, opinions, emotions and relationships of individuals.[16] This was not to try to prove a hypothesis but rather to explore an area where there has been little research in order to inform those in the field and offer a solution to any issues that came to light. These issues affect people who create programming today in the decisions they make and what they base these decisions on.

[13] See eg RP Hart, *Seducing America: How Television Charms the Modern Voter* (Thousand Oaks, Sage, 1999), JP Jones, *Entertaining Politics: Satiric Television and Political Engagement,* 2nd edn (Lanham, Rowman & Littlefield, 2010).

[14] L Freedman, 'Wit as a Political Weapon: Satirists and Censors' (2012) 79(1) *Social Research* 87.

[15] A rough-cut is a programme at the early edit stage, where all the elements of the programme have been put together in order.

[16] N Mack et al, *Qualitative Research Methods: A Data Collector's Field Guide* (North Carolina, FHI 360, 2005) 1.

The interviews discuss the day-to-day mechanisms of producing satire for broadcast. They include discussions about what satirical content is broadcast and why some ends up on the cutting room floor. It also considers to what extent those who work within the boundaries of the Communications Act 2003 and the Ofcom Code are guided by them when they make these decisions. The aim of the interviews was to illuminate and further the understanding of both the editorial and the creative processes in programme making.

The interviews focussed mainly on the rules for harm and offence, and the due impartiality requirements (generally referred to here as 'impartiality'). These rules come into play when programmes deal with 'matters of political or industrial controversy and matters relating to current public policy'. These will be further explained in the following chapters as participants discuss the impact of the Code when they are producing political entertainment for broadcasting.

The way in which these sections of the Ofcom Code and any editorial policies are interpreted and applied have a direct effect upon what can be broadcast. Ric Bailey, the Chief Adviser Politics at the BBC, wrote that British satirists felt constraints which came 'from a misunderstanding of impartiality and actual regulatory practice and should not prevent satire'.[17] These interviews, alongside my own background of working for many years in broadcast editorial compliance raised the questions,

> What regulatory (or other) considerations might affect editorial decisions about what content to broadcast (or not) in topical comedy and political satire?

and

> What influences creatives' (writer/performer) decisions to push boundaries or to potentially self-censor?

These questions then would lead on to consider if such decisions disproportionately affected the audience's right to receive information and ideas concerning political issues impacting on democratic engagement and knowledge.

III. Approaches to Data Gathering

Editorial rules can be open to interpretation. It is likely that some editorial decisions are made on a subjective basis. As the interviews are exploratory, a Grounded Theory[18] approach was used. The research considers how the participants understand and apply regulatory and editorial rules, the project aimed to see the world as the contributors did, 'from the inside'.[19]

[17] R Bailey, 'When journalism and satire merge: The implications for impartiality, engagement and "post-truth" politics – A UK perspective on the serious side of US TV comedy' (2018) 33(2) *European Journal of Communication* 33.

[18] B Glaser and A Strauss, *The Discovery of Grounded Theory: Strategies for Qualitative Research* (Chicago, Aldine, 1967).

[19] K Charmaz, *Constructing Grounded Theory: A Practical Guide through Qualitative Analysis* (London, Sage, 2006) 14.

The data collection was made easier because I was able to 'speak the language' of the participants. I had worked in editorial compliance for public service and commercial broadcasters for several years. I was able to empathise with the difficulties of making editorial decisions through my own experiences. It enabled me to engage in the process of the interview. There was no need for me to be 'objective' or 'detached'.[20]

I began contacting potential participants in April 2019 and completed my last interview in 2025. I contacted potential interviewees by sending them a 'briefing note' as well as a letter of introduction, explaining my research and my professional background. I attended a conference on Freedom of Speech in Comedy held by the satirical writer Charlie Skelton in November 2019. This event was attended by academics, comedy performers, producers and broadcast commissioners. I used this as an opportunity for approaching potential participants who were involved in comedy production and five agreed to contribute, although ultimately only four did. I checked which comedians, who were known for political comedy, were appearing in local comedy venues and left letters with contact details at reception for them.

During the interviews, several contributors, and one who could not take part, suggested other participants and passed me their contact details. In all 32 interviews were completed. On average the interviews lasted around an hour. Nine were carried out in person before the coronavirus lockdown. Two interviews were carried out by telephone, and the rest were conducted via Zoom. Each interview was transcribed and sent to the participant for approval with a deadline for them to request any changes. The transcripts were typed verbatim; many quotations have been edited for the purposes of clarity to remove repetition and incomplete sentences.

The interviews were as informal as possible. The interview questions were semi-structured and adapted to the participant's professional role. Whilst the discussion themes were similar, the questions were not necessarily worded in the same way for each participant or asked in the same order.

IV. Participants and their Status

It was necessary for all the contributors to be involved in the creation of comedy and (hopefully) be aware of Ofcom and the existence of the guidelines even if they had not read them. All contributors had worked on some political entertainment programming during their careers. The participants included those who had policy knowledge, 'hands on' editorial experience, and writers. In these interviews the participants talk about their daily decisions and so there is an element of

[20] P Collins, 'Negotiating Selves: Reflections on "Unstructured" Interviewing' (1998) 3(3) *Sociological Research Online* para 1.6.

'justifying what they do'.[21] Each of the participants was aware of their own power within the industry and the decision-making process. There were different levels of seniority, and those higher up the career ladder certainly had less concern about the potential consequences of their interviews than others.

It is important to consider the different roles of the participants within the context of the answers they provided. For example, the interviewee Lord Michael Grade has decades of experience and has held multiple positions in very senior roles across the BBC, ITV and Channel Four. He is now the Chair of Ofcom. This is in stark contrast to a freelance radio producer whose next job and mortgage payment depends on her or him keeping her or his job. As Lord Grade said in the opening to his interview, he was happy to be named as his career 'was not exactly hanging in the balance' and, commenting on some younger participants' preference for anonymity, said this was a 'good career move' by them.

Those who had long careers and were successful in their field have more worth to the broadcasters and can be more confident when dealing with editorial staff without fear of losing their job. These included Jon Thoday, the joint founder and Co-Executive Chairman of the television production and talent management company Avalon, the Former Controller, Comedy Commissioning, BBC Television Shane Allen and the well-known comedian and broadcaster Alexei Sayle. They can often use their status to push more contentious programming to air. They were confident in arguing against editorial strictures given their power gained through a track record of creating material which appealed to large audiences. Although even Thoday noted that there were limitations for the more powerful companies as, if they wanted to work with a broadcaster again, too much 'push back' might ruin a relationship. This then had financial repercussions. He believed this was a reason that writers and smaller production companies were more likely to capitulate to the broadcasters and edit content out even if the content was compliant with the rules and regulations. They needed the work to protect their income and create programmes and by doing so raise their profile and generate further work. It makes commercial sense not to jeopardise a relationship with a broadcaster.

The interviewees who included lawyers and compliance consultants could advise on risk, even someone as senior as Ric Bailey. Generally, their advice was held in high esteem and followed. However, time constraints and avoiding what one interviewee termed 'a fuss' meant advice was not always sought even though it could also be used by producers to mitigate responsibility, or 'share blame' as one contributor said. The further down the hierarchy one goes with the interviewees, the more worried they became about making a bad decision. Sometimes, at the bottom of this hierarchy were the writers. They were those who had no level of fame as a performer and no level of power to push back on editorial decisions.

[21] JM Berry, 'Validity and Reliability Issues In Elite Interviewing' (2002) 35(4) *PS: Political Science & Politics* 679, 680.

Most of those interviewed who worked for a broadcaster worked or had worked for the BBC. Many also had experience of working for other broadcasters. Those who worked for independent production companies and writer/performers had usually worked for both the BBC and commercial channels. The interviews tended to focus on BBC political entertainment output because the BBC is the UK broadcaster which currently produces the most comedy.

My professional background means that some interviewees are ex-colleagues in editorial roles, and some are comedy writers with whom I have worked with in the past. Five participants contributed to other studies I had carried out on aspects of broadcast regulation. The interviews were carried out on a one-to-one basis. There were two reasons for this, the first to give contributors the option of anonymity to counter concerns that their participation might impact on their career, and the second so they could speak more freely because they would not feel embarrassed or judged by other people. This latter reason was important as participants were at different career stages and different levels of seniority and freelance work is very precarious. As the subject of the interviews was about media policy and the law they may have been concerned about their level of knowledge and having one-to-one interviews left them less exposed. Those who worked for a broadcaster were generally more protective of their employer. Those who were in more senior positions, as opposed to those who freelanced, were generally more open in their answers. This was probably because they did not need to worry about their career progression and were confident in their status. It is notable that those who opted for anonymity were not in management positions and often employed on a freelance basis, so there was concern that discussing editorial decisions and their knowledge of media regulation might impact on their careers if they were a named participant.

Seven of the participants requested anonymity, therefore I am unable to give a breakdown of age, gender and ethnicity. As a broad overview, contributors were mainly white, male and middle-aged (between 40 and 60 years old). This is somewhat representative of the industry, as there are still more male comedy writers, executive producers and performers than female. Some women in senior roles who were approached did not wish to participate and suggested contacting someone else, who was generally male. In terms of the political skew, most participants said that comics, and those who worked in broadcast media, were generally politically on the left, or at least purported to be so. After the new BBC Director General, Tim Davie was reported as saying he wanted more right-wing comedy,[22] I purposefully sought out self-proclaimed right-wing comics and interviewed two with broadcast experience. One executive producer described himself as more 'right-wing' than his production team and one contributor described another as a 'libertarian'.

[22] B Gardner, 'Exclusive: BBC's new boss threatens to axe Left-wing comedy shows' *The Telegraph* (31 August 2020) www.telegraph.co.uk/news/2020/08/31/exclusive-bbcs-new-boss-threatens-axe-left-wing-comedy-shows/.

Many of the contributors knew or had worked with other participants, this was explained by one contributor as being because there was only a 'handful' of satirical and topical comedy writers in the UK. Three contributors asked for further details about which areas would be discussed during the interviews, two of them used prepared notes during the interview, with useful examples either of dealing with programme logistics and lawyers, or of former Ofcom breaches and rulings. The final contributor who had asked for the questions in advance withdrew from the interviews.

V. Ethical Considerations

Where requested, confidentiality has been respected. The interviewees all signed consent forms for their interviews to be used in a publication, and the research was conducted adhering to the Economic and Social Research Council's six key principles for ethical research.[23] The ethics board stipulated that I could not interview any participants if I were working for a company where they were also employed. Therefore, I stopped any consultancy work to ensure there would not be a conflict of interest, and I did not interview anyone with whom I had worked directly within a twelve-month period. This seemed sensible to me as I wished to lower the likelihood of having been party to any editorial decisions which were discussed in the interviews.

My career in broadcast editorial compliance had led me to the topic of the study and doubtless gave me an advantage to an 'outsider' in gaining participants. This was especially true in terms of access to participants in senior roles and creating a good rapport with many contributors. I explained my background to those participants I did not know as I wanted them to be aware that I had experience in making editorial decisions. This ensured that all participants had some knowledge about my own experiences. I wanted to establish that, whilst I was interacting with them as a researcher, I was also a practitioner with an understanding of the issues that they faced. I hoped that this might encourage the participants to speak more openly. Some interviewees, on returning their consent forms and transcripts, mentioned that they hoped I would represent them fairly in publication, that certainly is my intention.

To begin the interviews, I circulated my working title to the participants before the interview, it was framed in a way that I had hoped some interviewees might find provocative:

> Regulating Political Discourse: Curtailing, Controlling and Chilling Satire on Britain's Broadcast Media.

This led some contributors to assume that my hypothesis was that broadcast regulation stifled content (which it is not). This prompted some of them to tell me that

[23] Economic and Social Research Council Research Ethics, www.ukri.org/councils/esrc.

they disagreed. Some questions led to inconsistent or contradictory answers as we got further into the interviews. Interviewees would often note that they had contradicted themselves and I would assure them that they were not alone in this. I did not consider this as reflecting negatively on the interviewee's answers but rather thought it was a good thing, that they were thinking deeply about the questions and, in some cases, questioning their own answers as they considered different viewpoints.

If an interviewee did not know the Ofcom Code or said something which was incorrect, I would not immediately correct them. I did not feel it was my place to correct them but, in some cases, I would give them additional information about changes in the law or where previous complaints investigations had not led to a breach of regulations. Two interviewees came back to me for further information about regulatory and legal issues we had discussed in the interviews.

Participants could withdraw at any time before publication, but I did ask that they informed me within two weeks of approving the transcript. This was done to give them time to consider if they had included anything in the interview that might be problematic or damaging to their career. Any statements which may be defamatory have been removed. If they wished to make changes, they had to do this on their transcript and in their own words. Six participants made changes to the transcripts, removing names, correcting quotations, and clarifying points. No participant made substantive changes to their interviews.

VI. A Snapshot in Time

Although these interviews seek to demonstrate the difficulties production teams and writers face when negotiating the limits of humour, this comes with a caveat. They simply reflect a subjective account of an experience or experiences at a certain point in time, rather than a general 'truth'.[24] The bulk of data collection was carried out over a period of eight months from February 2020 through to September 2020 and during this time several news events shaped some responses in the interviews and impacted on editorial decisions and audience complaints. These, noted below, were touched upon in the interviews and are discussed in the following chapters.

Timeline of Key Events

23rd March
England goes into lockdown.

22nd May
The story breaks about Dominic Cummings driving to Durham in lockdown.

25th May
Death of George Floyd in the US.

[24] D Richards, 'Elite Interviewing: Approaches and Pitfalls' (1996) 16(3) *Politics* 199.

27th May
BLM protests break out in the United States and Europe.

4th June
Leigh Francis apologises over using blackface in *Bo' Selecta*.

10th June
Bo' Selecta is removed from All 4.

11th June
Fawlty Towers, *Little Britain* and *The Mighty Boosh* are removed from streaming services.

9th August
BBC apologises for using the 'N' word in a news bulletin.

27th August
Jamaica's Foreign Minister complains about stereotyping in the BBC show *Famalam*.

31st August
The Telegraph reports that the BBC Director General, Tim Davie, wants more right-wing shows.

Broadcasting Codes exist to require broadcasters to protect the sensibilities of their audience. Yet it seems from the interviews that the broadcasters and writers and performers sometimes make editorial choices to protect themselves from their audience. It seemed the audience could cause a crisis of confidence in the channels' and the creatives' output. As one comic said, 'The audience is the regulator'.[25]

It is this relationship with the audience and way in which contemporary makers of political satire interact with, interpret and apply the contemporary laws and regulations which is explored in the following chapters.

[25] Writer and Performer Dominic Frisby in interview.

6

The Interviews on Harm and Offence

I. Introduction

The opening chapters addressed what legal or societal boundaries historically affected editorial decisions and how writers and performers at the time were unable to reflect important political events. Those same themes are now addressed by exploring the influences which affect decision making in the production of modern-day socio-political entertainment and political satire on broadcast television and radio.

Existing research on comedy and political satire includes interviews with comedians or writers,[1] there is an established body of academic work on humour theory[2] and emerging work on humour and the law addressing the interpretative issues which judges face globally when dealing with humour related expression.[3] Much of the research into broadcast political entertainment, especially satire has tended to be US centric – or dealt with the effects or perceived effects of political satire on viewers' political engagement.[4]

The following interviews deal with the mechanics of the production of political entertainment and satire in the UK. The chapters consider the reasons that those in editorial positions cut or keep contentious programme content. This could be because of the potential of breaching the Code, broadcasters or producers censoring content for other reasons, or writers self-censoring. The interviewees are drawn from a broad base, with diverse roles, working within broadcasting. They include writers, producers, executive producers, compliance and legal professionals, from both the political right and left. This gives an almost complete picture of how decisions have been made.

The interviews are split across two chapters to separate the two sections of the Ofcom Code most relevant to British political entertainment and socio-political satire. These are the regulations on Harm and Offence[5] and Due Impartiality and

[1] 4 See eg S Wagg, 'Punching Your Weight: Conversations with Jo Brand' in S Wagg (ed), *Because I tell a Joke or Two: Comedy, Politics and Social Difference* (London, Routledge, 1998) 111, and P Keighron, 'The Politics of Ridicule: Satire and Television' in M Wayne (ed), *Dissident Voices The Politics of Television and Cultural Change* (London, Pluto Press, 1998).

[2] Leading figures include Salvatore Attardo and Victor Raskin, Mark Simpson and Villy Tsakona.

[3] See eg L Little, S Jacques, L Little and A Godioli, JP Capelotti, J Todd, A Godioli, J Young and BM Fiori.

[4] See eg Hoffman and Young, Holbert et al, Kumar and Combe, LaMarre et al.

[5] Ofcom Broadcasting Code, The (with the Cross-promotion Code and the On Demand Programme Service Rules) December 2020 (last updated 12 June 2023) s 2.

Due Accuracy.[6] This chapter examines the effects of the Ofcom Code's rules on Harm and Offence.

Both chapters begin with an explanation of the relevant section of the Code, followed by the contributors' comments and additional details of the regulations where needed. The chapters also explain the pertinent sections of the BBC Editorial Guidelines in more detail in connection with political entertainment when necessary.[7] The interviews provide the views and the 'lived experience' of the decision-making processes.[8] Rather than just considering and analysing contentious satirical content already in the public domain the interviewees reflect on and explain why some work never reaches the public domain; societal pressures and soft law shape editorial decision making.

II. Holding the Line

There are valid concerns that some participants in an interview may feel obliged to offer an account which either shows herself or himself in the best light, or to describe an account of what should happen rather than the processes that they honestly experience.[9] Reflecting on the interviews, most seemed to be speaking as individuals rather than as a representative of the organisation where they worked. They spoke mainly about personal experiences and decision making or writing and self-censoring. The contributors' comments are presented in a neutral way to avoid bias as much as possible, and, where more than one conclusion might be drawn from the participants' statements, it is left for the reader to reach their own conclusion.

III. Key Rules and Principles

What follows is an overview of the key rules and principles which broadcasters must follow so their programming complies with section Two of the Code on Harm and Offence. These regulations are underpinned by sections 3(4)(g) and 319(2)(a), (f) and (I) of the Communications Act 2003, which describe the general duties of Ofcom. Also relevant are Articles 10 and 14 of the European Convention on

[6] ibid s 5.

[7] Many of the contributors had worked at both the BBC and Channel Four so were aware of these regulations and, where relevant, this book differentiates between the Ofcom Broadcasting Code and the BBC Editorial Policy Guidelines.

[8] JL Hochschild, *Conducting Intensive Interviews and Elite Interviews* Workshop on Interdisciplinary Standards for Systematic Qualitative Research (Harvard University, 2009) jlhochschild.scholars.harvard.edu/publications/conducting-intensive-interviews-and-elite-interviews.

[9] P Bourdieu, *Outline of a Theory of Practice* (trans: Richard Nice) (Cambridge, Cambridge University Press, 1977) 37.

Human Rights which protect freedom of expression and the Convention rights and freedoms and, in the case of the BBC, the BBC Charter and Agreement.

The principle of the rule is to provide adequate protection for members of the public from the inclusion of harmful and/or offensive material in a programme. Ofcom regularly publishes rulings on content which has breached the regulations on harm and offence. Now Ofcom also publishes information on programmes which receive a large number of complaints but have not reached the threshold to breach the Code. This practice explains their reasoning and may have been driven by social media campaigns, with Ofcom wanting their practices to be more transparent. Publishing this information should help broadcasters in the interpretation and application of the Code. Ofcom also commissions and publishes regular research to help guide broadcasters further when making decisions about contentious content.

Broadcasters are free to make programmes about any subject providing they comply with the law and the Code. Ofcom states that 'the Code does not prohibit broadcast content from referring to any particular topic, subject or group of people.'[10] Ofcom does not ban words either, yet one of the comedians who took part in the empirical research released a song entitled *The Ofcom Song – 186 Words Not To Use*.[11] In this song he lists a number of words from Ofcom's Research, but at no stage in this research does Ofcom state that any of the words should not be used. This type of performance perpetuates a myth amongst creatives and the audience that certain language is not allowed rather than the content needing to be editorially justified, playing to the theories of 'woke' and 'cancel culture'.

Ofcom states that their rules and guidance are unable to 'anticipate every situation' and broadcasters need to be aware that 'social mores and sensitivities change both over time and in response to events.'[12] This is normally reflected in the rules on 'generally accepted standards'. These standards are informed by regular audience research.

Ofcom gives a non-exhaustive list of material which may cause offence which includes,

> offensive language, violence, sex, sexual violence, humiliation, distress, violation of human dignity, discriminatory treatment or language (for example on the grounds of age, disability, gender reassignment, pregnancy and maternity, race, religion or belief, sex and sexual orientation, and marriage and civil partnership).[13]

All offensive material must be justified by the context, and so a justification to broadcast controversial material must be considered by the production team during the creative and editorial processes. Editorial teams willing to challenge

[10] ibid.

[11] D Frisby, 'The Ofcom Song – 186 Words Not To Use' (25 September 2022) www.youtube.com/watch?v=q5ZoeYze-og.

[12] Ofcom Guidance Notes: Issue Twelve: Section Two: Harm and Offence (Ofcom, 18 July 2017).

[13] Ofcom Broadcasting Code, s 2.3.

and provoke their audience can look to these previous rulings by Ofcom to help them build this defence of justification.

Unfortunately, this is not failsafe, as Ofcom rules on potential breaches by weighing the measure of offence against current 'generally accepted standards', and these change over time. Therefore, a broadcaster could be found in breach of the Code when broadcasting content previously judged acceptable, if audience attitudes, or 'generally accepted standards', have changed since the programme was last broadcast.[14]

Ofcom's commissioned research into the public's generally accepted standards is a very useful tool for practitioners. Ofcom uses this research to judge programme content and to revise the Code, as directed under The Communications Act 2003.[15] Those who make editorial decisions need to do so within the framework of the Code and attempt to judge if their audience might find the content offensive, how offensive that might be, if it could be considered as contextually justified, and if it would fall within the margins of 'generally accepted standards'. It is not an easy task.

Ipsos MORI conducts audience research on behalf of Ofcom into public attitudes towards offensive language on TV and Radio. Their research indicates that the audience is aware of the importance of context when judging the level of offence in certain types of language.[16] Participants in the Ipsos MORI research considered that 'even very strong words or phrases, could be acceptable in the right circumstances, for example, if it was used to educate, raise awareness of issues or reflect reality'.[17] Comedy was one genre which divided Ofcom's research participants. Whilst some audience members considered strong language was acceptable in stand-up comedy (post watershed), they generally differentiated between swear words and the use of discriminatory language which could potentially harm individuals. Some considered that this harm would be heightened because of the audience laughing. Some of the participants actively avoided watching stand-up shows because they had been upset before by similar shows.[18]

It is not forbidden to broadcast offensive content, and the guidance which Ofcom publishes alongside section two of the Code recognises that programming might include material that some sections of the audience might find harmful or offensive.[19] The broadcaster is expected to consider the context (see the list below) of the offensive content and successfully argue it is editorially justified. This responsibility

[14] See eg the *TV Burp* ruling (resolved, as pulled from further transmission by UKTV) in Ofcom Broadcast and On Demand Bulletin Issue 313 (Ofcom, 26 September 2016).

[15] The Communications Act 2003, s 319(1).

[16] Ofcom, Ipsos MORI research, Public attitudes towards offensive language on TV and radio: Summary Report (Ofcom, September 2021). 14 www.ofcom.org.uk/siteassets/resources/documents/research-and-data/tv-radio-and-on-demand-research/tv-research/offensive-language-summary-report.pdf?v=326909.

[17] ibid 15.

[18] ibid 37.

[19] Ofcom Guidance Notes: Issue Twelve: Section Two: Harm and Offence (Ofcom, 18 July 2017).

generally falls to producers who must judge content against context, including 'the degree of harm and offence likely to be caused'. Given this is likely to be a subjective measure, it leaves the production team exposed to criticism for being either too careful or not careful enough about the content they choose to transmit.

Section Two of the Code states context includes (but is not limited to):

- the editorial content of the programme, programmes or series;
- the service on which the material is broadcast;
- the time of broadcast;
- what other programmes are scheduled before and after the programme or programmes concerned;
- the degree of harm or offence likely to be caused by the inclusion of any particular sort of material in programmes generally or programmes of a particular description;
- the likely size and composition of the potential audience and likely expectation of the audience;
- the extent to which the nature of the content can be brought to the attention of the potential audience for example by giving information; and
- the effect of the material on viewers or listeners who may come across it unawares.

The comedian Frankie Boyle believed this need for justification causes a chilling effect and softened challenging content.

> If you're any kind of writer these days the culture seems to be saying 'please challenge and provoke me, redefine how I see the world, while I scream my head off every time I hear something I don't like.' So now a lot of challenging stuff just doesn't get made. Good stuff that does get made is weaker because it has to contain the seeds of its own defence.[20]

This adds in a layer of simplification, having to explain the joke takes the edge off the joke. Ofcom is a public authority and therefore must balance protecting the audience from offensive material alongside protecting the broadcasters' right to freedom of expression and the audiences' right to receive information and ideas.[21] Audience protection is a theme which runs through the various regulatory bodies and institutions which historically censored socio-political content, but a democratic society needs challenging and thought-provoking expression. It plays a vital role in opening discussions on political topics and those in the public interest.[22]

[20] Frankie Boyle, *Prometheus Volume 02, The Promethiad* (3 October 2017) www.frankieboyle.com/prometheus-vol-2/.

[21] Ofcom Broadcast Bulletin Issue 284 (Ofcom, 27 July 2015) 46.

[22] 'The Court has observed on several occasions that satire is a form of artistic expression and social commentary which, by its inherent features of exaggeration and distortion of reality, naturally aims to provoke and agitate' *Eon v France* App no 26118/10 (14 March 2013) paras 60–61.

Whilst Ofcom recognises this, and the importance of satire, it also recognises that there are limits to provocative comedy.

> Comedy in particular has a tradition of challenging and even deliberately flouting boundaries of taste. Whilst such programming must have room for innovation and creativity, it does not have unlimited licence. Individual performers and presenters may sometimes overstep the line.[23]

It is the production team, along with performers, writers and broadcasters' legal and compliance departments who must judge where this 'line' lies. This must be done within the remit of the Code and any additional Guidance Notes. There is an additional guidance note for Section two of the Code. Here Ofcom specifically states that racist content should not be included unless it can be editorially justified and 'broadcasters should take into account the possible effects programmes may have on particular sections of the community'.[24] Thus, it falls to the broadcast media to take responsibility for promoting social cohesion much more so than the printed press. This is especially true for the BBC.

The BBC's mission is to 'act in the public interest' and 'help contribute to the social cohesion and wellbeing of the United Kingdom'.[25] This can be contrast starkly by various comments spoken and written by some British politicians. For example, Boris Johnson, the former Prime Minister was able to publish newspaper columns referring to women in niqabs looking 'like letterboxes', black people as 'picanninies' with 'watermelon smiles', and gay men as 'bumboys' and defend it as 'wholly satirical'.[26] It is unlikely Ofcom's editorial test of being justified by the context would be met had he said these comments on a television or radio comedy programme. His weak defence of – it was just a joke – would rightly not be acceptable under the rules of harm and offence.

Ofcom has referred to the 'long history on British television and radio of broadcast comedy tackling difficult issues and deliberately pushing against boundaries of contemporary taste'.[27]

The comedian Frankie Boyle believes offence has been given a 'social status' and 'is just a way of avoiding difficult conversations'.[28] He gives the example of when he wrote a routine about Britain's rape culture for *Live At the Apollo*. This is a pre-recorded programme on the BBC which showcases comedians in a live gig environment.[29] He was told before performing that 'the sentiments of the routine

[23] Ofcom Sanctions Committee statement on *The Russell Brand Show* (Ofcom, July 2010) www.ofcom.org.uk/siteassets/resources/documents/about-ofcom/bulletins/content-sanctions-and-adjudications/bbcradio2therussellbrandshow.pdf?v=334500.

[24] Guidance Notes Issue Twelve: Section Two: Harm and Offence (Ofcom, 18 July 2017) 5.

[25] BBC, 'About the BBC Mission, values and public purposes' (n.d.), www.bbc.com/aboutthebbc/governance/mission/.

[26] A Bienkov, 'Boris Johnson defends calling black people "piccaninnies" with "watermelon smiles" *Business Insider US* (1 July 2019). www.businessinsider.co.za/boris-johnson-defends-his-offensive-articles-about-black-and-gay-people-2019-6.

[27] Ofcom Broadcast and On Demand Bulletin Issue 313 (Ofcom, 26 September 2016).

[28] *Prometheus* (n 20) vol 2 @1hr 24'50".

[29] *Prometheus* (n 20) vol 2 @1hr 22'35".

were acceptable' but he was not allowed to use the word 'rape'. This seems an odd decision because the word 'rape' is unlikely to cause gratuitous offence per se, given it was in the context of discussing a topic as important as rape culture. Such a routine, to add to a debate about rape culture, is a world away from gratuitous rape jokes being told by men to amplify misogynist attitudes, normalise violence against women, intimidate and silence them.

Given the sentiments of the routine were acceptable – that rape culture is a difficult subject but is in the public interest to debate – this would be one example of censorship: going beyond the legal and regulatory boundaries on important socio-political matters. This creates a gap both in creativity and shuts down an opportunity for public debate. It illustrates the importance of understanding the key issues of context which producers must consider when it comes to the interpretation of humour which incorporates contentious subjects.

As Strasbourg's judgments indicate, a chilling effect on political satire is undesirable. Yet to decision makers the Code might seem contradictory, warning about protecting the audience from offensive material whilst stating at the same time:

> The Code places no prohibition on the broadcasting of offensive material – to do so would be an inappropriate restriction on a broadcaster's and the audience's freedom of expression.[30]

The decision makers must recognise the nuances of justification as they consider what is appropriate to broadcast. Whilst nothing is banned, writers do not have carte blanche to include provocative language or stereotypical portrayal in their work, all content must be justified.[31]

What follows are the interviews which focus on the understanding and opinions of content creators, and broadcasters' editorial teams about the Code and the way in which they apply these when considering contentious content. The interview chapters are sub-divided into *in vivo* headings (words or phrases spoken by a contributor during the interviews) which best encapsulate their answers around key subjects. The chapter looks at how much weight contributors give to the Ofcom Code and how they interpret and understand the Code in the light of the rules on Harm and Offence. Note not all contributors are named, some asked for anonymity, and they have been given a number to differentiate between them where they have the same professional role as others.

A. Not a Blueprint but a Framework

> The Ofcom Code … is sufficiently flexible … it does take into consideration … freedom of expression, … that's where I think the Code is quite good, because I know I can make a judgement[.] (Anonymous, Compliance Consultant 02).

[30] Ofcom Broadcast Bulletin Issue 292 (Ofcom, 9 November 2015).
[31] The Ofcom Broadcasting Code (January 2019) 5, as per the Communications Act 2003, s 319(4).

Each participant was asked if they had read the Ofcom Code and, where relevant, any broadcasters' editorial policies.[32] Overall, those who had been working in broadcast for decades, and arguably not so concerned about their career prospects, as they were established or in senior positions, were most likely to give responses that might potentially be construed as reflecting badly on themselves. For example, some contributors in editorial positions, when asked if they had read the guidelines would reply along the lines of, 'I really should say "yes", but no I haven't'.

It became apparent that many had not read the Code in any detail, if at all, unless they had worked in some capacity as a producer, and even then, some would not have necessarily read it. Those working in the editorial compliance departments (compliance) knew the Ofcom Code and their employers' editorial policy guidelines well, however they were in advisory rather than decision making roles. One expressed a frustration that some producers and most writers and performers did not know, and often did not want to know, what the rules were.

> [W]hy would you not want to know where the parameters are, so you know when you are up against them, so that you can navigate, like the side of a road, or what that sign means by the road? (Anonymous, Compliance Consultant 01).

Formal guidelines were not often referred to by any participant who was not a compliance consultant or in a senior editorial position. It became clear that producers are more likely to discuss issues with their peers than to refer to the guidelines, or to compliance or legal departments who had regulatory knowledge. Some editorial participants discussed how they did not necessarily feel that it was important that they should know the regulations because they could refer to the compliance or legal department when they needed guidance. It became apparent from the interviews that sometimes they do not refer content they are unsure about because it creates additional work. This point will be discussed in more depth later.

Those in senior positions recognise that a lack of up-to-date knowledge of the guidelines can lead to an overly restrictive attitude by some programme makers.

> I still get people quoting at me the rules that went out twenty years ago, as if they were still in existence, so I am sure that there is some self-censorship in some areas. (Ric Bailey, Chief Adviser Politics).

Regulations are regularly updated as is in-house policy. Not regularly reading updates could be self-limiting when making editorial decisions.

Those who had read the Code and/or the BBC Editorial Guidelines thought them 'mostly … sound, allow[ing] creative programme makers to create innovative programming'.[33] They were deemed flexible enough for writers to be able to create provocative and challenging content. Shane Allen, the Controller of Comedy Commissioning at the BBC (at the time of the interviews) and therefore

[32] It should be noted that where broadcasters have their own editorial policies, these incorporate the Ofcom Codes and can go beyond Ofcom requirements.

[33] Anonymous (Compliance Consultant 01).

one of the more senior participants, thought that the Code had 'got a little bit more nuanced and broader in scope' and been 'helpful … when we do the editorial justifications'.[34] He was aware of the importance of editorial justification and mentioned this without prompt, he also worked closely with Frankie Boyle.

Radio producer Laura Grimshaw believed the rules presented a framework within which she could make judgements about content on a case-by-case basis. She also talked about justifying the content without prompt.

> [T]hey make you think about what you're doing, who you are talking about and why you are talking about them, … you should be thinking about these things if you are making a joke …. So you are prepared to justify it. (Laura Grimshaw, Radio Producer).

When asked if he had read the Ofcom Guidelines, the writer and broadcaster Alexei Sayle replied, 'fuck no!', as if it were a ridiculous question. Sayle, like many other writers, feels he is guided by 'an instinct' about what is acceptable to broadcast rather than needing to know regulatory boundaries. It should also be acknowledged that it is likely Sayle's experience and level of fame would give him a greater ability to challenge editorial decisions. Steve N Allen, a writer and broadcaster who had worked on *The Mash Report*, *Late Night Mash* and GB News' show *Headliners*, had attended Ofcom training at the BBC and two training sessions at GB News but had not read the original source materials. Overall most writers and performers thought not reading the regulations was beneficial to their work, as doing so might curb their ability to write freely.

> [T]he more you worry about that [regulations], the more it stifles your thoughts, so sometimes it's better just to write what you think, and then leave the decision about whether or not it is allowed to someone else. (Christine Rose, Writer).

They are all aware that regulations exist which apply to their work, even if they do not know where the boundaries lie. This may have a chilling effect on their work if they believe that the Code is more restrictive than it actually is. Knowing the Code better would help guide them in their work and give them an opportunity to argue for their material to be retained if it complies with the Code, but in general the writers do not believe they have much power to challenge any editorial decisions about their work.

It is not just writers who do not know the regulatory boundaries, more surprisingly some editorial participants, even in senior positions, admitted that they had not read them.

> No, I have never read it [the Code] … I might have read bits of it. I've certainly done an online course in it. (Anonymous, Executive Producer).

Although, when pushed this participant could not remember if the online course was on a broadcaster's in-house policy or Ofcom's Code, and whilst in-house policies incorporate the Code, they are not the same thing. Another, who had worked

[34] Shane Allen (Controller of Comedy).

in a senior position in production for many years, thought it 'likely' he would have been given editorial rules and told 'you have to go through this' but could not remember doing so. One, with many years of editorial experience, did not realise there was such thing as an Ofcom Broadcast Code.

Several participants believed those in editorial positions who know the regulations well are more permissive. Writers and producers thought editorial decision makers could be divided into two groups. The first group is those who cut content, rather than referring it 'up' for various reasons, and the second is those people who are happy to rework content to get it to air.

> There are some people who say 'look, we can't do it like this, but how about we try and work like that?' and there are some people who just say 'no'. (Jolyon Rubinstein, Writer and Performer).

> [T]he higher-up lawyers at Channel Four used to be weirdly the most relaxed. They would be, 'oh that'll be fine'... they tend to be more relaxed about things the higher up the chain you went. (Anonymous, Executive Producer).

This indicates that the better one knows the regulations the easier it is to understand how to build in that all important justification for contentious content and get it to air. Rubinstein, creator of *The Revolution Will Be Televised*, has a track record in making particularly provocative, 'high risk' content which needs the involvement of legal and compliance departments and so would be better versed in what needs to be done to get his work transmitted.

Many producers feel they had a good relationship with editorial departments. Some producers see themselves as the arbiter between the writers and performers and the compliance departments and their role is to enable writers to express themselves. Grimshaw believes that everyone was working towards a common goal.

> [T]he head of compliance at Radio 4 is brilliant. Very keen for funny people to be funny ... even though he represents the regulation, I'm in the middle and the comedians are the chaos, all of us just want to make something that's good and funny. (Laura Grimshaw, Radio Producer).

It would be better for those who just say 'no', to talk regularly with those 'higher-up lawyers' and editorial compliance advisers who know the regulations. This would give writers and production teams a clearer idea of where the limits to comedy lie, making them better equipped to argue for material which could be broadcast. It would draw a line against which they could push, should they wish to do so. It was recognised that those who know the regulations best are the Compliance and the Legal Departments.

B. Compliance and Legal

> Of course, you've got to have regulation ... I think 'hurting people's feelings' sometimes gets mixed up with legal reasons[.] (Jon Holmes, Producer and Writer).

Often the legal and compliance departments are grouped together in the minds of those who make editorial decisions, although they might perform different roles depending on the broadcaster's structure. For example, compliance departments handle matters of harm and offence and protecting the under 18s, whilst the legal department (or an external legal company) would be more likely to deal with potential defamation, contempt, or privacy issues. Sometimes compliance and legal 'sit together', sometimes they are entirely different departments. Few writers have any interaction with the compliance and legal teams unless they also work as a producer and, therefore, cannot generally get advice on their content. In terms of complying and 'legalling' programming, some content – like Rubinstein's – is considered more high risk than others. It is likely that programmes like this would be referred to compliance and/or legal departments at pre-production stage.

Content issues for programmes can be raised at any point in the production process. This might include scripts and rough cuts getting checked by commissioners, executive producers, producers and then potentially referred to compliance and legal. Whilst there is no longer statutory need for broadcast content to be pre-vetted, as it was with the IBA, in much the same way as scripts were submitted to the Lord Chamberlain and the Comptrollers, some production teams submit programme scripts and rough cuts to the commissioners, executive producers and sometimes to the compliance department who may give notes. At any stage these notes might request changes to the programme. If compliance advisers ask for changes these generally have to be agreed with the commissioning editors or executive producers, as compliance acts in an advisory role only. This is the same for someone as senior as the Chief Adviser Politics at the BBC. Their role is to clarify the regulations and/or policies, leaving the programme makers to make the final decision.

> [M]ost of the time, they [programme makers] want to know how the guidelines apply. … And most of them are asking people to make quite subtle and acute judgements. So, my role really is to help them make those judgements, it's not really to hand down tablets of stone that say, 'you can, or you can't do this'. (Ric Bailey, Chief Adviser Politics).

The executive producers or producers normally have ultimate editorial responsibility for making decisions over provocative and potentially offensive programme content, except in the cases of mandatory referrals (see below). They can ignore advice given, but in the event of a breach or adverse publicity over a programme then they would have to take responsibility. If they had taken advice, then the blame could be shared with others.

Some production staff feel they can rely solely on the advice of the compliance or editorial team rather than read the guidelines themselves. This could be problematic in two ways, first, if producers are not versed in the guidelines, they will not always know what needs referral. Second, some in advisory roles might exaggerate potential problems to deter programme makers from taking risks, so that they would not be held accountable for allowing provocative content to air.

> I think there are some people … who build in the fear factor when they are giving advice, because they don't want to take responsibility for the advice that they are giving … and they [the producer] will then just go away and think 'well I am too frightened of doing that, so I won't'. (Anonymous, Compliance Consultant 02).

If those in advisory roles exaggerate potential problems to steer the production teams away from risk taking and producers do not know the boundaries of the legislation and regulation well, then they will come to believe that the boundaries are more restrictive and so continue to rein in writers' work more than necessary.

Producers who regularly worked on high-risk programming are generally very happy working with the compliance and legal departments. For example, the long running British satirical panel show *Have I Got News For You*, (HIGNFY) has a series of checks by compliance and legal before transmission. Its producer Jo Bunting appreciates this process. It ensures that decisions are made as a team effort rather than one person. As she has no legal qualifications she thinks lawyers play an important role in ensuring factual accuracy. She illustrated this with an example from an episode which transmitted shortly after Boris Johnson's Special Adviser, Dominic Cummings had travelled to Durham and was accused of breaking strict Covid lockdown measures.

> I was just looking at the Dominic Cummings toing and froing of emails there and the things we had to nip out were things in terms of pinpoint accuracy, so that everything was accurate and fair, and we weren't saying 'somebody lied about something deliberately' when we don't know that. (Jo Bunting, Producer).

Jolyon Rubinstein considered this relationship with the legal team can improve the content.

> [T]here's been times when, as a result of being told that you couldn't do it in the way you were planning version A, version B is a lot better as a result. [T]here can be a really positive interaction between the legal departments and the creatives. (Jolyon Rubinstein, Writer and Performer).

This pre-emptive approach by compliance and lawyers is unusual as most programmes are not considered high risk. Some performers wish there was more interaction between producers and legal or compliance teams, or that producers were better versed in legal issues so they can be more confident in allowing provocative content to be transmitted. The experienced writer and performer Andy Parsons thinks having lawyers involved in the pre-production process would be useful.

> [There's] nothing worse than having a slight change in phrase that suddenly makes it actionable, when, had you talked beforehand, it wouldn't have affected the joke at all … Often with comedy … it feels there's a slight after-thought that they don't work as closely … with the lawyers as they might. And maybe the comedy producers don't know the law quite as well as they might, and they might be slightly shy as to what they could possibly put out. (Andy Parsons, Writer and Performer).

Whilst in-house lawyers are sometimes considered overcautious, in general the participants think that the compliance and legal departments are supportive, almost to the point where content can be approved which could be deemed inappropriate.

> I think some things are still getting by in terms of compliance, I think there are lots of things you can say that will get waived on through compliance but that doesn't mean you should say them. (Anonymous, Writer and Performer 09).

C. The Chain of Worry

> Creative people are like explorers, they set off to find the source of the Zambezi and deal with all the leopards and the crevasses along the way, and failure is part of creativity. The whole business of being creative in any field is making mistakes and correcting them. (John Lloyd, Executive Producer).

Lloyd, who has worked in comedy for many decades, feels that there is no longer the freedom within the broadcast industry for programme makers to fail, or for producers to make mistakes. He believes this attitude stops experimentation in programme formats and commissioners taking risks which might stray from the tried and tested because innovative and challenging programming takes longer to build an audience.[35] This was echoed amongst many creatives, who thought there was a nervousness amongst broadcasters in making challenging programmes. This was described by one anonymous writer and performer as the 'chain of worry'. This chain of worry also illustrates the hierarchy of the roles of the participants, starting with writers without any degree of fame at the bottom, and the head of the broadcasting corporation or company at the top.

> I think it's almost impossible to properly make biting satire in the world of broadcast now, that's nothing to do with guidelines and that's nothing to do with compliance, it's to do with the politics of it and it's to do with a sort of chain of worry that goes from producers upwards. Producers worry that they will annoy their execs who worry they'll annoy their editor, who worry that they will annoy the departmental heads, to their channel boss, to the owners or controllers of the company or corporation. There's just so much fear … it's like we've become frightened of emotion. A lot of satire that's good comes from an emotion, generally a negative one … really good comedy takes on something very toxic, and frightening or worrying or upsetting, and finds a way to neutralise it in your mind. (Anonymous, Writer and Performer 09).

Although whilst the contributor stated that 'it's nothing to do' with guidelines or compliance, it is to do with the referral process. This chain of worry is integral to checking everyone is happy with content when it might be unorthodox or

[35] SP Hargreaves Heap, 'Television in a digital age: what role for public service broadcasting?' (2005) 20(41) *Economic Policy* 112.

provocative. As many said, the higher up the chain one got, the more relaxed the person tends to be about approving the transmission of contentious content.

Most participants believe that compliance and legal departments judge content against the regulatory boundaries, rationally weighing up the material, or applying the legal limits to it, rather than taking a subjective stance and applying ethical or moral standards. The same was not necessarily true with the approach that some in production took. Jon Plowman OBE, another veteran Executive Producer in the world of comedy who had also been Head of Comedy Entertainment at the BBC, believes many producers need 'a bit of lead in their pencil' insomuch as producers should not be so worried about taking risks or innovating. Like Lloyd, he feels there is a greater need for innovation within programme making. This claim is supported by a senior figure in independent comedy production who explained how broadcasters wanted to do satirical programmes 'but they are really too scared of it.'[36]

It is less precarious for broadcasting veterans to encourage risk-taking than it is for a producer starting out in their career to do the same. Producers have hands-on control of the production and are held responsible if they have approved content for transmission which breaches the guidelines. The editorial referral process, this 'chain of worry', was described by another contributor as 'manifold'. To help in understanding the process of getting a script to air, a producer describes the procedure as follows.

> [W]e start off with the initial draft of scripts ... if there's something that isn't ever going to be suitable, I will give notes early on to withdraw that, so that's my contribution to editorial. I also work with an exec [executive producer], so that's someone who has oversight on a production. On TV we sometimes have two execs and on radio we often have an exec internally who we will go to with any editorial questions on stuff which may be problematic, whether it's language or subject matter, or treatment of a particular subject matter. There's no hard and fast moments where I will necessarily escalate up, some of it is just a judgement call on what fundamentally you are going to be able to broadcast. And then also we have editorial oversight from the broadcasters themselves, so for example I might go to editorial policy if I have a query. So it's a dialogue with them, it's not censorship, it's me going to them and saying, 'I have a question over this', and I would rather use them as a positive recourse and get them on board rather than treat them like a censor, it's more, 'can I get this on air?' if I feel it is appropriate. (Anonymous, Producer 02)

It is time consuming, but it is right that contentious content should go through layers of producers and execs, lawyers and compliance before it is transmitted. It is never ultimately the responsibility of the performer or the writer. They rely on the production team to decide what is appropriate to transmit. Even so, often it is the performer who is blamed if something contentious is broadcast, especially if this is picked up by the press.

[36] Jon Thoday, Avalon.

For example, the comic Jo Brand joked about throwing battery acid rather than milkshake at politicians on a Radio Four programme called *Heresy*. On the programme Brand qualified her comments by adding that they should not be taken seriously and were not a call to action. The incident received a great deal of press coverage, with calls for the BBC to 'sack' Jo Brand. The (currently) Reform UK MP Nigel Farage demanded police action.[37]

> It must have been incredibly stressful for all concerned. These pile-ons work, they do gag people, they do shut people up. (Jo Bunting, Producer).

Twenty people complained to the BBC that the comments were offensive and amounted to incitement to violence. The BBC defended the programme as 'deliberately provocative' and not supposed to be 'taken seriously'. It added the programme was 'carefully considered … before broadcast'. Their statement noted that comedy will 'always push boundaries' yet they decided to edit any repeats and regretted any offence caused. The BBC upheld the complaints about offence but not incitement.[38] Six complainants were not satisfied and further complained to Ofcom. Ofcom did not uphold these, nor consider the complaints worthy of investigation. This type of scenario is another reason why Christine Rose (Writer) suggests that writers self-censor, they have no confidence that the broadcaster will back them if there is an issue with a contentious joke.

> There's a whole chain of people that make a TV show and I just think that once you've made a show you've got to stand by it. 'We made it, we thought it was good, people didn't like it but soz'. I think people do get hung out to dry now, so people are too scared to do too many edgy things because – is it worth it? (Christine Rose, Writer).

Even though they did not investigate the programme, Ofcom published a statement explaining their reasoning. Ofcom acknowledged that *Heresy* was a 'long-running comedy programme, which aims to challenge generally accepted ideas through satire'.[39] Within this statement Ofcom disagreed with the BBC's conclusion, believing Jo Brand's comments would likely have fallen within listeners' expectations. The BBC had not given detailed reasons for their conclusion, leading Ofcom to raise concerns about the transparency of the BBC's decisions.[40] The production team decided to retain the joke, but it was Brand who suffered the public fallout, and this creates a chilling effect and furthers the potential for self-censorship amongst writers and performers.

[37] K Rawlinson and H Siddique, 'Police to take no action against Jo Brand over battery acid comments' *The Guardian* (14 June 2021) www.theguardian.com/media/2019/jun/14/police-to-take-no-action-against-jo-brand-over-battery-acid-comments.

[38] BBC Statement on *Heresy* (*BBC*, 28 November 2019) www.bbc.co.uk/contact/ecu/heresy-radio-4-11-june-2019.

[39] Broadcast and On Demand Bulletin Issue 395 (Ofcom, 27 January 2020) www.ofcom.org.uk/__data/assets/pdf_file/0025/190294/Broadcast-and-On-Demand-Bulletin-Heresy,-BBC-Radio-4,-11-June-2019,-1830.pdf.

[40] ibid.

With scripted programmes producers can decide from a very early stage what to remove, what is deemed appropriate and which content is worth referring for further approval. This first step of judging content as 'appropriate' is subjective if the producers are not versed in the Code. Writers discuss how this approach can be overly restrictive because, on paper, jokes may not be what they seem.

> [I]t could be conceived to be in bad taste to do a joke about coronavirus if you just go, 'I am doing a joke about people dying'. People would go, 'sorry what?' and then you'd go, 'no, it's not about people dying of course, it's about the underfunding that's leading to people's deaths, the joke is here, the point of the joke is on the Government', or wherever that might be. So there's all these nuances within every joke, it's all of that context, … but often executives aren't necessarily that humorous … Transcripts of jokes don't necessarily leap off the page like they'd be delivered … [I]t's a massive juggling act when you get close to the line. (Jon Holmes, Producer and Writer).

These lines for broadcasters are drawn both by Ofcom and by their own Editorial Policy Departments (Ed Pol). Broadcaster and producer John Lloyd describes those in Ed Pol as highly intelligent people who put a lot of 'care and thought' into creating guidelines. He believes that 'is then interpreted further down the line by people who are just kind of "Argh! We've been told this!"'.[41]

Those further down the line are in production roles. Whilst the writers do not concern themselves with the Code, they do rely on the production team to make sure their material is compliant. This is only effective if the team knows the rules, applies them, and has the confidence to allow content to air which pushes against those rules when necessary. If, rather than referring to the regulations, producers rely on their own opinion or past experiences of what has been judged appropriate, they may be limiting creative content. Worse still, if they had not kept up to date with any regulatory changes then, as Bailey says, they could be working to defunct rules.

As an example, Taste and Decency regulations were replaced with Harm and Offence by The Code in 2003. Yet, during the interviews some participants would still refer to 'Taste and Decency' rather than 'Harm and Offence' when discussing contentious content.

> 'Taste and decency' is the phrase I hear more than anything else. It doesn't even mean anything, one person's taste and decency is different from another's, it's all up for interpretation and it all depends on who is feeling braver on that day. (Christine Rose, Writer).

Knowing what one might feel brave about and knowing what should be referred to senior editorial staff is helped by knowing what the current regulations are. If a producer is unsure how brave they can be some contributors believe that

[41] Note Lloyd's 'Argh!' was one depicting panic.

producer is likely to err on the side of caution. It was frustrating for some writers and performers that sometimes producers are not willing to take a risk on contentious material. It appears to them that a fear of 'messing up' drives some producers to say 'no'.

> [C]omedy is difficult, topical comedy or satire is more difficult still, because you've got all these pitfalls and people watching you to make sure you don't cross the line … to manage that you need somebody of iron integrity and toughness and somebody who knows where the line should be drawn … Creative people are basically driven by bravery, as they are explorers, and management people are driven by fear, nobody wants to be seen to fail. So, the easiest thing to say is 'no' because at least then you can't be blamed for it. Saying 'yes' is very difficult. (John Lloyd, Executive Producer).

It does seem that the BBC at least is aware of this – there was not enough information from other interviewees to make the same comment about other broadcasters. Concerted efforts have been made at the BBC to give those in production more confidence to push at the boundaries, the most recent BBC *Editorial Guidelines* had been 'designed to nudge people back towards the idea of permissiveness rather than restriction as a starting point'.[42]

Jon Plowman refers to 'timid producers'. He had 'been asked to talk to producers to say, "come on, be a bit more daring" because I think that there is a sort of inbuilt worry that isn't real'.[43] He feels attitudes are self-perpetuating and self-limiting in terms of programme making.

> '[Y]ou only can't do it if you tell yourself you can't do it. I think it's sad. I mean I do think that there is quite a lot of self-censorship that we never know about'.

Lloyd thinks the same and gave an example where producers stopped content transmitting which would have been acceptable.

> [N]ow you've got people coming in and they say, 'Oh no! Don't do that! Don't do that! Stop! You can't say that!'. A thing came up on the radio show, … Danny Wallace …. he's written a book with an asterisk in it which is obviously with an F. U. C. K. It's got an asterisk on the title and it's about rudeness, and I put in the script 'who the effing hell do you think you are? You've got an asterisk in your damn title', and you're not allowed to say 'effing' on the radio, let alone the 'f' word, you can't bleep things on the radio, 'we know what you mean!', who thought that up? (John Lloyd, Executive Producer).

Unlike television, radio does not have a watershed as such, and there is no hard rule about language beyond that of judging it within context and being aware of periods where there may be more children available to listen, such as the 'school run'. Bleeping certainly is not proscribed, and section five of the BBC Editorial Guidelines specifies this.

[42] Ric Bailey (Chief Adviser Politics).
[43] Jon Plowman (Executive Producer).

5.4.15 Radio does not have a watershed.

Bleeping and Obscuring Strong Language and Offensive Gestures

5.4.36 Generally, content that includes strong language and offensive gestures should be appropriately scheduled, used with editorial justification and signposted.

However, where strong language is editorially justified but the slot, channel or context are not appropriate, it may be necessary to edit out, dip or bleep language, even occasionally post-watershed on television

One radio presenter and writer, who had worked as a producer, spoke about similar situations. He knew the broadcaster's policies and was able to argue the material was compliant but still could not get the content to air.

> I have had fights with producers where I have said 'this is fine I know this is fine', and I know [*name of person removed*] has had huge rows with producers. Both of us have worked as producers, and we have read the producer guidelines, and we have said 'this is fine, this is absolutely broadcastable' and the producer said, 'well, not on my watch'. (Anonymous, Writer and Performer 09).

Some producers go further than the requirements both in statute and in policy and, if they are in a more senior position than a writer, can refuse to broadcast content. The only way to push back is to go over the producer's head, which can have career-limiting consequences, especially where people are freelancers and their employment is precarious.

There are many other producers who are flexible in their approach. For example, writer and broadcaster Alexei Sayle feels he is able to 'get away' with more working on Radio Four, he is aware the station lacks appeal to children and has no watershed. He recounted a story where he was working with his producer and he got a story to air in which he originally used the phrase 'Santa Claus Faced old motherfucker'. They changed the word to 'bastard' and it was transmitted. 'Motherfucker' is a mandatory referral and considered in Ofcom research to be one of the strongest swear words/insults, and at the time the programme was broadcast it placed 'bastard' as strong language, and 'effing' as 'medium language'. Whilst potentially unacceptable pre-watershed, effing was, '[o]ften seen as humorous',[44] and given there is no watershed on radio, it is the producer's personal decision rather than policy to remove 'effing' from John Lloyd's script. What makes the edict for Lloyd more irrational is that Radio Four commissioned a show called *Where's the F in News?*, an obvious play on the euphemism 'effing'.[45]

Sayle feels he can push boundaries in his radio work but noted others' reticence to do so. 'I think it's easier, because everybody else is being such a

[44] Attitudes to potentially offensive language and gestures on TV and Radio Quick Reference Guide (Ofcom, September 2016) 5, 6.

[45] 'I did the show *Where's the F in News* and I can't tell you how offended some Radio Four listeners were by the title, I mean probably 20 of them out of the two million that listen every week, who knows?'. Jo Bunting (Producer).

cowardly shit'. But, of course, Sayle is famous, has a long track record of attracting audiences by not conforming and is certainly not shy.

The former Controller of Comedy, Shane Allen, believes that it is not the broadcaster being timid but rather a shortage of talent with 'something very vital and important to say'. He thinks there are fewer performers who want to push the unorthodox. Another contributor believes this was 'bollocks', arguing that the talent was there but again it is producers who are reluctant to be adventurous.

> It might be that voices can't get to him [Shane Allen] via producers who are frightened of putting something out there that goes too far, and so by the time it gets to him all the rough edges have been sort of smoothed off it. (Anonymous, Writer and Performer 09).

If Plowman is correct and some producers need more 'lead in their pencil' then a better knowledge of the regulatory boundaries would serve them well. As established earlier, the more senior the person making an editorial decision, the more likely challenging material will be approved. To get to that point the producer needs to overcome ascending 'the chain of worry'. This requires perseverance and a willingness to raise one's head above the editorial parapet.

> If a thing was so contentious or potentially contentious, it would escalate up potentially to the top of the BBC … sometimes you think 'oh, let's not bother, let's leave it, it's not that funny'. … You don't want to upset people for something that's not that funny, or have people think you've broken the rules and in short … get into trouble and have loads of fuss about something that was never that funny … but if something is really funny and you think it is really funny and deserves to be heard and make people laugh, then it's worth … fighting for the thing. I mean, you're not fighting, sending some emails … it's about how funny you think it is at the end of the day as to whether it is worth doing anything. (Anonymous, Executive Producer).

There are issues here with working from a script, as writers have said, what is on a page can be very different when performed. Steve N Allen gave the example of *The Mash Report*, which was filmed in front of a live audience, as a better way to judge content.

> [I]f you record everything and then think about it at the editing stage, that's better than just thinking that there are some things we daren't go near. (Steve N Allen, Writer and Broadcaster)

Allen found what made the edit 'interesting', but he was not in the edit suite or part of discussions around what was to be cut from the programme.

Potentially one person decides if material is subjectively funny enough to warrant escalating and by doing so creating additional work for themselves and those around them as well as taking responsibility for the material. It often came back to someone having the courage to be accountable for contentious content rather than checking it complied with the Code.

> It's just cogs in the chain. At the end of the day, someone's neck is on the line here and nobody wants it to be them, so everyone plays safe. (Jon Holmes, Producer and Writer).

It should be noted that several people were named at the BBC, including two participants, who would likely push for contentious programming to be broadcast, and these were both in positions of senior management. It is not easy for a producer or executive to make the decision to potentially annoy managers by repeatedly referring content, of course they may not think them annoying, but referrals are time consuming. Ultimately it is quicker and easier for everyone just to remove it. It is not always simply a question of being 'brave' and taking a decision to retain contentious content.

> You have to justify the context of it, get special permission from the king or queen of the channel and it's just, 'you know what, I can't bothered, let's just take it out'... It's just easier to leave it out. (Anonymous, Compliance Consultant 02).

This may start at the commissioning stage. An independent production company will be asked to produce challenging content but when that is delivered, the commissioner may no longer wish to defend it. Slowly those edges are softened as it goes through the production stages. These editorial decisions may be painted as regulatory requirements when they are not. This can cause a disagreement between the independent production company and the broadcaster.

> So quite often ... particularly the BBC who worry about their licence fee and what politicians think of them, they will sometimes flag something up which the regulations will allow, but they will try and hide behind the regulations to either take a personal view or a broadcaster view. Because their editorial policy people don't just think about the regulations. I've had a few occasions where we have spoken to somebody at Ofcom, before Ofcom was running the BBC actually, where they've said 'there's absolutely no problem with this', where our lawyers have said 'there's absolutely no problem with this' but where the broadcaster, usually the BBC, will say there is a problem.[46] (Jon Thoday, Co-Executive Chairman Avalon).

Others believe producers also use the regulations as an excuse to remove content when the material is compliant.

> It's an easy blame isn't it? 'Oh compliance won't let me'... commissioning editors clearly just blame compliance because it is easy to do so. (Anonymous, Compliance Consultant 01).

If this happens often, it will create confusion around what the real limits of expression are under the regulations. How much it is countered depends on the power of the production company. Jon Thoday is the Co-Executive Chairman of Avalon, a large and established comedy production company. He is in a strong position to defend retaining compliant contentious programme material.

> For small companies it can be very difficult. We have quite a lot of opportunity for pushback, but I would say that it is limited, and it damages your relationship with the

[46] *nb*. Jon Thoday qualified this by saying that it was more likely to be the BBC because the BBC was more likely to make satirical and contentious programming than other broadcasters.

> broadcasters … So if you have something where the regulations definitely allow it and they really don't want it, if you go against that, they will possibly want to work with you less in the future … it's a very important thing for the many small independents that exist that are thinking 'they're not going to commission my next show'. So that is a significant part of the broadcasting industry, partly because the BBC, albeit it's under attack at the moment, is very powerful. (Jon Thoday).

This was reiterated by a lawyer.

> I think what is tending to happen is that the broadcasters are taking a very conservative view of what the Ofcom rules will allow. … [W]here broadcasters [are] not prepared to run the risks of being complained about and they want to see off the complaints before they happen. (Anonymous, Lawyer).

With the smaller production companies not pushing back on material which the broadcaster does not want to show, this creates a chilling effect and self-censorship. The impact being that in the future the independent production companies will produce content which is less contentious, so that they can get their programmes recommissioned.

Whilst producers must navigate the slippery subjectiveness of offensive humour, as mentioned above, there are also mandatory referrals for some words, depending on in-house policy.[47] These words must be approved by someone in a senior position before they can be transmitted. Sometimes requested permissions do not materialise. Departments are busy and waiting for an answer could be an issue if the production is under time pressure. This might be frustrating for a producer who wants to push at the boundaries, leading to a censorship by omission. The writer, Jed Mercurio, tweeted about how he wished to use strong language which needed mandatory approval for broadcast.

> Never a more pre Covid moment, than in #LineOfDuty S1 Ep5! After the spit, Neil Morrissey's character called Kate Fleming a word so rude we needed permission from a BBC executive. After weeks without ever getting a reply, we had no choice but to cut it from the final version. (Posted on Twitter 18 August 2020 by @jed_mercurio).

It might seem to some inconsequential that there was one word missing from a programme, but if it was used to illustrate the character of the person and his total disdain for another by using language to shock, the lack of it might just make the scene a little less satisfying. It might additionally make writers think twice about using provocative language because of the process of trying to get it to air and it potentially not being approved.

Whilst there is a protocol for certain language, it is always judged on a case-by-case basis with context being the key defence.[48] Swear words, such as the word Mercurio wanted to use, are not the most problematic types of offensive language.

[47] See BBC Editorial Guidelines, ss 3.2, 5.2, 9.2 and 10.2.
[48] ibid s 5.2.2.

Ofcom research indicates audiences are more concerned with strong, discriminatory language used as insults than with swear words per se.[49]

Most participants recognise that precluding discriminatory stereotypes and language, even within the context of creating a bigoted character from which the audience might draw a moral lesson, might be done to promote inclusivity and equality. But some writers feel that this might make sections of society or figures feel excluded from comedic treatment and thus feel they were not reflected within society. Additionally, broadcasters' concerns about the over-sensitivity of the audience could de-target those legitimately deserving of satirical treatment because of fear of being seen as prejudiced.

Stereotypes and caricatures around minority communities may be construed as offensive by 'creating a false impression of that minority'.[50] This is particularly problematic for comedy writers who, to some extent, rely on using caricatures.[51] Such concerns can make writers shy away from incorporating certain topics and characters within their comedy.

D. Just Because Someone is Offended by Something doesn't Mean they are Right[52]

> You've got to say the right thing, … woke culture is always changing. … who knows what it's going to be in twelve months' time, …, with progressive stuff, it's always progressive, so I don't know how they can say that their attitudes at this moment in time is the absolute perfect version. (Leo Kearse, Stand Up Comedian).

Kearse (who styles himself as a 'right-wing comic') is correct: that which is progressive, by its very nature, progresses. It is defined as ideas that are new, modern and encourage change in society or the way in which things are done.[53] Things that were once acceptable become less so and vice versa, the line of offence constantly shifts which is why judging that line is so difficult. He is also reflecting the issues which writers and performers have in trying to judge audience expectations and generally accepted standards. Where is the line with harm and offence?

More recently, research indicates that discriminatory behaviour and language are more unacceptable to most people than concerns about other types of offensive content.[54] If this is 'woke culture', a concern about the negative effects that words

[49] Attitudes to potentially offensive language and gestures on TV and radio (n 44).

[50] ibid.

[51] M Busby and L Bakare, 'Famalam criticised for sketch of Jamaican People' *The Guardian* (22 August 2020) www.theguardian.com/world/2020/aug/22/bbc3-show-famalam-criticised-for-sketch-of-jamaican-people.

[52] Christine Rose (Writer).

[53] *Cambridge Dictionary* www.dictionary.cambridge.org.

[54] Audience Expectations in a Digital World (Ofcom, last updated 16 March 2023) 14 www.ofcom.org.uk/siteassets/resources/documents/research-and-data/tv-radio-and-on-demand-research/audience-expectations-in-a-digital-world/audience-expectations-in-digital-world-report.pdf?v=324723.

may have on minority communities, then doubtless it is beneficial for societal cohesion to use such language carefully. This benefit can be contrasted with disparaging humour utilised by those in power to reinforce structural imbalances which harm historically vulnerable groups.[55] On the other hand being overly concerned about offending some sections of the audience is problematic in comedy. It is here often where writers and performers want to experiment, push the boundaries of taste and seek innovation. It is possible to do this whilst conveying a message to promote diversity and tolerance, but writers can be accused of stereotyping or racism or blasphemy whilst trying to approach socio-political issues through comedy involving targets from minority groups.[56] Writers do not want to alienate their audience and are aware that the audience needs to be complicit with the aim of the joke for it to land properly.

> Unless you're setting out to offend, which I don't think you should … that's absolutely not the purpose of satire, you don't want to offend your audience, your audience is on team you. In the world of satire, there's you and there's your audience and surely together both of you poke fun at them, the authority, the higher up figures, and if they're offended then that shouldn't matter. (Steve N Allen, Writer and Broadcaster).

Many participants are also concerned about the changing nature of audience attitudes because of the permanency and accessibility when clips of their work are uploaded to the internet. This affected decisions about how close to the limits of generally acceptable standards a piece of work could go.

> Comedy's about driving stuff as close as possible up to the line without going over the edge but the line constantly changes position, so if you did something that was up to the line in 2005, but the line has changed position in 2020, and then you get judged by the current position of the line on what you did 15 years ago, you're doomed, you're just doomed! (Dominic Frisby, Stand-Up Comic and Broadcaster).

Ofcom's research on generally accepted standards tries to establish this ever-shifting line, but each outcome is a snapshot in time. Ofcom's definition of context might now include when something was made or broadcast originally. The audience could be asked to consider its historical nature; however current standards apply to many broadcasts regardless of a wider temporal context.

> [A] comedian [recently] said [to me] 'the joke that will destroy my career is already out there'… [T]his is quite a young guy, this shows how different the atmosphere is now to how it was just a few years ago. A lot of comedians are kind of just waiting for the hammer to fall. I would say that nervousness must be reflected in the BBC and Channel Four, I would be astonished if it wasn't. (Graham Linehan, Writer).

[55] R Pérez and G Ward, 'From Insult to Estrangement and Injury: The Violence of Racist Police Jokes' (2019) (63)13 *American Behavioural Scientist* 1810.

[56] L Spoliar, 'Learning from laughter: Implicit Religion, satire, and power in two British TV situation comedies' (2022) 43(1) *Journal of Beliefs & Values* 68.

With the shift in audience attitudes to offence, there potentially comes a chilling, not only in what can be said in that moment, but also how it might be judged in the future. The broadcaster and performer Robin Ince thinks this is not a bad development, but it does impact on expression.

> I think the positive side of it [permanence of content via social media] is that it's made us more aware, that we go, 'hang on a minute, how many different ways can these words be interpreted and I think that's an interesting thing … to … judge your own level of privilege, judging all those different things and using empathy to going into as many mindsets as possible, the negative side of that is that sometimes your kind of internal homunculus is watching so actively, …, you just go 'I've realised, I've stopped saying that, I was going to say that and now I'm not saying that because I am so worried it might be taken in the wrong context'. (Robin Ince, Writer and Broadcaster).

Ince understands that performers must consider not only what is said, but also the ways in which it could be [mis]interpreted. Additionally, it was not only the way in which one's words might be interpreted in the present and the future, but also the imagined demographic of an unseen audience which affects editorial decisions.

> [Y]ou're self-censoring all the time because you're thinking, 'that is just not broadcastable' and as a BBC guy, you have the sense that you are broadcasting to the nation, all of them, all genders, all ethnicities, all ages, and you're not there to offend. (John Lloyd, Executive Producer).

This is an additional consideration, which not only the writers and performers self-impose but also the broadcaster imposes, especially the BBC, because of the unique way in which it is funded. The corporation is expected by the audience to be all things to all people. This is borne out by Ofcom research; research participants had more conservative expectations of mainstream TV channels' output (especially the BBC) than specialist TV channels.[57]

It is impossible to create comedy which will appeal to everyone, just as it is impossible to create biting satire which is not going to offend anyone, even if you set out not to offend anyone. To spark debate, one needs to talk about debatable subjects. Audience expectation should be managed through pre-programme announcements, and additional context should be used as tools to help push boundaries and to spark those conversations around difficult subjects.

The performer's reputation is one useful context when it comes to managing audience expectations, but this does not stop audience complaints. Take the example of Frankie Boyle, a comedian who has fallen foul of both Ofcom regulations and BBC editorial policy.[58] He has a level of fame and reputation which gives him

[57] Attitudes to potentially offensive language and gestures on TV and radio (Ofcom, September 2016) 29.
[58] Ofcom Bulletin Issue number 179 *Tramadol Nights* (Ofcom, 4 April 2011) and 'BBC apologises for Frankie Boyle joke' (*BBC News Online*, 28 April 2010) news.bbc.co.uk/1/hi/8650254.stm.

more leeway than other lesser-known performers. The audience should expect challenging content from a challenging comedian.

> Frankie [Boyle] is going to say something that is quite hard hitting, quite challenging, deals with all sorts of taboos, race, sexuality, mental health, all kinds of things that a lot of people are very sensitive around … the whole Channel Four mantra was always 'How can we do this in a way that we can justify it?', rather than 'you can't do this, you can never do this'. … Frankie always talks about the subject of the joke and the target of the joke, so the subject can be around race and sexuality but without that joke actually being racist or demeaning to some individual or minority. It's being able to do satire where you know exactly where the subject, the target of the joke is and that's to undermine, or to challenge something that feels like it is sexist or racist, or horrible in some way. [S]ometimes people hear a subject and … take things out of context and they will use that to say that he's 'a racist comedian'. He's not a racist comedian. He's a comedian who deals in issues of topics of race at one point for one of his jokes … [T]hey end up at the high court sometimes, these decisions, so you want to process them to make sure that he's getting the full support as an artist.[59] It's all about the creative freedom and artistic licence that being a comedian has, because you get to say things and do things that other genres and forms of expression don't get to do … [I]n the end you get the blandest, vanilla comedy if you worried about any joke that is going to offend any person. (Shane Allen, Controller Of Comedy).

Even within the genre of comedy, writers do not necessarily use their full creative freedom and edge towards blander comedy. Some writers consider there is a certain type of material which is acceptable to broadcast and for them it was better to create content which does not stray from this.

> [A] lot of writers write what they think they should be writing, because most of the gag writers … tend to be white men over forty-five, … they need to keep working so they produce material that they think will get used. (Richard Wilson, Executive Producer).

The former Senior Standards Officer at Ofcom, now a compliance consultant, explained that the regulator wanted to encourage freedom of expression within a comedy content, even comedy which some might find offensive.

> Ofcom [is] very, very keen always to give the maximum latitude to comedy and satire because there is a very rich tradition of this in Britain and freedom of expression means nothing if it doesn't mean the right to offend people. We always said to [those] who complained about harm and offence issues that … there is no right not to be offended at all, and the ECtHR has made this clear that political speech is very important, you must be able to offend people … if you have a comedy programme or a satirical programme, you should be able to create programmes that really, really cause offence, … provided the broadcaster has scheduled that properly, possibly after nine o'clock, possibly given warnings to members of the public and they respect what probably the ultimate barriers were. (Trevor Barnes, Compliance Consultant).

[59] *Boyle v MGN Ltd* [2012] EWHC 2700 (QB).

Some creatives described their surprise when they had put in contentious material which they considered very controversial and it was broadcast, and more surprised still when there were no complaints. Three contributors noted the same example.

> [W]e had one at Christmas [2019] … it was a joke about Prince Andrew, 'the rapist formally known as Prince', a play on 'the artist formally known as Prince'… and I thought 'oh, this is going to get complaints' and nothing, not a single thing on that. Whereas something about him [Frankie Boyle] being too left leaning got a complaint. (Shane Allen, Controller of Comedy).

Jon Plowman also described a similar example of content he thought would offend a section of the audience, but which received no complaints. This programme was created by the writers of *The League Of Gentlemen*, another well-established programme known for pushing the lines of taste.[60]

> We once did a show called *Psychoville* … and in episode one there was a character … called David, who might or might not have had mental deficiency problems and we're in a hotel … and at one point … the David character rushes into the restaurant area and says, 'come quick, come quick, there's been another murder!' and they go through. 'Look, the murderer has written the word 'fuckpig' in his or her own excrement'! I thought, well, we'll at least get twenty comments of 'how dare', not 'how dare you' but sort of offended, … and I looked at the duty log. … There were two comments on *Psychoville*, one was that at the beginning of the show there had been a number of locations and the locations had been identified, so London, Bristol, Avon, and one of the complaints was 'Do you people do no research? Bristol is not in the county of Avon', and there was another one which was to do with the way in which somebody had held something, there were no complaints about 'come quick, come quick, there's been another murder, the murderer has written the word 'fuckpig' in his or her own excrement'. So, I give up! No, I don't give up, but you know what I mean, it looks like you're pushing the boundaries, and that's how it should look but sometimes you're not. (Jon Plowman, Executive Producer).

These examples illustrate that the audience is not as easily offended as some in editorial control imagine. Of course, different people get offended by different things, but comedy and satire sometimes need to be offensive when tackling challenging societal issues, as was the case with programming such as *Till Death Do Us Part* discussed earlier. Offensive characters are needed to illustrate the stupidity of prejudice and bigotry. However, according to most participants, a programme like *Till Death Do Us Part* would not be broadcast unedited today due to the heavy-handed way it deals with certain social issues which could potentially perpetuate discrimination. This should not stop the broadcast of an updated satirical programme highlighting the hypocrisy and small mindedness of modern

[60] In June 2020 Netflix removed the series from its platform because of its use of blackface, whilst the BBC retained it on iPlayer, alongside another surreal comedy, *The Mighty Boosh*. 'League of Gentlemen stays on BBC iPlayer after Netflix removal' BBC (11 June 2020) www.bbc.co.uk/news/entertainment-arts-53009761.

bigotry, especially given the rise of the far right across the globe. It would serve a social purpose and potentially illustrate both the dangers and the idiocy of such ideology.

A concern about offending a section of the audience should not play a significant role in editorial decision making if most of the audience is not offended or even enjoys offensive material, if it lies within the boundaries of regulation and is not simply to gratuitously offend sections of society or promote discriminatory beliefs. It is better for freedom of expression and a pluralist society if boundaries are pushed, tested, and explored to keep a healthy level of debate alive in a democracy.

Trevor Barnes goes further, believing that broadcasters should not shy from occasionally breaching the guidelines. This would help others judge the boundaries of acceptability.

> I've got a feeling it's self-censorship within broadcasters. They are trying to say 'well, I want to play safe, we don't want any breaches of the Code by Ofcom because we'll get it in the neck from higher up, so what we'll do is that we will play safe'. Now, one of the things that I and other senior colleagues at Ofcom would say to broadcasters, … and some people may find this controversial, but it's true, 'if you don't have the occasional breach then you are really not doing your job properly'. Your job arguably, and particularly in the area of political speech, is to always kind of keep pushing slightly at the boundaries, and provided you, the broadcaster, has thought it through, and have a good set of reasons as to why you have put out this programme, which might at the end of the day, breach the Code, Ofcom is not going to go and sanction you. (Trevor Barnes, Compliance Consultant).

Most participants who discussed offence agree with Barnes that no one had the right not to be offended, but that one should not create offensive material simply for the sake of creating offence. They mostly thought that this is why it is important to consider what editorial justification there is for including offensive material.

There are tools that broadcasters can put in place in the form of pre-programme announcements that alert the audience to offensive content. If the viewer then chooses to watch the programme, any resulting offence would be foreseeable and would delegitimise the complaint (as long as the content complied with the Code). Plowman believes that the audience should take more responsibility for their choices.

> [W]hoever said that the BBC doesn't have a right to offend you? … Why do you feel the right not to be offended? The BBC are pretty damned good at signalling programmes, they put out trails, they put out announcements … I defy the audience to find a programme by accident, that they are then offended by. I think that's careless. (Jon Plowman, Executive Producer).

If a complaint about being offended by content which has been flagged as offensive, but is within the regulations, is taken seriously by the broadcaster, this gives an extraordinary power to the audience.

> I am always amazed by how sensitive broadcasters are to complaints. You know, you think 'well twenty people have complained but that is not very many compared to the number that watched the show'. Why does that have to be the thing that dictates whether you can say it or not? (Anonymous, Lawyer).

It also puts the onus onto the programme maker to consider adverse audience reactions when they make editorial decisions.

> The problem … with making strong, powerful jokes, is the audience, that people have just become too sensitive, or the vociferous ones are too sensitive. I think maybe the majority of people would be fine whatever. Everyone's sense of offence is absolutely massively heightened now, and they've unfortunately got an easy means of articulating it … [The BBC] and companies [listen to them], you'll get a big powerful company kow-towing to about three hundred Twitter protesters … It's terrible, it's the death of, not just political and satirical comedy, but a lot of comedy. … the thing is nobody has a right not to be offended. As long as you're not breaking the law and you're not inciting hatred I just think people should be able to joke about anything, whatever they like, the idea that someone is offended means nothing. 'Oh, I was really offended by this', so what? I'm offended by lots of other stuff, I just let it go. (Richard Wilson, Executive Producer).

Most interviewees find it odd that audience members do not just turn off their televisions or turn over the channel but rather seem to be waiting for an opportunity to complain.

E. Inclusivity Creates an Exclusivity

> Satire in general is a satire of the world … if you're not allowed to make fun of people then you're excluding them from comedy. … Inclusivity can be exclusive sometimes. (Graham Linehan, Writer).

This next section considers discrimination and contains discriminatory language. It should be contextualised within events happening at the time of the interviews. As the legal scholar Stanley Fish notes, when it comes to language, 'We are never not in a situation'.[61] Although Fish is discussing text, the same logic can be applied when it comes to audio-visual media. Like text, it is 'always set' but similarly 'it is set not for all places or all times but for wherever and however long a particular way of reading is in force, it is a text that can change.'[62]

Whilst I was carrying out most of these interviews in May 2020, George Floyd, a black American, was killed by a white American policeman. This triggered protests globally under the Black Lives Matter movement. A couple of months later a British black man who worked for the NHS was subjected to a racial attack which left him hospitalised. On reporting the attack, a BBC newsreader repeated in full

[61] SE Fish, 'Normal Circumstances, Literal Language, Direct Speech Acts, the Ordinary, the Everyday, the Obvious, What Goes without Saying, and Other Special Cases' (1978) 4(4) *Critical Inquiry* 625.
[62] ibid.

the racial insult shouted during the attack (the '*N*' word). The word was included in the news report at the specific request of the victim's family to reflect the bigoted nature of the attack. Following the report 18,600 people complained to the BBC. The BBC first defended the inclusion of the word but later apologised.[63,64]

Such events have repercussions in all aspects of broadcasting.[65] Some writers and performers publicly reflected on how they had portrayed certain characters, acknowledging that routines and jokes which they had performed had potentially been harmful to the targets. This raised issues about discriminatory language, stereotypical characters, and white comics using black face.[66] Netflix took some programmes off their platforms, and the BBC and Channel Four did the same on their streaming platforms. An episode of the classic comedy *Fawlty Towers* was briefly the centre of controversy as it contained dated, strong racist language. It was removed from streaming services whilst the platform updated the programme guidance before reinstating it.[67]

The comedian Leigh Francis, who created a character called Keith Lemon and the show *Bo' Selecta* made an emotional apology on social media on 4 June 2020 for using prosthetic masks which caricatured black and ethnic minority celebrities.[68] He also caricatured white celebrities using similarly grotesque masks. Andrew Newman, who runs the production company Spelthorne Community Television with the satirist Sacha Baron Cohen, was Head of Comedy and Entertainment at Channel 4, at the time. He participated in these interviews two days before Francis publicly apologised.

> *Bo' Selecta*, … was certainly puerile, but it was also sort of joyful and silly, but I think now there would be a whole thing about, is it okay to black up and pretend to be Michael Jackson? And I think, 'yeah, but it's a bloke from Leeds, who … looks nothing like, he's like ginger haired and he's portraying Michael Jackson as some kind of almost Richard Pryor character, it's so odd, that it's got more in common with Vic and Bob than it has with Jim Davidson. But I think that that is lost on people … it means that a show that lots of people liked at the time and didn't find racist at all, they might now be worried, 'oh, is it? Should I laugh or should I not?' and that self-censorship makes it possibly difficult for comedians. … and *Bo' Selecta* was for … the youth audience … and there

[63] D Sillito, 'BBC Apologises over racial slur used in news report' BBC (9 August 2020) bbc.co.uk/news/uk-53715814.

[64] It should be noted that Ofcom's research argues that news, drama or documentary programme could use the strongest racist language 'to explore or expose prejudice' in Attitudes to potentially offensive language and gestures on TV and radio (Ofcom, September 2016) 54.

[65] D Olusoga, 'David Olusoga: his Edinburgh television festival speech in full' *The Guardian* (24 August 2020) www.theguardian.com/media/2020/aug/24/david-olusoga-his-edinburgh-television-festival-speech-in-full.

[66] L Morris, 'All the TV shows removed from Netflix, HBO Max and other platforms over blackface controversy' *Radio Times* (30 June 2020) www.radiotimes.com/tv/comedy/tv-shows-removed-blackface/.

[67] BBC News, 'Fawlty Towers: The Germans episode to be reinstated by UKTV' BBC (13 June 2020) www.bbc.co.uk/news/entertainment-arts-53032895.

[68] BBC News, 'Keith Lemon actor sorry for playing "offensive" black characters' BBC (5 June 2020) www.bbc.co.uk/news/newsbeat-52935412.

> was that tradition of late Friday night 'God I can't quite believe they put this on TV, what are they thinking of?!' and now there is probably not as much of that. And that probably is the little bit that is maybe broadcasters being a bit worried, performers being a bit worried, maybe fashion has changed, but I don't think it had any malice in it and I don't think it was particularly worried about whether things were going to be offensive. I don't think that it was saying 'we only want to do things that are offensive' but C4's remit was to do things that other people wouldn't and give people a voice who wouldn't be given a voice on the BBC really and I think Leigh Francis, at that time, would not have been given a voice on the BBC. (Andrew Newman).

Francis parodied both black and white celebrities, men and women. The masks were grotesque and the portrayals sometimes derogatory. As a white man he wore masks depicting black men and women but also wore masks depicting white women and men. Does this equate to punching out with equal force at equally legitimate targets, or does Francis being a white male make the situation more problematic? Black argues that the form of apology and the self-reflection of comedians such as Leigh Francis, Matt Lucas and David Walliams (who also portrayed characters using blackface) is indicative of attempts for them to distance themselves from the racist and stereotypical tropes they used and rather blame the attitude of the time which found such comedy acceptable. As he notes, David Olusoga argued that it was not just the comedians but also the producers and commissioners who were also to blame for the content.[69]

Ofcom research shows that in terms of older programme content, which might contain discriminatory language and material generally considered acceptable at the time of its original broadcast, the audience is unsure of what broadcasters should do if they were to show it to a modern audience. Older audience members tended to think that the content should be judged within the context of the original broadcast and that older programmes should not be censored.[70] It was recognised that editing such programmes would make them more acceptable for a modern audience if the material was not integral to the programme. Broadcasters were expected to do this to avoid gratuitous offence. On the flip side there was also concern that this might lead to a sanitising of the past, meaning there were missed opportunities for educating the younger generation, in which case a pre-programme announcement could provide context to the offensive content.[71] Even within this context those in editorial positions consider that blackface would be unacceptable now.

When asked if there were any unacceptable subjects, all the interviewees agree that there were none but that there should be editorial justification when using contentious content. This might include the tone and delivery, timing and

[69] J Black, 'On Reflexive Racism: Disavowal, Deferment, and the Lacanian Subject' (2020) 48(4) *Diacritics: A Review of Contemporary Criticism* 76.

[70] Ofcom, Ipsos MORI research, 'Public attitudes towards offensive language on TV and Radio: Summary Report' (Ofcom, September 2021) 37.

[71] ibid 41–42.

mannerisms of a performance. Again, as pointed out by Holmes, these things cannot be judged from words on a page, and because of this some writers and creatives believe content about challenging subjects is removed too early in the production process. This stymies a free flow of creative work around themes which it is in the public interest to debate. These are subjects which needed to be treated with sensitivity, but they are not banned in any way. Some in editorial positions believe addressing taboo subjects through comedy could be done in a way to inspire a positive change in societal attitudes.

F. Broadcasting the Taboo. Are you *Really* Going to Go There?

> I genuinely do think, whatever topic, in the right hands, with the right comic mind, you can get comedy out of that … be illuminating and impactful and hopefully help change people's perspective [.] (Shane Allen, Controller of Comedy).

Overall, participants in both creative and editorial positions think regulating broadcast programming is a good thing. They believe the broadcaster, if not them personally, has a responsibility to the audience, not to cause unnecessary offence. The writer and performer Alexei Sayle was not alone in considering regulation was important in linear broadcasting, as the content was 'beamed' into the audiences' home and should be held to some kind of standard. When given the opportunity to refine content to make it comply with the regulations, writers often said they became more creative. Many writers and performers believe this produces cleverer content which forces them to be more artful in their writing.

> The restrictions that it [the Code] puts in place, sometimes are … quite useful as a framework to work out the area that you can use to get your point across in satire. If there were no restriction then some of the art might be lost, you'd simply just say a thing, be insulting, go for it, and some people would love that, and maybe we're living in a media age where people would love that more than they used to when I started, but I think that might take away some of the artistry of using that space to actually get a point across. (Steven N Allen, Writer and Broadcaster).

Exploring taboos is an opportunity for comedians to challenge the audience on prejudiced or intolerant views. Many participants feel comedy is the perfect vehicle by which to tackle taboo subjects and create discussion around controversial ideas.

> I would like to think that comedians, writers, producers, could bring us programmes around race, gender fluidity, inequality, social demographic concerns, international issues, religion, whatever it might be because I think it is all about … what the context is. [C]omedy can be a massive, positive tool to break down barriers and to generate conversation and spark debate around a lot of those kind of areas. (Steve North, General Manager UKTV).

When asked what, if any subject, was considered taboo for broadcast media, writers who considered there were still taboos, raised race, religion, and gender. The comment below is from the satirical writer and script editor Charlie Skelton.

> So, there's, in inverted commas, taboos that you can sort of push against and there's sort of real taboos, that you can't go anywhere near, and I would put race in there.

Some writers and performers think there are certain aspects of these issues that would not be countenanced on broadcast media, not only in the way in which these topics might be discussed but also by whom they can be discussed.

> [T]here is a chill around what you could potentially say or what you think you could get away with now, certainly .... Huge topics which are very important, like race for instance in Britain, are not off limits to comedians who are of immigrant families themselves. If you're a second generation, Indian immigrant doing comedy, you will almost be expected to simply address that ... virtually impossible for a white comedian to talk about that. It would be expected that you would simply have to express abject self-abdication, guilt and shame ... but you're best just to steer away from it altogether and accept that it's nothing to do with you. Even though I would argue it is a lot to do with you, we all experience those effects, and it would be irrational or implausible to suggest that anyone who is not white British but living in Britain is affected by issues of race, but that people who are white British are not affected by issues of race. If it is happening, then it is happening and it is an equal and opposite reaction. If that isn't the case, then I think that certainly needs to be explored and explained. (Simon Evans, Stand-up Comic and Broadcaster).

Sometimes it is just the mention of colour.

> [R]ace is, it's just such an uncomfortable subject. You just talk about black taxi drivers or something, you just say the word 'black' and you can see the audience visibly get uncomfortable. So, race is very taboo. (Dominic Frisby, Stand-Up Comic and Broadcaster).

If this discomfort around race is apparent when in front of a live audience, it is likely to inform the way that broadcasters imagine a television audience reacts to taboo subjects.

> [Y]ou can't see them [the audience] ... so you have to be mindful that you can't just say 'because we're all edgy we can joke about anything and everyone is in the same position to receive it' because I don't think that's quite true. There are certain things that I personally as a producer would be less comfortable putting on air, whether that's because I don't find it funny, I don't say as a blanket thing that certain things aren't funny, ... there's certain things that I feel like the bar to clear as a performer is so much higher then maybe it's almost not worth it. ... [I]t has to be really clever, really satirical, and not make people feel massively uncomfortable .... [I]t's not a case of censorship, it's a case of ... how skilful is the performer and how clever is the joke? ... [G]ood satire is on the edge of what is acceptable, but not so much that it is needlessly offensive, it's a real tricky one to pull off and probably because of that, what happens is people can play it safe. (Anonymous, Producer 02).

As Evans said above 'there is a chill around what you think you could get away with'. However, one can potentially 'get away' with offensive material, if it can be argued as justified, as Shane Allen commented above, comedy can 'hopefully help change people's perspectives' for the better. Comics are censoring themselves because some conversations are not being had with producers and compliance advisers which might help frame traditionally taboo content in a broadcastable manner.

> I do think that there is an element of self-censorship there ... they're worried about the reaction of their imagined audience or the people around them and I find it slightly depressing that they are not saying 'right, is it really funny? Then let's put that together and talk to the compliance people and at that stage see if we have to take it down and change it.' ... [B]ut you shouldn't be self-censoring too much at the beginning. (Trevor Barnes, Compliance Consultant).

This is something which is happening, as one producer explained.

> It's not necessarily that I'm always saying 'no' and the comedian is always pushing forwards, it's quite often that I get to say 'no you can say that, that would be fine', or 'maybe if you said it like this maybe we could get this through'. [J]ust actually considering what you're doing and why you're doing it all the time, and the process of actually articulating that between the people that you're working with is a useful thing. (Laura Grimshaw, Radio Producer).

This approach seems to be entirely dependent on the producer being willing to work through contentious issues.

A compliance consultant believed that there had been an audience shift in the ability to openly discuss some subjects. Certain topics were considered off limits because performers were afraid of being accused of bigotry.

> [T]he lexicon has now moved on and it serves to shut down proper discourse. Phobes, any kind of phobe words, shuts down debate. (Anonymous, Compliance Consultant 02).

This 'shutting down of debate' concerns some of the participants. Whilst most think that the shifting of language away from intolerance and towards an inclusivity of all sections of society is positive, some felt that it potentially has a chilling effect on the way in which they can tackle issues, taking away the nuances of debate. It was part of the 'smoothing' of the edges previously discussed.

However, some in editorial roles thought that writers often say they 'weren't allowed' to say something when, actually, content is cut because it is simply not funny enough.[72] But 'funny' is subjective, it is the comedian's job to make people laugh, so cutting a joke on the basis that a producer does not think it is funny, rather than on the grounds of a compliance or legal issue, means sometimes decisions are based on personal taste rather than regulatory limitations.

[72] Anonymous (Producer 02).

> [O]n some shows they [producers] might just give you the script from the commissioner and it'll say 'no, what does this mean? No thank you!' Underline underline! I have done shows years ago with [comedian's name removed] where the commissioner went through and wrote 'not funny! What does this mean?' and it went down the line and it accidentally got in front of [comedian], and he saw the notes and he was really unhappy about that … particularly for professional comedians, they're sort of, 'what do they know if a joke is funny or not? That's what I do for a living', so there's a line between 'we don't want you to say this on our channel' and 'it's not funny'. I'm not sure you get to decide what is not funny, you get to decide what is not fitting for your channel, that's fine. (Christine Rose, Writer).

Like any editor, a producer needs to make decisions about the content of their programme. It is down to them what to cut, what to retain, programmes have a running time, someone has to decide what is in and what is out to keep to their scheduled duration. As Lord Michael Grade commented, 'Everything you broadcast is a choice … "do we cut there?", "do we use that bit or do we cut the sentence there?"'.

Therefore, it is a choice that the producers have, if they have to cut for time,[73] they can cut the sections which they think are controversial, to avoid a fuss, or it might be that they are cutting the jokes which they think the audience will find the least funny. After all, it would make no sense for a broadcaster to transmit content which would upset its audience en masse. Broadcasters need to keep audience numbers to retain commercial revenue, or, as in the case of the BBC, to retain relevance and an argument for public funding, so to some it makes financial sense not to make waves.

As the Ofcom research shows, the audience understands nuances in language. It differentiates between general swear words and discriminatory language, considering the latter more problematic. In addition to this ability to differentiate between the levels of offence, there is an expectation that comedy as a genre can be outrageous. Producers need to tread a thin line if they are concerned with attracting and retaining a mass audience. As we have seen above, many contributors to these interviews felt the opinion of the audience (or at least the section which complains) is given greater weight than it deserves.

G. The Court of Public Opinion

> The media used to be unassailable before social media, you could quite boldly put something out that perhaps felt quite partisan and biased. … [T]he people who didn't like it would sit at home and tut, and the people who liked it would cheer …. now that all discourse and discussion … is so public, and then amplified by the media saying, 'Twitter erupts as BBC broadcast sketch about Boris Johnson', it becomes impossible,

[73] Programme material usually needs to be cut to fit in a specific transmission slot.

> you're literally kind of hobbled by the Lilliputians clinging to your ankles. (Anonymous, Writer and Performer 09).

Just as the audience influences Ofcom guidelines, so too does it influence editorial decisions and writers. Ofcom's audience research into generally accepted standards informs the Code on Harm and Offence. Audience feedback, using either 'official' channels or taking to social media, affects writers and creates a chilling effect, encapsulated as 'the Heckler's Veto'. Although the Heckler's Veto has its roots firmly in First Amendment Jurisprudence, its meaning has been more recently broadened to capture the process of audiences being able to veto certain aspects of speech. It is used predominantly by both right-wing and more mainstream media to 'describe the act of one group attempting to silence the controversial speech of others'.[74] This is especially problematic when political expression is silenced in a democratic society.

A multitude of people make up an audience; all these people have different expectations depending on their cultural and socio-political backgrounds which in turn affect their viewing and listening patterns. When Ofcom carries out its research it includes a broad range of participants and many of them have some level of media literacy. For example, the majority of research participants understood the importance of context. At the same time, they may not know the finer detail, for example the audience is unlikely to know what regulations are in place regarding discriminatory language. Research indicates some audience members believed that homophobic, racist and antisemitic content would be censored by the broadcaster.[75] The audience also generally differentiates between discriminatory language which might be editorially justified and that language which is used as an insult. Disciminatory language is considered a particularly sensitive area, and to reflect this Ofcom specifies,

> Racist terms and material should be avoided unless their inclusion can be justified by the editorial of the programme. Broadcasters should take particular care in their portrayal of culturally diverse matters and should avoid stereotyping unless editorially justified.[76]

Ofcom research participants had an expectation that comedy might be offensive and 'outrageous'.[77] According to Simon Evans, such audience expectation was not reflected in the writers' room.

> Half of the writing team are kind of on the side of the Lord Chamberlain, half of the writing team are going 'well, you can't say that, well that's a bit offensive, I think that

[74] BG Johnson, 'The Heckler's Veto: Using First Amendment Theory and Jurisprudence to Understand Current Audience Reactions Against Controversial Speech' (2016) 21(2) *Communication Law and Policy* 175.

[75] Ofcom, Ipsos MORI research, 'Public attitudes towards offensive language on TV and Radio: Summary Report' (Ofcom, September 2021) 11.

[76] Ofcom Guidance Notes: Issue Twelve: Section Two: Harm and Offence (Ofcom, 18 July 2017).

[77] Audience Expectations in a Digital World (n 54) 24.

> marginalises X or Y'. They're not trying to get the funny out, they are quite self-policing, it's been absorbed, it's been internalised, that kind of puritanical mindset[.] (Simon Evans, Stand-up Comic and Broadcaster).

However, given the changing nature of generally accepted standards, it might be that marginalising X or Y is no longer considered funny or could breach the guidelines. Alternatively, too much is being read into a joke which would be different on paper to one being performed. There is a difference between using justifiably offensive content and insult and this is the line that writers need to tread. Broadcast satire needs to be framed within the constraints of the Ofcom Code and so should not be gratuitously offensive or racist as the Ofcom Code requires editorial justification for discriminatory language and stereotyping. The Code is not overly restrictive. The following example is a programme which Ofcom did not find in breach of generally accepted standards but there appears to be no editorial justification beyond ridicule.

In January 2020 the British weekday breakfast news show *Good Morning Britain* broadcast a segment discussing members of the British Royal Family using their position for personal financial advantage. They showed an advertisement in which a minor member of the Royal Family promoted Chinese State milk. The advertisement was narrated in Chinese and finished with the minor royal speaking in English. Afterwards the presenter, Piers Morgan, mimicked the Chinese language. He mispronounced words and used the phrase 'ching chang' and said, 'Can you imagine on Christmas at Sandringham is like, "I'm sorry your majesty but I only drink 'yeng yeng dong dong yong ming ming' milk … milk" and "Ching chang chojo. Okay. I got it. I got it. I got it"'.

His co-presenter behaved in an exasperated manner but was laughing along which rather endorsed his behaviour. She pointed out that 'taking the mickey out of foreign languages is rather 1970' and 'Piers do you not realise the kind of woke times we're living in?'. Rather than saying that the behaviour was inappropriate she blamed 'woke times' for it being problematic. In its defence statement to Ofcom, ITV said her words should be interpreted as 'he should appreciate that some viewers might be offended by mimicry of a foreign language for comic effect.'

In response to the segment 1,600 viewers complained but the complaints were 'not pursued',[78] although nor was the content editorially justified. The broadcaster argued that Morgan was mocking the minor royal for appearing in an advertisement rather than mocking or denigrating 'Chinese people, their language or accent' and added that Morgan was attempting to mimic the wording of the Chinese to comically juxtapose the Chinese voiceover with the incongruous spoken English from the minor Royal Family member. Both ITV and Ofcom agreed that the phrase 'ching chang' was a racist trope targeting people of Chinese heritage.

[78] Ofcom Broadcast and On Demand Bulletin Issue 400 Good Morning Britain (Ofcom, 6 April 2020) www.ofcom.org.uk/__data/assets/pdf_file/0025/193525/Good-Morning-Britain,-ITV,-21-January-2020,-0630.pdf.

In the bulletin Ofcom referred to the judgment in *Redmond-Bate v DPP*[79] stating that Ofcom needed to take account of both the broadcaster's freedom of expression rights and the audience's right to receive information and ideas without undue interference under Article 10 ECHR. Quoting Sedley LJ, Ofcom stated that these rights enable views that may include

> the irritating, the contentious, the eccentric, the heretical, the unwelcome and the provocative.[80]

On the face of it, the outcome goes against the principles of the Ofcom regulations on Harm and Offence given there was no justification for the mimicry. If the minor royal was the target of the joke, then that target was missed.

In coming to its conclusion Ofcom considered ITV's rights and included its 'freedom to express potentially offensive views' and defended its decision on the grounds that there was sufficient challenge and context from the co-presenter. This included the steps the broadcaster took, which included meeting with Morgan to discuss the complaints, and apologising in a press statement. The reasoning is somewhat conflicting – a conclusion which could be drawn from this example is that one can be offensive and provocative, and use stereotypes or racist tropes, if you apologise for it afterwards.

The interviewees are aware that the use of stereotypes is problematic, however they consider that it is difficult to avoid in comedy, because

> [C]omedy does rely to some extent a little bit on stereotypes and sending people up[.] (Shane Allen, Controller of Comedy).

Linehan, a writer of several very popular comedies discussed how he had been accused of being misogynistic because of creating a flawed female character, but stated that all his characters are flawed.

> I remember when people would criticise me for *The IT Crowd*, their argument was that Jen didn't know anything about computers and was portrayed as an idiot, she was the only female character. The thing is that they were all portrayed like that and if you don't let me portray a woman like that then there's not going to be a woman in the show, because that's the only way I know how to make funny people, is to make them all deficient in some way. (Graham Linehan, Writer).

Banning offensive material because some audience members feel offended by it undermines the broadcasters' right to freedom of expression. Some contributors consider the *Heckler's Veto* of the audience has the same effect and protects some high-profile figures from comedic treatment. This is not because of the regulations but because of the audience's vociferous reactions to jokes which had targeted certain figures. Contributors think this then led to false accusations of prejudice by the performer and created a chilling effect.

[79] *Redmond-Bate v DPP* [1999] 7 BHRC 375.
[80] ibid [1999] 7 BHRC 375 at para 20.

> [T]his idea that it was racist to have a go at Meghan [Markle], which is so fucked up … it's bonkers that she's been sort of 'de-targeted' I would say, by satire, … when I say satire, … it's interesting isn't it, I am then using it as 'the satire that's allowed'. You know, or the satirical parameters that are in place and that some of them are unspoken and you just sense it, although some of them are shrieked. Like Meghan's quite a good example of seeing a, seeing a kind of, I don't know what the word would be, an Overton window of possibility being moved, you certainly go 'oh fuck, what? I'm saying this thing and I'm suddenly being racist?'. (Charlie Skelton, Writer and script editor).

Some participants felt figures such as Diane Abbott and Meghan Markle were untouchable in satirical terms, on grounds of racial heritage, but it was not the same for the Conservative politician Priti Patel. Possibly because Patel, at the time of the interviews, was in a more powerful position, and so seen as more deserving of satirical attack. Yet, whilst not a cabinet minister, Abbott as a member of Parliament is likewise a powerful figure but the executive producer of *Have I Got News For You* felt Abbott had been delegitimised as a target.

> Diane Abbott, the vanguard of people around her that cried foul any time people made fun of Diane Abbott, but nobody is doing that for Priti Patel, no one is claiming we are racist for having a go at Priti Patel. Whereas you make a joke about Diane Abbott then that is racist. 'You're picking on a black woman with diabetes', and it's not that. … Anything you say about Meghan Markle that's negative is now racist, and the fact that she is a product of Hollywood, whether she is black or white, she is going to have airs and graces that other people don't have, not that she's 'getting above her station' because she is a black woman. But, Ian [Hislop][81] has found it difficult on a number of occasions, because he tends to be on the side of the free press, so they should be allowed to write what they want, especially if they [Harry and Meghan] are tabloid hounds themselves and using the media as a way to publicise themselves. He thinks it's fair game to have a go at them and for the press to have a go at them. But he's done that a couple of times, and he says that it is not worth it for the post bag that he gets, the hostility that he gets. (Richard Wilson, Executive Producer).

This seems to indicate a left-wing/right-wing divide in terms of tolerance to certain people being targeted, it would follow that an audience which does not agree with a viewpoint or feels more aligned with the target, is more likely to cry foul and complain. Yet, this does not seem to be as much the case when right-wing figures are targeted. Since the interviews Meghan Markle has come under increasing satirical attack, so the Overton window which protected her from being targeted may now be firmly shut.

It is better for promoting tolerance within society by using a range of characters who are diverse and equally targeted, on the condition they are not targeted for their protected characteristics. Otherwise, some sections of society could be further excluded from comedic treatment. Those who are already bigoted might

[81] Ian Hislop is a broadcaster and editor of the satirical magazine *Private Eye*.

then feel that they are vilified and consider that others' rights are better protected from satirical attack than theirs are. For example, middle-aged white men have been described as 'male, pale and stale', or labelled as 'gammon' and it is unlikely the writers fear reproach or to be labelled as racist.[82] Ultimately this could create a backlash against a more liberal society when certain sections of society feel they are being targeted and others are not. It is important for a diversity in comedy, not only in writers and performers, but also a diversity of targets of satire. Comedy should be challenging, in its complaint assessment for *Heresy* Ofcom stated, 'The editorial premise of this programme is to discuss challenging ideas, through comedy, that may differ from the generally accepted consensus.'[83] Whilst the opportunities to discuss challenging ideas through comedy are available from a regulatory perspective, they are not necessarily fully utilised because of writers and producers fearful of the audience's reaction. I should reiterate that the argument is not that people should be targeted for their protected characteristics, but their flaws are legitimate subjects for comedy. Yet this seems to be happening less because of writers', performers', or broadcasters' concern about their image, and the nature of the audiences change.

> I sometimes think, oh wait, is everything a bit too nice? What's being challenged here? Who's challenging authority? How are we pushing boundaries and is everything being slightly blanded out, that's a genuine worry and that's not coming from the broadcaster perspective, that's from a kind of a generational perspective … (Shane Allen, Controller of Comedy).

Many participants commented that audiences were divided by age. Older audiences want more challenging material, and younger audiences seem to prefer less contentious content.[84] One Executive Producer referred to research carried out by Channel Four with participants aged between 18 and 19 years old which concluded that younger people were quite conservative in their tastes.

> [W]hen you look at what people are saying about comedy shows, they talk about 'oh it was so cringe', like cringe comedy … [W]e would think of that as like David Brent, characters that are embarrassing, and that's funny, but young people find it too embarrassing to watch, because it feels like you are taking the piss out of those characters, and you are to some extent, and so comedy is quite a hard-to-navigate minefield for making it, hoping to appeal to younger people, because it does involve laughing at people quite a lot of the time.(Anonymous, Executive Producer).

Whilst Ofcom research has found older people were more likely to find content offensive, this seems to be more to do with younger people finding disparaging

[82] *Gossip and Goddesses with Granny Kumar* Episode 3 Radio 4 (Transmission date 24 February 2021) 'Granny Kumar decides to host her own series, born out of frustration at seeing or hearing the same old parade of guests on chat shows (mainly male, pale and stale)'.

[83] Ofcom Broadcast and On Demand Bulletin Issue 395 (Ofcom, 27 January 2020) www.ofcom.org.uk/__data/assets/pdf_file/0025/190294/Broadcast-and-On-Demand-Bulletin-Heresy,-BBC-Radio-4,-11-June-2019,-1830.pdf.

[84] Jon Thoday (Managing Director).

humour more uncomfortable. Some jokes rely on othering.[85] Often there is an exclusiveness and maliciousness in humour and, as mentioned, satire does not have to be 'funny' but can be uncomfortable and cruel.[86] This can exacerbate a sense of callousness and seem 'unfair'.[87] If unpleasant things are said about bad people the audience might feel the element of cruelty fairly dealt, but the audience may not be in agreement as to who deserves this kind of treatment. Some may take a different reading of the character or the situation and therefore consider the target is unfair and interviewees find this frustrating.

> There is so much that we should be so fucking angry about, but you know I don't think there's some great conspiracy with people who have executive or legislative and political power, telling broadcasters what they should or shouldn't do. I don't think that. But I think that there's a vested interest for everybody at the moment in keeping everyone docile and laughing giddily at all the silly funny silliness. Nobody wants … *let's all just be nice*. That whole hashtag *be kind*, that has been applied to satirists. It's not our jobs to be kind, it's our job to be slayers – but we should all be kind. And maybe it's the goldfish bowl of social media. I don't know what it is. (Anonymous, Writer and Performer 09).

It is impossible to #BeKind whilst creating satire, to fulfil its remit it needs to provoke the audience. If satire upsets an audience member, then they can immediately express their dissatisfaction, or outrage, through social media, and this may cause a chilling effect. It is to social media that this chapter finally turns.

H. The Minefield of Social Media and (Self) Censorship

> [W]ith Twitter [X] … you could tread on a landmine more easily now without knowing it …. that's why broadcast, more stuff gets dropped … you end up with a comedy which is more inverted … it becomes more orthodox in the sense that it just follows the kind of moral and political line of the chatterati. (Charlie Skelton, Writer and script editor).

As seen with Ofcom's statement on *Heresy*, there is licence for comedy to deviate from the orthodox. Yet offending an audience has potential consequences for the broadcaster, the production teams, and the performer. It could have career repercussions, create a media storm or cause audiences to turn off, damaging those all-important ratings.

[85] Defined by Jean-Francois Staszak as 'transforming a difference into otherness so as to create an in-group and an out-group' in 'Other/Otherness', in R Kitchin and N Thrift (eds), *International Encyclopaedia of Human Geography*, vol 8 (Oxford, Elsevier, 2009) 43–47.

[86] S Lintott, 'Superiority in Humor Theory' (2016) 4 *The Journal of Aesthetics and Art Criticism* 347 and J Bicknell, 'What is Offensive about Offensive Jokes?' (2007) 51(4) *Philosophy Today* 458.

[87] EM Dadlez, 'Truly Funny: Humor, Irony, and Satire as Moral Criticism' (2011) 45(1) *Journal of Aesthetic Education* 1.

For the performer especially, the fear of an orchestrated social media attack impacts on how far a performer is willing to tackle controversial issues. These attacks can be personal, brutal and, in some cases, threaten their safety. This informs the material writers produce and the routines that comics perform.

> You get people [performers] rolling their eyes and saying 'eurgh, yeah, I'll say it because people want me to say it, but I don't really think that'... it's self-preservation, they don't want to lose their career and their livelihood. [As a comedy writer] you're not writing for yourself, you're writing for someone else, to help them not get cancelled ... Sometimes I will be half-way through a sentence, and I'll go 'no, delete that'. (Christine Rose, Writer).

Many describe how it is increasingly difficult to predict how audiences might be offended. This offence then leads to some audience members demanding people lose their jobs. This can be exacerbated through orchestrated social media pile-ons, not just through audience demands but also by it being picked up and amplified by certain newspapers. Whilst not all such pile-ons make headlines, it appears that even the possibility of one has a chilling effect. Skelton talked about writing controversial material as not being worth the repercussions anymore.

> It's just come to pass that ... the juice isn't worth the squeeze. (Charlie Skelton, Writer and script editor).

A few participants thought that previous social media campaigns illustrate how some people actively want to be outraged by content rather than trying to understand its nuances.

> [S]o much of social media does revolve on 'how can I possibly impute the worst possible motives onto this person for doing something that in another light might be interpreted as being entirely innocuous?'. (Anonymous, Writer 11).

In some cases, audience interaction with comics gets exceedingly personal and aggressive. One interviewee talked of his female (comic) friend receiving death and rape threats for stating her political opinion on Twitter. Although this is not an isolated occurrence, women who actively engage with politics are often targeted to try to exclude them from the political arena.[88]

Even with the *Have I Got News for You* Twitter/X account, where the text of a tweet cannot be taken out of context, the writers avoided certain subjects due to the fear of an audience backlash. This frustrates the executive producer.

> We just do jokes, and the people that run the feed for us, they send me the jokes every day and ... I'll say, 'should we not do something about that?' and they'll say 'no, we'll get terrible blowback if we do that'. And I am thinking, 'this is the *HIGNFY* Twitter feed, we should be upsetting people on a regular basis, not getting cheers from other like-minded Twitter users'. (Richard Wilson, Executive Producer).

[88] See the concurring judgment of Judge Motoc in *Patrício Monteiro Telo de Abreu v Portugal* App no 42713/15 (ECtHR, 7 June 2022) in which she discusses semiotic violence against women in politics.

Online campaigns and newspaper reports are effective in encouraging people to complain to broadcasters in large numbers. However, it is impossible for a broadcaster to know if a complainant has been outraged by hearing a joke on a programme or outraged by seeing a tweet or a report telling them they should be outraged and that they should complain.

Many interviewees believe it is a false equivalence when broadcasters give the same weight to the number of complaints via social media and to the number who write a letter or call the duty log. They believe it is 'too easy' to complain.

> [I]n the old days, if you wanted to protest against a show or a film … you'd have to actually make placards and go and stand outside the theatre … And now anybody can just do it, they don't even have to put trousers on, they can just do it from their phone. They can lie in bed and they can tweet that they were offended and 'this is disgusting' and then if enough people do that, then action is taken. (Leo Kearse, Stand Up Comedian).

Performers and writers talked about those on social media who sought to 'cancel' people. These cancellations might mean them being sacked by broadcasters, lose bookings from venues, or sometimes have venues cancel their performance because of social media campaigns. Whilst such campaigns may not necessarily lose a performer their job, the threat of reprimand may potentially influence the type of material which they create. Frisby commented that 'The audience is the regulator',[89] and whilst this has always been true with live performance, now the broadcast audience uses social media to get their voice heard.

Those who complain may be in the minority but were considered vociferous and effective. This, again, gives the audience a lot of influence in the creative process and the choice of what to broadcast and what to cut.

> [T]he result is that everyone's really watching what they say all the time because they don't want to lose their jobs. And the effect is censorship, it's like a new form of censorship. (Dominic Frisby, Stand-Up Comic and Broadcaster).

Although it has been noticed that comedians can use cancellation to their advantage. Being reported as having been cancelled for saying something outrageous can lead to newspaper reports, writing newspaper articles and boost ticket sales to their stand-up shows.

> Comedians are almost the one group that shouldn't talk about cancellation. You do hear stories about people who express a point of view and they work in a museum or something and then they lose their job, if you actually lose your main earning job, then that is a proper cancellation, but comedians, and not even just comedians, but actors will go on Question Time and say something and then manage to get interviews, book deals, their own TV show off the back of their cancellation, it's not what the word cancellation means really is it?
>
> Saying 'you can't say anything anymore' [whilst appearing] on national TV is something of an anathema. (Steve N Allen, Writer and Broadcaster).

[89] Dominic Frisby (Stand-Up Comic and Broadcaster).

The current situation, where writers are self-censoring because of worrying about their audiences' reactions, and producers and broadcasters are concerned about taking risks, narrows the range of ideas being pitched. Writers and producers talked of how sometimes neither the broadcaster nor the audience knows what kind of programmes it wants until it gets them. Indulging the outrage of a minority of the audience, or not giving those in production the opportunity to fail, restricts innovation. This stops new and challenging content.

In the future broadcasters should be more forceful in their defence of provocative comedy programming, especially those which deal with contentious issues around important socio-political themes. Done in the right way, without gratuitous offence or needless obscenity, comedy can benefit the public discussion and should help tease out the nuances around current polemic taboos. Although this is easier said than done, as John Lloyd said, 'you need somebody of iron integrity and toughness and somebody who knows where the line should be drawn', but the lines are constantly shifting and hard to judge. If no one steps up to take the challenge to innovate and test the limits, broadcasters will end up like the theatre managers of old, who simply put on re-runs of Shakespeare and played it safe.

7

The Interviews on Due Impartiality

I. Introduction

By tracing the origins of the harm and offence laws and rules which impacted on socio-political entertainment we can also trace the relaxing of censorship surrounding subjects once considered taboo. These subjects used to include depicting politicians on stage. Once the great and the good could finally be represented in political entertainment on stage, the laws and rules of impartiality were applied to broadcasting. This then impacted political satire on television and radio.

The impartiality requirement in news and current affairs media has been the focus of attention for a long time.[1] All channels which hold an Ofcom licence to broadcast must adhere to the impartiality requirements. The BBC states that impartiality is a 'core BBC value' and that their approach to impartiality as set out in the BBC's Editorial Guidelines 'is more demanding than the Ofcom Broadcasting Code'.[2] It is not unusual for there to be some sort of media storm around broadcasters, especially the BBC, and impartiality obligations. For example, a leaked internal memo written by Michael Prescott, an external adviser to the BBC's editorial standards committee, accused the BBC of editorial failings, listing bias in reports and senior management not taking criticism seriously. Among other things Prescott highlighted the clumsy editing of a documentary about Donald Trump and his role in the US Capitol Hill insurrection. This led to accusations of left-wing bias in the corporation. The memo itself was problematic, and Stephen Cushion considered that it was not 'transparent or robust in design or approach'.[3] Nevertheless, the events led to the resignation of Tim Davie, the BBC's Director General, and the Head of News Deborah Turness. The BBC admitted to an error of judgement over the documentary edit and apologised. For this editorial lapse, Donald Trump has threatened to sue the BBC for up to $10 Billion. After this incident, and following legal advice, the BBC edited out Rutger Bregman's comment in a Reith Lecture that Trump was 'the most openly corrupt president in American

[1] See eg the excellent research output from Stephen Cushion, Cardiff School of Journalism.

[2] BBC Guidance: Impartiality (BBC, 23 June 2025) www.bbc.co.uk/editorialguidelines/guidance/impartiality.

[3] S Cushion, 'BBC bias? The Prescott memo falls well short of the standards of impartiality it demands' (*The Conversation*, 14 November 2025) www.theconversation.com/bbc-bias-the-prescott-memo-falls-well-short-of-the-standards-of-impartiality-it-demands-269576.

history'. This was ironic given the subject of Bregman's lecture was the cowardice of institutions in the face of authoritarianism. This then led to accusations of the BBC demonstrating right-wing bias.

Impartiality is something that the BBC prides itself on and the corporation requires due impartiality across all output, including political entertainment. The BBC voluntarily imposed impartiality on itself until it was incorporated into the licence agreement of 1996.[4] The BBC is the only broadcaster which must comply with a due impartiality requirement in its online output as well as its broadcast output. The argument given for this is two-fold, first that it 'maintains a reach and immediacy that remains unrivalled by other media' and second that it provides 'a counter-weight to other, often partial sources of news'.[5] Impartiality was imposed on commercial broadcasters in statute by the Television Act 1954. Newspapers, on and offline, can be as partial as they want to be, and generally are.

Like the harm and offence requirement, it has been recognised that the due impartiality requirement interferes with freedom of expression and, as with the harm and offence rules, it is argued that there are legitimate reasons. As mentioned at the beginning of this book, after Ofcom imposed a financial sanction on Autonomous Non-Profit Organisation TV-Novosti (the Russian state-owned broadcaster, known as Russia Today/RT), RT called for a judicial review. The case concerned the proper interpretation of due impartiality provisions in the Communications Act 2003 and the Code, and the compatibility of those provisions with Article 10 of the ECHR.[6]

RT argued that the sanction was a disproportionate interference with its right to freedom of expression. However, as per Article 10(ii) of the ECHR, the three-part test applies, meaning any limitation to freedom of expression must be prescribed by law, pursue a legitimate aim and be necessary in a democratic society. The Court found the sanction was proportionate and the limitation was legitimate. The Court stated that,

> [T] he due impartiality requirement is the preservation of the democratic process itself, which is safeguarded by providing a level playing field for competing views and opinions so that those views and opinions are expressed, heard, answered and debated.[7]

Whilst this might be appropriate for news, as shall be shown, the misinterpretation by production teams when making political entertainment means it can have an adverse effect on satirical content. An over-zealous application and a misreading of the impartiality requirement by the makers of political satire

[4] E Barendt, 'Judging the Media: Impartiality and Broadcasting' (1998) 69(B) *The Political* 108.

[5] *R (Autonomous Non-Profit Organisation TV- Novosti) v. The Office of Communications* [2020] EWHC 689 (Admin).

[6] ibid.

[7] ibid para 36.

produces a negative effect. This is especially when the rule is interpreted by programme makers as a need to create 'balance' within a comedy programme. The unintended consequence is that it causes a chilling effect in the production of satirical entertainment. The impartiality requirement can, in effect, protect politicians from scrutiny. This has not gone unnoticed, for example, in 2006 the then Italian Prime Minister and media mogul Silvio Berlusconi, introduced the Italian version of due impartiality, the *par condicio law*, to prevent Italian comedians and satirists from deriding his administration on television networks that were beyond his editorial control.[8]

In terms of the impact on writers and producers trying to create political comedy, it can be frustrating and sometimes make topical commentary on controversial political subjects nigh on impossible. For example, the comedian Sophie Duker quit a television show because parts of her routine were edited out. A section was removed from a monologue in which Duker had discussed Israeli-Palestinian violence in Jerusalem, and antisemitism among liberals. This section was not broadcast, even though it had already been 'edited for tone and balance'. She described this as censorship.[9]

The Code stipulates that due impartiality may need to be applied in all programming genres, including cinema films shown on television, comedy programmes, or televised dramas.[10] Although if these same films, comedy programmes or televised dramas were to be shown on media platforms other than traditional broadcast (except for the BBC online services) then they would not need to adhere to a due impartiality requirement.

Often satirical programmes engage the due impartiality requirement because they contain content which includes 'matters of political or industrial controversy and matters relating to current public policy' being debated by politicians, industry and/or the media, or relating to a policy 'under discussion or already decided by a local, regional or national Government or by bodies mandated by those public bodies to make policy on their behalf'.[11] What sometimes seems to be forgotten by production teams is that the word 'due' is very important, especially when it comes to impartiality outside news programming.

This final section explores how the impartiality requirement might impact editorial decisions, potential censorship decisions and self-censorship in the production of political entertainment, satire especially. Section Five of the Code lays out the regulations on Due Impartiality and Due Accuracy and Undue Prominence of Views and Opinions.

[8] WR Jones, '"People Have to Watch What They Say": What Horace, Juvenal, and 9/11 Can Tell Us about Satire and History' (2009) 36(1) *Helios* 27.

[9] 'Comics quit Comedy Central's all-female panel show' (Chortle.co.uk, 27 May 2021) www.chortle.co.uk/news/2021/05/27/48529/comics_quit_comedy_centrals_all-female_panel_show.

[10] Guidance Notes Issue Six: Section Five: Due Impartiality and Due Accuracy and Undue Prominence of Views and Opinions (Ofcom, 20 October 2025) 1.4.

[11] Ofcom Section Five: Special Impartiality Requirements: news and other programmes (Ofcom, 20 October 2025).

II. Key Rules and Principles

The legislation underpinning the rules on impartiality can be found in sections 319(2)(c) and (d), 319(8) and 320 of the Communications Act 2003, and the BBC Charter and Agreement. The principles of the section are foremost to ensure due accuracy and due impartiality in news.

Ofcom defines impartiality as 'not favouring one side over another' and specifies that the qualification 'due' means 'adequate or appropriate to the subject and nature of the programme'. So 'due impartiality' does not mean an equal division of time has to be given to every view, or that every argument and every facet of every argument have to be represented.'[12] It is worth noting that 'the subject and the nature of the programme' should mean that satirical comedy would be given more scope to use the 'due' in 'due impartiality' than a serious news programme. The BBC's definition of impartiality goes further and emphasises the importance of a range of views 'When dealing with "controversial subjects", current public policy or political issues, the BBC must ensure a wide range of significant views and perspectives are given due weight and prominence, particularly when the controversy is active'.[13] This leaves room for the producer to determine what is significant and how much representation any one view might be given in any programme.

As with the requirements on Harm and Offence, broadcasters need to consider audience expectation and context when deciding what approach they take to the content they transmit to ensure compliance with the due impartiality requirement. The due impartiality requirements become stricter around election times.[14]

Due impartiality does not need to be achieved within one programme but can be reached over a series, editorially linked, discussing the same or related issues. The Ofcom Code stipulates this must be 'within an appropriate period and aimed at a like audience'. So, for example, a broadcaster could not transmit a partial programme at 7pm on a Monday evening and argue that the programme they transmitted three months later, on a Friday at midnight, which put an opposing view to related issues was 'within an appropriate period and aimed at a like audience'.

Whilst Ofcom does not require due impartiality to be achieved within one show, the BBC's rules on impartiality specifies programmes in strands which are 'widely disparate' from one edition to the next should 'normally' achieve impartiality within one show.[15] Referring to 'Impartiality in Series and Over Time' the editorial guidelines state:

> In such strands, due impartiality should normally be achieved within individual programmes, or across a specific number of explicitly editorially linked programmes. However, across a whole series or over time these strands will also need to

[12] The Ofcom Broadcasting Code, s 5 (Ofcom, last updated 20 October 2025).

[13] BBC Editorial Guidelines, s 2.4.7.

[14] Ofcom Guidance Notes: Issue Six: Section Five: Due Impartiality and Due Accuracy and Undue Prominence of Views and Opinions (Ofcom, 22 March 2017) s 1.14.

[15] BBC Editorial Guidelines, s 2.4.28.

> demonstrate due impartiality, for example through a consistent application of editorial judgement.[16]

It is the producer who uses his or her editorial judgement to decide how the programme might demonstrate due impartiality. Additionally, on long running or continuous output such as rolling news, an appearance by a politician, or other contributor with partial views, should not normally have to be followed by someone taking a contrary view, although it may sometimes be necessary to offer the opportunity to respond.[17] This negates the need for 'balance'. The BBC states that 'Audiences expect artists, writers and entertainers to have freedom to explore subjects from one perspective and to create content that reflects their own distinctive voice'.[18] Therefore one would expect them to be able to express their potentially partial opinions. Additionally, it is important to remember that Ofcom specifies that the qualification 'due' means 'adequate or appropriate to the subject and nature of the programme'. A satirical programme is not hard news, therefore it should not be judged in the same way either by the audience, or by Ofcom, if it is not politically balanced. Bringing together all these elements, comedians should not have to be neutral, or balanced, with their material.

The Royal Charter has stipulated that the BBC should provide programming to

> build people's understanding of all parts of the United Kingdom and of the wider world .... championing freedom of expression, so that all audiences can engage fully with major local, regional, national, United Kingdom and global issues and participate in the democratic process, at all levels, as active and informed citizens.
>
> [T]he BBC should help everyone learn about different subjects in ways they will find accessible, engaging, inspiring and challenging.[19]

A BBC report into impartiality, written in 2007, discussed how the BBC should look 'to widen the intellectual, social and political perspectives' in drama because 'comedy … has been painting in the blanks' given that the topical shows take 'no prisoners of any political stripe' and can therefore evade any accusations of bias.[20] This no longer appears to be the case with audience expectations. Some audience members now believe that topical, political entertainment shows should be impartial and if they perceive them as being biased, they complain. In an accusation of pro-Israel bias by the BBC in the comedy programme *The News Quiz*, the BBC's Editorial Complaints Unit stated that 'the requirements for impartiality differ significantly between news and comedy'.[21] It is surprising that there is any audience expectation that satirical programming should be impartial, but

[16] ibid.

[17] BBC Editorial Guidelines, s 2.4.29.

[18] BBC Editorial Guidelines, s 2.4.33.

[19] The Royal Charter for the continuance of the British Broadcasting Corporation Cm 9365, s 6(1) and (2).

[20] *From Seesaw to Wagon Wheel: Safeguarding Impartiality in the 21st Century* (BBC, June 2007) 52.

[21] *The News Quiz*, Radio 4, TX date 16 February 2024 (BBC, 29 August 2024) www.bbc.co.uk/contact/ecu/the-news-quiz-radio-4-16-february-2024.

reassuring that the Complaint's Unit differentiates between the genres regarding the due impartiality requirement. Unfortunately, this has not always been the same within the production teams across all broadcasters.

A. Impartiality is a State of Bliss

> [I]mpartiality is a state of bliss to be attempted. There is no definitive impartiality, there isn't, it doesn't exist … Everything you broadcast is a choice … 'do we cut there?', 'do we use that bit or do we cut the sentence there?'… and so inevitably sometimes you make the wrong choice, and it's interpreted as partiality whereas in fact it's just a wrong choice. (Lord Michael Grade).

On 29 September 2020 the BBC News website published a story with the headline 'Tim Davie: BBC boss "prepared to fire stars who break impartiality rules"'.[22] Such a statement from the Director General of the BBC might have a chilling effect on staff speaking about political events, even if they were not 'stars'. It could lead producers to over-apply the impartiality regulations by not considering the 'due' nature of the requirement, or simply avoid certain political or controversial content altogether.

At the time of his interview in 2020, Ric Bailey stated that there was little satire referred to him in his role as Chief Adviser Politics at the BBC and considered that the interpretation of the due impartiality requirement might be the reason

> There is no one in the UK who has made the impact with satire in the same way as in the US and this may be down to a misconception of the due impartiality requirement …. If there were lots of budding talent, expecting to do political satire, at the cutting edge of wherever the rules are, then I am not seeing it'. (Ric Bailey, Chief Adviser Politics).

Although, more recently (January 2026) Bailey noted that there has been an upturn in political satire referrals to him.

Section 2 of the BBC Editorial Guidelines states that the BBC 'is committed to achieving due impartiality in all its output' and '"due" means that the impartiality must be adequate and appropriate to the output', depending on the context. It specifies the range of perspectives or opinions need not be covered in 'equal weight' and that there is no requirement to give minority views the same prominence as the 'prevailing consensus'.[23] No views on subjects must be excluded, and programme makers should apply 'consistent editorial judgement, about whether to include or omit such perspectives.'[24] Satire should be an opportunity to give voice to minority or unorthodox views in a way that hard news cannot.

[22] 'Tim Davie: BBC Boss "prepared to fire stars who break impartiality rules"' (BBC, 29 September 2020) www.bbc.co.uk/news/entertainment-arts-54263754.

[23] BBC Editorial Guidelines, s 2.4.3.

[24] ibid s 2.4.4.

When discussing impartiality requirements, most interviewees talked of 'balance' when creating political comedy, rather than 'due impartiality'. Maintaining due impartiality mainly falls to the producer and from many interviews it seems there is a misconstruction by some that due impartiality and balance are the same thing. Ric Bailey was very clear that balance did not and should not equate to due impartiality, 'I never use the word "balance", I am very anti the word "balance"',[25] believing that the application of the due impartiality requirement upon satire should not be restrictive.

> Satire is a part of political communication, and I don't think we should be looking for any more constraints than are necessary. In the context of BBC impartiality … it's not about balance or anything like that, it tends to be about range and consistency. … So, my basic approach is not less but is more. The more satire and the more range you have, then the easier it is to satisfy the requirements of impartiality. (Ric Bailey, Chief Adviser Politics).

At the time of the interviews these concepts of balance did not appear to have filtered down to those in production. One anonymous producer thought the opposite was true.

> Impartial isn't a word that's used … a word we use all the time is 'balance'. … So instead, what we often talk about is 'balance', trying to get a balance of viewpoints across a series, and in that way achieve some level of fairness … So, as I say, 'impartial' is not a word we really use, more balance. (Anonymous, Producer 02).

Ofcom refers to 'balancing' programming,[26] and to the potential for 'significant imbalance' to breach the code regarding undue prominence of views and opinions.[27] Importantly Ofcom uses the qualifier 'significant', and from precedents in previous breaches only considerable oversights to a major viewpoint trigger a breach. Satire needs this significant leeway to be effective.

> How do you square impartiality with political satire? Because as a writer I can imagine, you can't be writing a gag and then think 'right, I've got to balance that with the other opposing view', I mean I don't think that's how satire works. … that doesn't make sense to me, impartial satire, I think those terms are mutually exclusive. (Anonymous, Compliance Consultant 02).

Partial satire should be possible under the regulations given the genre of political comedy and taking in the considerations of a series of programmes transmitted over time and the 'due' qualifier.

There was a general agreement that whilst satire played an important part in political discourse it was not 'hard news', and this should be considered when applying the impartiality requirement. For example, during an interview with Sky News, the former MP Huw Merriman complained about the BBC satirical game show *The News Quiz* as being completely biased against the Government, the interviewee

[25] Ric Bailey (Chief Adviser Politics).

[26] Ofcom Guidance Notes: Issue Six: Section Five: Due Impartiality and Due Accuracy and Undue Prominence of Views and Opinions (Ofcom, 22 March 2017).

[27] The Ofcom Broadcasting Code, s 5.13.

checked that he understood that the programme was comedy and not actual news.

Writers differentiated between the importance of due impartiality in the news and in satire more so than those in production.

> [T]here was a sort of tacit understanding [in the eighties and nineties] that the people in power were the people that you lampooned, now lately … I have been in meetings or in production situations where I have heard people saying, 'well we need to get someone right-wing on, you know for balance' and you're talking about a satirical comedy programme, no you don't. It's not Newsnight, it's not about a right to reply, this isn't about, well it is about fairness, in the sense that this is our little window this is our space to point out hypocrisy and tyranny in the world as it is governed and whoever is in power, they are the ones who need to get that kicking. … the idea that it should be balanced is disgraceful actually. Our job as satirists, actually whatever your political persuasion, is you have to attack whoever it is in power and you have to call out hypocrisy. (Anonymous, Writer and Performer 09).

The writers discussed how they were asked to write jokes for 'balance', but this was not something considered appropriate by Bailey, who holds a very senior editorial position. He also pointed out that the audience should be aware of what had happened in political entertainment programmes during previous political administrations.

> [I]mpartiality over time is a much under-analysed aspect of it … If I am being told in 2020 that we are not being even handed or balanced between Government and Opposition, I like to point people back to 2005 or 1998 or whenever it is, to say that actually, impartiality over time means consistency of approach. And often with satire, in particular I think, you are satirising the people who are doing things and that, by definition, is the people in power and that is therefore the Government. And opposition parties tend not to be in power. But that doesn't mean that you can't satirise them because they all do daft things, but do you have to do it equally? Do you have to have 'balance'? Absolutely not, I think you can satirise according to what deserves satirising and that can be a definition of impartiality. … If you're always satirising the same target and you're always coming at it from the same view, then I think you have a problem, but does that mean you have to satirise all politicians for some false balance? Absolutely not and I don't think we ever do that. (Ric Bailey, Chief Adviser Politics).

This had not been filtered down to the production teams. Writer and script editor Charlie Skelton, who has written on shows for Frankie Boyle, Jimmy Carr and Charlie Brooker thought there was very little 'real' satire on television.[28] He talked of getting 'notes' to write jokes for 'balance' where there was no satirical material. Others, both writers and producers, echoed this. It should be noted that the interviews took place whilst there was a Conservative Government in power.

> [T]here was a really weird thing … we would write monologues and stuff, the main note that would come back was 'there aren't enough jokes knocking the Labour

[28] Charlie Skelton (Writer).

> party' … in the great cacophony of voices … say Piers Morgan isn't chastised for the same thing and I think comedy is a weird one where people are scared, or broadcasters are scared of comedy because it's easy to cause offence and because there's such a fight for the BBC to keep the licence fee and that massive battle, so you have to keep the Government on side, they're terrified of causing offence[.] (Neil Webster, Writer and Producer).

The BBC was often the channel most often referred to as being 'worried' about impartiality. Again, this is doubtless because they produce more socio-political comedy content than other broadcasters. As mentioned, Bailey believed there were no real constraints on satire outside election periods but 'people think it's all a bit tricky and so avoid it'. Several writers expressed their frustration of being asked to 'balance' their output.

> Boris Johnson will do something stupid like go and hide in a fridge or something[29] and then you'll do a load of jokes about that and they'll go, 'now, we'll need the same amount of jokes about Labour', and you understand, but he's just gone and hidden in a fridge! That's why this is news, it's not a hatred of the Conservatives, it's a 'look what this guy is doing!' (Christine Rose, Writer).

Rather than 'balancing' jokes, the balance of political power should be taken into consideration when deciding on how 'duly' impartial material is. The Ofcom code does not require ridiculing a Labour politician to be countered by ridiculing an opposing one or vice versa. Balancing political satire undermines the power of satire to expose hypocrisy and foibles and levels political behaviour.

Demanding an equal amount of satirical attack against each different political party could lead to an electorate disenchanted with the political system by painting a picture with the message that all MPs and all political parties are as bad as each other. This sentiment could protect those already in power.

> Impartiality is one of those wet words … it means, 'now don't upset anybody', but what it usually means is, impartiality means don't upset the Government … I am all in favour of partiality. If somebody is doing something outrageous and appalling, and they need to be made serious fun of, so people don't take them seriously, then that's important to do. You don't then say, 'let's pick on somebody totally innocent and give them a hard time as well', that's not impartial, that's ridiculous. (John Lloyd, Executive Producer).

If both the political left and the right are made to look equally foolish through satire when one side is more deserving than the other, this is not duly impartial.[30]

[29] C Duncan, 'Boris Johnson hides in a fridge on live TV while dodging interview on eve of election' *The Independent* (11 December 2019) www.independent.co.uk/news/uk/politics/boris-johnson-hides-fridge-general-election-piers-morgan-good-morning-britain-live-tv-a9241631.html.

[30] It is difficult to give a definition of left- and right-wing comics/comedy in the context of these interviews where each contributor who uses the terms did so without defining what it meant to them. It was described by Shane Allen as a 'nebulous' concept. According to Thorisdottir et al, Western European right-wing ideologues would resist change and accept inequality, whilst placing a high value on tradition and rule-following, whereas left-wing ideologues would prefer change and reject inequality.

It appears to be more of a 'false balance' to ask for jokes ridiculing politicians if they have done nothing ridiculous (that week). Lloyd's point about impartiality meaning 'don't upset the Government' implies he believes it gives a Government a layer of protection. It may be used to protect ministers from further ridicule, to stifle rather than further political debate. One case which illustrates this is the satirical panel show *Have I Got News for You* [HIGNFY]. The producer, Jo Bunting, discussed due impartiality requirements when booking politicians as participants.

> The BBC wants to see a range of views expressed from people clearly allied to political parties, now what we have got is a [Conservative] Government who simply don't put people forward. I don't blame them obviously, why would you come on HIGNFY if you are probably a mediocre, rubbish politician? … That means we can't have other people who would come on and I find that very frustrating. I think if you have given them the opportunity to come on and if you have asked endlessly, 'will any Tory politician come on HIGNFY this series on any of the shows?' and if they simply say 'no', I don't see why therefore we can't have Labour politicians who are willing to come on. … We're not going to invite a Labour politician on for a nice chat and a Tory in to be given an absolute grilling, it just doesn't work like that. … But if they're willing to come on, it frustrates me that they are shut up and silenced and gagged and unable to come on because we can't get right wing politicians to come on as well, but that's the rule, so is what usually happens. … That is something I think that needs to be looked at. (Jo Bunting, Producer).

If it is considered a rule, then it is a self-imposed rule. Ofcom does not put similar restrictions upon broadcasters. This is illustrated by Ofcom's investigation into Channel 4 News Climate Debate transmitted on 28 November 2019.[31] The debate was entitled Emergency On Planet Earth, and all the party leaders were invited to appear on the programme to discuss their climate-related policies. Both Nigel Farage and Boris Johnson did not appear, and Channel 4 refused the Conservative party's request that Michael Gove, a senior Cabinet Minister, could take Johnson's place. They were 'empty chaired' and melting ice sculptures put in their places. The Conservative party complained to Ofcom before the programme was transmitted that Channel 4 was failing to comply with Sections Five and Six of the Code on due impartiality.

H Thorisdottir, JT Jost, I Liviatan, PE Shrout, 'Psychological Needs and Values Underlying Left-Right Political Orientation: Cross-National Evidence from Eastern and Western Europe' (Summer 2007) 71(2) *Public Opinion Quarterly*. I asked Leo Kearse for his definition as he styled himself as a right wing comic and he described right wing as believing 'in smaller Government, lower taxes, less Government interference in people's lives', rather than what many would associate with right wing comedy as leaning towards homophobic, misogynistic or racist humour, see M Sienkiewicz and N Marx, 'Appropriating Irony: Conservative Comedy, Trump-Era Satire, and the Politics of Television Humor' (2021) 60(4) *Journal of Cinema & Media Studies* 1.

[31] 'Decision of the Election Committee on a due impartiality complaint brought by the Conservative Party in relation to Channel 4's Channel 4 News Climate Debate' (Ofcom, 28 November 2019) www.ofcom.org.uk/siteassets/resources/documents/about-ofcom/how-ofcom-is-run/election-committee/decision-election-climate-debate.pdf?v=324397.

Ofcom responded with this statement:

> If a broadcaster is unable to agree participation in a programme with any particular politician or party, it is then the broadcaster's editorial decision whether to proceed with the programme or not.
>
> Depending on the particular circumstances, a broadcaster may decide to proceed with an election debate programme and to 'empty chair' a political party or politician who decides not to participate. In any event, the broadcaster must ensure that the programmes (including linked programmes) as broadcast comply with the due impartiality requirements of the Code.

It should be noted that there are additional requirements to observe due impartiality during election periods. Therefore, empty chairing a major political party in a political debate would be under more regulatory scrutiny than would empty chairing politicians on a comedy panel show outside an election period. This incident was also commented upon by a lawyer.

> Channel 4 did that … ice sculpture during the elections debate, … that was a real light the paper and run-away moment. The Government went mad about it and Channel 4 may still suffer repercussions about that, because they're public service, and part of the funding comes from the Beeb. [C]riticising someone for not turning up to a debate, that in itself is enough to cause huge, potential political fallout and how can that not have a dampening effect? (Anonymous, Lawyer).

Not only is it potentially problematic for the broadcaster when politicians decide not to do media appearances, but also broadcasters may want to avoid financial repercussions from ministers. After the incident, the funding of Channel 4 came under review and the then Culture Secretary Nadine Dorries discussed potentially selling the broadcaster.[32] Broadcasters are aware of the power politicians have over them. This potentially influences editorial decisions. There have been incidents of writers being told that they should tone down their satirical attacks on politicians, which they have found surprising.

> [The BBC] were saying 'we can't do a joke about the Prime Minster like that, he's the Prime Minister' and we were going 'what?! Since when have we not been able to do a joke about the Prime Minister?'. …
>
> This [joke] was for the film BAFTAS … they like us to incorporate several of the nominated films in a joke, you've got the elements of all the films you've got to put together, with a topical element, it's like a terrible puzzle. It was, *the biggest film nominations tonight really do sum up Britain over the last year, there's 1917, Marriage Story and Joker, a fight with Europe, a messy divorce, all led by a psychopathic clown*. They [BBC] said, 'well we can't call him [Johnson] a psychopathic clown' … And then we try and change it and nothing sounds as good as *psychopathic clown* because it also has to sound like *The Joker*. Sometimes they don't seem to understand jokes very well, which is fine, it's

[32] 'Channel 4 News didn't do itself any favours, says Nadine Dorries' (BBC News, 19 May 2022) www.bbc.co.uk/news/uk-politics-61508170.

> not their job, but when you are changing jokes, it helps if you understand them and some people are like, 'why can't we say, 'horrible man'?' and you say, 'well it doesn't work', 'or why can't we say 'bumbling buffoon'?', and you're 'because the Joker in the film is not a bumbling buffoon, he's a psychopathic clown, and these two things have to work as comparisons'. (Christine Rose, Writer).

This joke could have been transmitted under the regulations. It is an example of how misinterpreting due impartiality creates a chilling effect on material. Another misinterpretation which caused participants needless problems was that impartiality had to be achieved within each show.

> Argh, fucking impartiality. I think it hamstrings things, I really do … Frankie [Boyle] is a self-confessed, working class, left wing/leaning, Scottish comic. And the idea that he then gets slightly his wings clipped within a show, I get that for balance, we should have other people representing other perspectives, and all of that across the board, but within a show it is very difficult. I find it very difficult that he, that we have to achieve a sense of equilibrium within each and every show. When actually you are hiring someone … because of his comic ability in the first place and part of that is enshrined in his own personal views and perspective on the world. And then the impartiality, I get round it and it's you know, it's workable, but it's a constant that becomes slightly wearying. The idea that everything has to have balance within the show in terms of that punching in all directions[.] (Shane Allen, Controller of Comedy).

As an established performer, context, especially that of audience expectation, would give Boyle's political voice more leeway. Boyle is known to be left-leaning, therefore the audience should expect the satire to be from a left-wing perspective, and should people choose to watch him they would be prepared for this. By insisting that the show should be impartial, the audience who would enjoy seeing political satire solely through the filter of a left-wing comedian loses out. This does not fulfil the requirement of preserving a democratic process. As mentioned above, there should be greater scope for contentious authored programmes, provided the authorship is clear, and that over time there is a balance of opinion across the intellectual and political spectrum. This should create opportunities for comedians with differing political views but, since the interviews *Frankie Boyle's New World Order*, *Mock the Week*, *Unspun* and *The Mash Report* have not been recommissioned, so there are fewer satirical voices on broadcast television.

Regarding the potential harm in misinterpreting the due impartiality requirement, the following contribution by John Lloyd illustrates how it results in some programme content never being made. He described working on a comedy project under the umbrella campaign *Make Poverty History*, where the producer Richard Curtis was told in a production meeting,

> 'Richard, you have to put the other side as well, because some people might quite like world poverty'… They said, 'you know, there's always somebody who may say, "you may be against child labour, but it gives a lot of poor people some serious employment, if the children didn't work …"'. (John Lloyd, Executive Producer).

In a civilised society, perpetuating poverty or the benefits of child labour, should not need to be argued. Creating a 'balance' which could downplay these issues is an example of how information and ideas would be skewed because of a misinterpretation of the rules.

The more those in production misinterpret and over-reach with the rules on impartiality, the more ineffectual broadcast satire is at checking Government and policy. Interpreted in this way the misapplication of these regulations gives a better protection to the powerful than either the vulnerable, or the audience's rights to hear new ideas from a different perspective. It is a lost opportunity to raise contentious issues, educate audiences and provide the chance to instigate positive societal change.

Some decision makers find it hard to judge where the line of 'due' lies. Instead, they 'play it safe', and limit themselves in transmitting programming that might challenge the Government or public policy. This creates gaps in both broadcasting and public debate which can be filled within the boundaries of statutory requirements, and a false 'balance' could be avoided.

The pressure on writers to 'balance' satirical attacks on political targets perpetuates the belief that there is a statutory need for balance. It creates not only weaker jokes but also a weaker programme, this could turn viewers off and continue the belief that all politicians are as bad as each other. Ian Hislop, the editor of satirical magazine *Private Eye* commented on the shortcomings of impartiality during an appearance on the panel show *Have I Got News For You*. The programme was discussing the Brexit Party and UKIP candidates for the 2019 Peterborough by-election and the host said,

> I should point out in the interest of balance that all other candidates in the Peterborough election are equally shit.

Ian Hislop replied

> That's what you get if you apply rigidly those supposed guidelines, you don't make any distinction between rubbish and the truth or if people are any good or if people are not any good, you just say 'it has to be the same amount of time' I mean it is just nonsense.[33]

If the impartiality requirement is misinterpreted in this way, then it could then lead to a disenchantment of politics. It would give out the message to viewers that change was pointless, all politicians were as bad as each other.

The BBC has previously argued that 'balance' is not equivalent to impartiality, that there are more than two sides to an argument, and all voices should be given the opportunity to be heard. It is somewhat telling that the BBC more often than not refers to 'impartiality' in its output rather than due impartiality. It might be better for democratic debate if the 'due' is given more emphasis. When all voices are given equal weight, outliers could become as accepted as the mainstream, and truth will be harder to discover. In this scenario the impartiality requirement is counterproductive to democracy. Audiences might believe that there is an equal

[33] *Have I Got News For You*, BBC (TX, 17 May 2019, 21:00).

split between all points of view, all views being as valid as each other when they are not, and some given greater credibility than deserved.

Some producers realised due impartiality did not require balance but were aware that others had misinterpreted it.

> I think people feel, 'if I say something particularly left wing they'll have to balance it' and I don't know if that is necessarily true ....we have quite a lot of political comedians coming in for interviews and they express their political views and that's totally fine and it doesn't need to be balanced and we don't have to have our presenters stepping in all of the time to try and balance the views of guests, opinion has a place within comedy. (Laura Grimshaw, Radio Producer).

One anonymous producer explains how he tries to counter his own bias by booking people from across the political spectrum.[34] Of course this is only possible when people from the political spectrum make themselves available to be booked. If it is impossible to get a required range of political voices that could mean eventually there will be fewer programmes with political voices beyond serious news.

Jon Thoday produced the satires *Last Week Tonight with John Oliver* in America and *Unspun with Matt Forde* in the UK, and he felt due impartiality was a stumbling block to producing good, satirical comedy in the UK.

> [I]n the UK … it's very, very difficult, weirdly, it's very difficult to do satire full stop here …. The biggest reason is impartiality … The problem with impartiality is that it doesn't allow a point of view … you cannot do a satire show which leans either to the right or to the left, you have obligations to impartiality which just don't exist in America. Now whether that is a good thing or a bad thing, I don't know, but it's definitely anti-satire. Although weirdly, those kinds of rules should lead to more satire[.] (Jon Thoday, Co-Executive Chairman, Avalon).

Applying impartiality means there could be a wider range of voices in satire, both from the right and the left. Andrew Newman, ex- Head of Entertainment at Channel 4 and CEO, Spelthorne Community Television, felt that the regulatory flexibility was there to create a wide range of comedic views across a channel, but the broadcasters did not use the opportunity.

> A channel should be able to say, 'this show is quite right-wing, but this show is quite left-wing, in the round we are impartial'. That seems to be a difficult thing for broadcasters to do and to articulate … (Andrew Newman, CEO, Spelthorne Community Television).

As due impartiality can be achieved across a series or strand of programming this would lead to more political satire, across a wider political spectrum. The BBC was actively trying, and had been for several years, to get more right-wing voices onto satirical shows.[35] This seems to be proving difficult.

[34] Anonymous (Producer 02).
[35] Anonymous (Producer 02).

> When we're doing *Unspun* at UKTV, ..., [the broadcaster says] 'you've got to have a right-wing comedian as one of the regular comedians' and ironically it is pretty hard to find one. ... I think it would have been quite good to have a right-wing comic on it but if you haven't got one, I don't think you should have it. (Jon Thoday, Co-Executive Chairman Avalon).

B. Right Wing Comedians

> [It's] like when they wanted to find more female comedians and they kept looking for them, but no one ever asked the question 'why are there so few in the first place?', ... And the same with right-wing comedians. Why are there so few? ... [A]s a producer of topical comedy, you aren't overwhelmed by the number of really sharp comedians who focus on politics of any hue. ... I wish the BBC well with its efforts to find more overtly right-wing comedians, but I'm not holding my breath. (Jo Bunting, Producer).

It seems unlikely that fewer right-wing comics wish to come on the radio or television. There is a gap in the market, and it is also unlikely they are not being booked given the contributors' comments. A *Guardian* newspaper article quoted an anonymous source which said that many right-wing comedians were just not funny enough to appear on shows.[36] It was not necessarily that right-wing comics were not funny but rather that the pool of talent was smaller. There were fewer comics who were right wing and commissioners often found it frustrating that a broadcaster required 'balance'; to achieve this a few comics are booked on a regular basis to fulfil the requirement. When a contributor is not 'very good' it is detrimental to a programme, the programme will be less appealing to the audience and, in turn when the audience numbers are not delivered, will be less appealing to the broadcasters to recommission. It could hasten the demise of satirical programming rather than widen its appeal.

Yet many producers believed a range of voices would make programmes more interesting, especially when contributors challenge the general consensus on political issues.

> [re BBC Radio programme *The F in News*] I had to make sure that the chat involved criticism of both Government and opposition over the course of the series – it doesn't have to be during the course of one particular show – but at one point I really did need to have an overtly right-wing voice. So, I booked [Julia] Hartley-Brewer, who is very much a right-wing voice. I have booked Julia over the years ... there is a lot about her that makes her a brilliant panel show guest, and because she is actually funny, witty, bright, very articulate. [S]o I booked her on ... and she absolutely was fine, she was prodding the audience a little bit about how predictably anti Brexit

[36] J Waterson, 'Right-wing comedians not funny enough for BBC shows, says insider' *The Guardian* (1 September 2021) www.theguardian.com/media/2020/sep/01/rightwing-comedians-not-funny-enough-for-bbc-shows-says-insider.

> they were, but I thought 'that's alright, it's so refreshing to hear a different view'. (Jo Bunting, Producer).

Is there a reason for the right to be under-represented in comedy which goes beyond a lack of talent or the number of comics? Kearse thought broadcast talent scouts were just not looking in the right places.

> [T]here was a BBC insider saying, 'we can't book any right-wing comedians because they're not funny, there's no funny ones'. And how would they even know? None of the BBC come and look, they don't come to the working-class club circuit that I do. (Leo Kearse, Stand Up Comedian).

Shane Allen thought it was increasingly likely that talent was spotted online, especially because of covid, rather than on the club circuit.

> The paucity of right-wing comedy isn't about there not being awareness or an appetite, any half decent right wing comic mops up because of the need for balance on shows. The only barrier to careers being progressed is one of talent and ability.[37]

Again, this self-imposed, rather than regulatory requirement, need for balance should work in favour of a right-leaning comic. Dominic Frisby, a comedian and composer of *Libertarian Love Songs*, and the pro-Brexit song *17 Million Fuck-Offs*, thought there was not a shortage of good, right-wing comedians but rather a shortage of comedians who wished to admit publicly to being right-wing.

> The clever comedians just keep their politics to themselves unless they are a political comedian. You just make so many enemies … why alienate half your audience by twatting on about Brexit? … I get so many messages from closet right-wingers [comedians], … 'Really like what you're doing, really admire it, totally agree with you', but then will keep their politics to themselves. It's a form of censorship and suppression and it is this tiny, vocal and extremely influential minority with their magic spell words.[38] (Dominic Frisby, Stand-Up Comic and Broadcaster).

Other contributors echoed this idea of 'closet right-wingers', those who were politically on the right but did not want it known publicly. This was because the 'eco-system' of the comedy circuit was more supportive to left-leaning comics.[39] This shy approach to admitting to being right-wing meant that there were fewer publicly right-wing comedians.

> [Y]ou have less to choose from, so maybe you are hearing from the same few right-wing voices. … People may have right-wing opinions, but they don't necessarily want to go on air and stand by those because they almost don't think it's worth the hassle … but if you're say a more apolitical comic who said, on a satirical show, 'actually let's give Boris Johnson a fair crack at the whip', then people would probably castigate you for

[37] Shane Allen (via email 19 January 2021).
[38] Frisby's definition of 'magic spell' words was, 'sexist, or racist, or whatever it is'.
[39] Anonymous (Producer 02).

> that … It is not as simple as saying … we're not booking the right-wing people, or they are not being given a shot, sometimes the culture in which we all exist … people don't want to raise their head above the parapet. (Anonymous, Producer 02).

There is a flip side, Bunting believed that some comedians had purposefully styled themselves as right-wing when in fact they were not.

> I don't know any right-wing comedians, I know some that call themselves right-wing and I have never ever heard them say anything right-wing, they are very clever, because it is a good little niche to build on. … If a comedian said something supportive about the Government's immigration policy or said they felt that the pay for care workers was perfectly adequate … that would be really interesting. (Jo Bunting, Producer).

However, often right-wing comics seem more intent on attacking what they perceive as left-wing 'wokeness' and cultural sensibilities, rather than promoting right-wing politics. It seems that finding suitable 'right-wing' voices which will enhance programming can sometimes prove difficult.

Whilst Bunting had found the right-wing broadcaster Hartley-Brewer a refreshing change, this was not universal.

> What is interesting is that the panelists [for HIGNFY] … who would be slightly, more right of centre, … tend to be really generally objectionable and what you're after is a good atmosphere between five people. (Richard Wilson, Executive Producer).

There is no statutory requirement of having to include a right-wing contributor. Trevor Barnes talked of how Ofcom had noticed that most comedy output on broadcast tended to be from the political left but thought that this should not be restrictive.

> [D]ue impartiality does not mean, by any means, fifty/fifty … You are perfectly entitled, with freedom of expression, to have a programme, whether it is satire, comedy, anything else, which puts forward a very, strong point of view … [B]roadly, if you are within the parameters of what people think of as kind of the limits of political discourse, you can go very much to one side or the other and provided you know what the alternative point is, and you kind of nod to it, you only need the smallest nod, that's duly impartial. (Trevor Barnes, Compliance Consultant).

Many participants believed more than 'the smallest nod' was necessary to fulfil the due impartiality requirement, with two stating that impartiality 'hamstringed' satire and stopped it from being hard hitting. They believed that satire played an important role and that broadcasters should be prepared to produce it, push the boundaries and to protect it.

C. Upsetting the Apple Cart

> Stuff that is punchy is risky, can … cost people their jobs, their reputations, their livelihoods if they get it wrong, … it's right for these things to be difficult to make, the ones

> who can really suffer I guess, is the audience, because they are not given those shows ultimately. (Jolyon Rubinstein, Writer and Performer).

Satire can be risky for several reasons, not just because it can cause offence, or problems with impartiality but it can be very expensive as it may need to go through complex legal checks before transmission. Satire can incorporate content which might, for example, border on the defamatory and statements could trigger an individual or a company to initiate legal action against the broadcaster and/or the writer. Therefore, risky satire is not the most attractive genre of programming for a broadcaster to commission. In addition to being expensive to make, it is not easy for a commercial broadcaster to 'monetise'. It normally has a quick turn-around from production to transmission because of its topicality, and a short shelf-life. Political satire has no repeat value as it dates quickly. Satires which challenge British political hegemony are only 'culturally relevant at that moment in time, they're not going to be relevant in three months' time, let alone three years' time.'[40] It does not sell well internationally in a global market of streaming services as it has a single geographical political focus so does not have as wide an audience appeal as a drama. For a commercial channel, the audience numbers ultimately decide what will be recommissioned.

In this respect, out of all the British broadcasters, the BBC is perfectly placed to take a risk because it does not have to rely on commercial factors to drive the value of its programming.

Cost was considered an overarching factor in whether satire was commissioned in the first place, which would over-ride any editorial issues in what might or might not be broadcast. Plowman thought the decrease in comedy production was a financial decision the BBC made in the light of the rise in popularity of streaming services such as Netflix and Amazon.[41],[42] Others agreed,

> [C]omedy doesn't travel. It's much more regional than drama, so we'll do a show and all funding for shows is based on distribution, you can't get a show paid for anymore, so it's got to be able to sell around the world and comedy just doesn't sell like drama. Now all comedies are becoming dramas … Comedy with bite is contracting. (Neil Webster, Writer and Producer).

This then leaves a satire shaped gap in the schedule which only a public service channel might be willing to fill. However, by 2019 the BBC's funding was cut by 30 per cent in real terms from that in 2010.[43] Rubinstein thought there should be funds 'specifically earmarked for legal support' for satirical programmes, but even with that it would be problematic given the political climate.

[40] Steve North (General Manager UKTV).

[41] Ofcom's Annual Report on the BBC 2019/20 (Ofcom 25 November 2020) 53 www.ofcom.org.uk/__data/assets/pdf_file/0021/207228/third-bbc-annual-report.pdf.

[42] Jon Plowman (Executive Producer).

[43] P Barwise and P York, *The War Against the BBC: How an unprecedented combination of hostile forces is destroying Britain's greatest cultural institution … And Why you should care* (London, Penguin, 2020) xv.

> I believe that we are living at a time where broadcasters are more concerned with upsetting the apple cart, and the potential ramifications that would have for their funding … [Y]ou have a very aggressive, fact-blurring, really almost dystopian [Conservative] Government, who seem hellbent on making the end of the licence fee some sort of form of … libertarian freedom. (Jolyon Rubinstein, Writer and Performer).

Many participants believed satire was important in uncertain political climates as it enhanced democratic debate. It was considered a valuable vehicle to add context to political commentary and encourage critical thinking.

> [I]f all your politics is kind of very serious and po-faced, you're not really getting all the landscape … And I think satire at its best, gives you some of the tools to help you understand politics. … [I]t [satire] felt a bit more central to the art of political communication in the States. Not necessarily as informing, but in terms of analysis ….it is following that pattern of a way of analysing politics from a different angle, which is potentially constructive. (Ric Bailey, Chief Adviser Politics).

Many interviewees commented that whilst satire often deals with news stories, its playful and challenging nature creates opportunities to open discussions on what otherwise might be considered taboo subjects. Andy Parsons, the stand-up comic and a contributor to the long running satirical panel show *Mock The Week*, thought that satirical programmes served as a valuable source of information for younger people because it worked to encourage the audience to think critically about political issues. Lloyd thought satirical programming was in the public interest and helped progress society.

> Roger Law[44] and I … used to call ourselves 'Her Majesty's Loyal Opposition'. …. [W]e engaged young people in politics, and we educated people, and we made them think without realising they were thinking about it because most people's opinions are very bipolar … [T]hat's what comedians do, they point out things you haven't noticed before. … So, it's all fresh thinking and a lot of jokes, of course, are a way of looking at the world which is surprising and unusual. And so it influences people in that way, it loosens them up, it makes them less prejudiced, but without realising it. (John Lloyd, Executive Producer).

Contributors talked about how there were few real challenges to what might be considered mainstream political ideology in both news and comedy. One reason was programmes which some might frame as satirical were long-running and considered relatively toothless.

> [T]hat's the danger sometimes, you get a marginal frisson sense that something's been satirised when it hasn't really, it was just a silly voice and it was a bit of fun and I'm very uncertain about how well satire works in the mediums that we have. (Robin Ince, Writer and Broadcaster).

[44] Co-creator of satirical show *Spitting Image*.

Another interviewee considered there was no incentive for new talent to write broadcast satire, because those shows and formats would not be appealing to up-and-coming younger writers.

> [I]f you're twenty now, what are you trying to get on? *The News Quiz*? Fuck, if you're aiming for that at twenty, then already you've got the mental age of a 65-year-old, haven't you? (Neil Webster, Writer and Producer).

This problem of attracting new talent was compounded because broadcast satire did not consider the issues that young people faced.

> I don't think they [satirists] are really trying to challenge anything because [politicians] went to Oxford and Cambridge and studied PPE, but you [the satirist] were at Cambridge ... in the footlights, so your perception of society and your perception of what needs to change is very cosy. [I]f you talk to a twenty three year old now, who can't get a job and has no prospects of getting a house, ... there's not as much speaking to that, as there is to very cosy London based, rich, 'oh Boris Johnson is fat' or 'Keir Starmer looks like a cushion', this isn't satire is it? This is all just parlour games. (Anonymous, Producer 02).

Skelton believed this was problematic and modern broadcast satire was running the risk of preaching to the converted, rather than challenging preconceptions.

> [T]here's a particular kind of smug which has now crossed into television more ... *The Last Leg*, ... [I]t's a catastrophe, a political and artistic catastrophe[.] (Charlie Skelton, Writer and Script Editor).

Preaching to the converted is easier than challenging audiences. If writers produce content that they know agrees with their audience's ideology, then they know there is more chance of them returning to the programme next time or buying tickets for live shows. It makes financial sense for comedians to find an audience, either right or left wing, and just reinforce their preconceptions, rather than challenge them. But this is not necessarily good for satire.

> Chris [Morris] ... wanted people to examine why they were laughing and think about the things that he was doing. ... So his job as he saw it, was to make people question and make people unsettled. I think people were very, very nervous about that now and I wouldn't be surprised if there wasn't a lot of self-censorship going on. (Graham Linehan, Writer).

If satire is there to prick pomposity and to expose hypocrisy, there is little point if it simply reiterates the opinion of those who already believe their politicians to be pompous hypocrites. But there may be another point to it, it might affect the behaviour of the target of the satire (for the better one hopes). They are certainly affected by it, when politicians have been the target of satire, there are examples where they have complained to the broadcaster.

> Politicians have complained about their representation to the BBC. Politicians are threatened by satire. It is a way to scrutinise politicians. (Ric Bailey, Chief Adviser Politics).

If negative media coverage concerns politicians, the level of concern depends on where the coverage appears. Lord Grade, who has experience of working across the BBC, ITV and Channel 4, illustrated the difference in attitude politicians have between broadcasters.

> We did a programme about Mrs. Thatcher's husband Dennis being involved with the mafia in America. He was a non-executive director of a waste disposal company in Florida, and they were under investigation by the Un-American Activities legislation, it was a good story. I spent hours going through with the lawyers and the transcript and the script and the cut, and I said, 'get onto Downing Street, you give them the whole story of what is in the film, and you give them whatever they want in order to respond'. So, they rang Downing Street, and we got no statement back, so we transmitted the programme, and we had tin hats on ready for the backlash, nothing happened, there was no backlash at all. Years later I told this story at his memorial service and Tim Bell,[45] … told me … 'Dennis and Margaret rang me in a state of panic, and I said "forget it, it's only Channel 4, ignore it! It'll go away"'. And that's exactly what happened, we could get away with murder. If the BBC had done that it would have been very, very different, there would have been blood on the moon … [The BBC] don't want to aggravate the politicians unnecessarily, they are quite prepared to tweak the Government, but I think that they would take more care than anyone else would take. It wouldn't stop them putting the programme out, I am sure of it, because the staff just wouldn't stand for it. (Lord Michael Grade).[46]

As discussed in chapter two, we have seen how Donald Trump has followed a long line of authoritarian leaders to use his power and influence, sometimes successfully, to get rid of satirists mocking him and his presidency. The popular and long running US satirical show *The Late Show with Stephen Colbert* has been cancelled. Whilst the broadcaster CBS claims this is to do with financial considerations, the announcement came a few days after Colbert criticised CBS's parent company Paramount for settling a lawsuit with Trump, calling it a 'big fat bribe'. This was alluding to the fact that the settlement was agreed at the same time as Paramount sought the US Federal Communications Commission's approval for a billion-dollar merger with another media company. Another US satirist, Jimmy Kimmel was also taken off air following a comment he made criticising Donald Trump and his MAGA supporters after a right-wing activist was shot dead. Trump took to his Truth Social Platform on 18 September 2025 to congratulate the broadcaster for their actions, writing

> Great News for America: The ratings challenged Jimmy Kimmel Show is CANCELLED. Congratulations to ABC for finally having the courage to do what had to be done. Kimmel has ZERO talent, and worse ratings than even Colbert, if that's possible. That

[45] Timothy Bell is Baron Bell who advised Margaret Thatcher on communication and public relations.

[46] This may not be the case now, two Panorama programmes were dropped, one regarding Vote Leave's activities during the 2016 EU referendum and the other on Vote Leave's spending and use of Cambridge Analytica. See Barwise and York (n 43) 154.

> leaves Jimmy and Seth, two total losers, on Fake News NBC. Their ratings are also horrible. Do it NBC!!! President DJT.[47]

This cancellation led to a backlash with subscribers in turn cancelling their subscriptions to ABC's parent company Disney, wiping billions off its share price. This forced them to reinstate Kimmel, much to the disgust of Trump who reminded ABC of the payout they gave him last time he sued the channel. All the decisions made, who to cancel, what to broadcast, what to commission and what to write ultimately have an impact on the audience in terms of their right to hear information and ideas. The health of a democracy can be judged on the way it treats dissent, especially satirical dissent.

Trump was not the first President to use his power to get satirical shows pulled from broadcast.

> [S]o there's regulation and then there's politics/commerce that dictate what you can and can't do. … [W]hen *Spitting Image* was on NBC in the eighties … it was allegedly cancelled because Ronald Reagan called the president of NBC because he didn't like his puppet. So you have to think, 'what's the politics and who's saying this and who's paying them?' because those are the things [broadcasters] are bothered about …. In the BBC they're worried about the Government, so they want to say they're taking risks, they want to say they are doing satire and they can point to things like HIGNFY which, because … it's reasonably well established, they can get away with some stuff, but could they do a show like *The Daily Show*? They definitely couldn't, they might say they want to, which is sort of what that thing, the *Mash Report* is trying to do, but they can't. They can't get somebody who's got a real point of view doing a show which is a great shame … Frankie Boyle has significantly had his wings clipped over time because they gradually get to learn what they can and can't do.' (Jon Thoday, Co-Executive Chairman, Avalon).

Since these interviews (under the previous Conservative government) neither the *Mash Report* nor *Frankie Boyle's New World Order* were recommissioned.

In the United Kingdom it is the Government which holds the purse strings of the BBC and holds sway over the ownership of Channel 4, so has a part to play in potentially having a chilling effect over what is broadcast. One contributor described this as an 'existential threat'.

> [T]he BBC always, for quite understandable reasons in many ways, seem to be a lot more nervous about things than perhaps other channels or services would be, which to an extent I understand when you have spent the last decade under constant existential threat from a [Conservative] Government that is not particularly fond of you, I can understand why you might be a bit more of a stickler in your interpretation [of the Code], and they are always going to be interpretations of course. (Anonymous, Writer 11).

[47] 'Jimmy and Seth' are references to the late-night show satirists Jimmy Fallon and Seth Meyers.

D. An Existential Threat

The British Government has considerable control over the BBC. It can set the licence fee, thereby controlling its funding, it can choose the chair and the non-executive members for the board who have editorial control, thereby controlling editorial principles.[48] If a Government is not supportive of Public Service Broadcasters they could be less likely to criticise the Government, especially if some board members are appointed by Government Ministers.

These are several factors which call into question the independence of the BBC from the Government. It is written in the BBC Charter article 20(2), in accordance with article 3 (independence of the BBC), that each member of the Board must uphold and protect the independence of the BBC, act in the public interest, exercise independent judgement and neither seek nor take instruction from anyone, including Government Ministers.[49] But if politicians are the ones who appoint them, it is likely they will be connected in some way to Government Ministers.

Politicians can potentially appoint people to the position of BBC Chair, Director General and to the BBC board, who are sympathetic to the Government. The Government can also attempt to influence the appointment of the Head of Ofcom, which is an independent authority. Tim Davie, the Director General who has just stepped down amid concerns over the BBC's impartiality, was chairman of the Hammersmith and Fulham Conservative Party in the 1990s before unsuccessfully standing as a Conservative councillor in Borough Council elections in 1993 and 1994. Richard Sharp, a Conservative Party donor with connections to the then Chancellor Rishi Sunak, was appointed the new Chair of the BBC before resigning, having been caught in a controversy when the *Sunday Times* claimed that he had secured a loan guarantee agreement for the Prime Minister Boris Johnson.

Sir Robbie Gibb, Former Downing Street communications director for the Conservative Party is on the BBC Board, he was also an editorial adviser for GB News. For a period of time there was a strong possibility that the Conservative Government would attempt to interfere with the selection process for the new Head of Ofcom to ensure that Paul Dacre was appointed, but the position was given finally to the Conservative peer Lord Michael Grade.[50,51]

Thus, politicians can wield influence internally and externally, by creating media laws, setting funding, and appointing amenable people into prominent

[48] BBC, 'About the BBC', www.bbc.com/aboutthebbc/whoweare/bbcboard.

[49] The Royal Charter for the continuance of the British Broadcasting Corporation Cm 9365 (December 2016), s 6.3.

[50] BBC, 'Richard Sharp: Who is the former BBC chairman?' (BBC 28 April 2023) www.bbc.com/news/uk-64368677.

[51] V Thorpe, 'Johnson poised to appoint Paul Dacre Chair of Ofcom' *The Guardian* (3 January 2021) www.theguardian.com/media/2021/jan/31/johnson-poised-to-appoint-paul-dacre-chair-of-ofcom.

positions. This can create tensions around editorial choices. Lord Grade believes that the Government has a chilling effect on editorial decisions.

> [T]here is always a political, subliminal political dynamic to editorial decisions at the BBC [.] (Lord Michael Grade).

Might such a dynamic cause a censorship by omission, programmes are never made, and so the audience misses out on seeing programming from different perspectives? Lord Grade thinks this political dynamic is heightened when there were 'moral panics'.

> [T]hey have to look around for 'something must be done, there's widespread public concern, so something must be done'. So, you end up with tightening the rules on the watershed, you end up with the IRA not being allowed to broadcast … you can't interview Gerry Adams or Martin McGuinness, … we made such fools of them, it's that ghastly political 'we must be seen to be doing something'.[52] (Lord Michael Grade).

One such political knee-jerk reaction happened following the infamous 2001 *Brass Eye* Special *Paedogeddon*. It satirised the media's hypocrisy of creating moral panic around paedophilia whilst simultaneously carrying stories hinting at the sexuality of teenagers.[53] Three politicians had unwittingly appeared on the programme, two of whom complained to the media regulator (at the time the Independent Television Commission – ITC) of unwarranted infringement of privacy, and unjust and unfair treatment. It was reported that many Ministers considered the programme 'unspeakably sick' and the programme whipped up a moral panic. The Child Protection Minister, Beverley Hughes, condemned the programme without having seen it. The Prime Minister's Official Spokesperson stated that the then Culture Secretary, Tessa Jowell, would be speaking to the Chief Executive of Channel 4, and the Chair of the ITC.[54] Jowell's call was to see if the ITC might respond more swiftly to potential breaches so they might not be retransmitted, as this programme was, before the adjudication was passed. It was emphasised by the Prime Minister's Spokesperson that the Government did not wish to tell the broadcasters 'what they should or should not broadcast' but if that were the case, it rather beggars the question as to why the Culture Secretary spoke with Channel 4 rather than just with the regulator. It is somewhat telling that there has not been a satirical programme by a traditional broadcaster since which has caused so much controversy. Some people might think that is a good thing.

As with issues of harm and offence, audiences need not wait for Ministers to condemn programmes, or for the media to be outraged on their behalf. They do not need to seek out a broadcasters' or regulators' contact details to complain about a

[52] This refers to a UK broadcasting ban on the voices, but not the words, of Sinn Fein activists and certain other Irish republican and loyalist political groups between 1988 and 1994.

[53] E Ferguson, 'Why Chris Morris had to make Brass Eye' *The Guardian* (5 August 2021) www.theguardian.com/uk/2001/aug/05/news.film.

[54] J Deanes, 'Regulator warns against 'knee-jerk' legislation', *The Guardian* (23 May 2002) www.theguardian.com/media/2002/may/23/broadcasting.communicationsact.

programme. Audience members can publish content directly to the public online, to politicians, production teams, and broadcasters. This too has a chilling effect. A seemingly lower tolerance of contentious material is demonstrated through performative outrage from sections of the audience on social media. Add this to a misinterpretation of impartiality requirements by some production teams and this means that broadcast content does not offer as much innovative or contentious programming to the audience as it potentially could. As Jolyon Rubinstein says, the ones who really suffer are the audience. They never get a chance to experience those shows, or those lines, left unwritten because of the various influences which burden writers, producers and broadcasters when deciding what to write, what to cut and what to transmit.

E. Her Majesty's Loyal Opposition

Many interviewees, although not all, believed the main stumbling block, in terms of producing biting, challenging political satire within the confines of the Code was the due impartiality requirement. There should not be an expectation that satire needs to be impartial within a programme or across a series but rather over time. It certainly should not be balanced but rather duly impartial. If broadcasters focus on seeking a 'balance', programmes potentially give politicians or policy more credibility than is warranted. Misinterpretation or over application of a due impartiality requirement may leave programmes lacking in innovation, leading to bland content, and an unchallenged Government because of over-cautious actors.

As seen through the examples throughout, politicians do feel threatened by satire, and have complained to broadcasters about their treatment, and this has happened all around the globe. If a broadcaster is under attack from the Government this will stop it from commissioning more biting satire for fear of losing their licence to broadcast, or because of the threat of a court case, as seen in the US with President Trump's actions.

Some interviewees in this book thought it was considered more important to those in editorial positions to keep the Government on side than to write content which provoked it. This is a lost opportunity to hold a Government to account. If a concern of Government interference clips satirists' wings, then threats are an effective way for politicians to control the editorial process. This chilling effect goes beyond changing media regulation laws, appointing like-minded management, threatening funding cuts, or lowering their funding by other means. In the case of Channel 4, they can threaten to sell the channel.

If a broadcaster's fear of having funding cut ultimately stops writers being able to satirise politicians and avoids making satire that has any political bite that is problematic, not only for the writers' and the broadcasters' freedom of expression rights but also for the audience's right to be informed. If a producer feels this fear, amongst all the other pressures not to create a fuss, then one person can still make a subjective decision to remove content, a modern-day Lord Chamberlain.

The regulations are flexible enough for satirical production but the interpretation of the requirement for due impartiality on satirical production is over-reaching. The regulation is often misinterpreted, and the unintended consequence of this regulation is that it chills political entertainment and therefore political debate in the public sphere.

Whilst due impartiality is considered important for the preservation of the democratic process of news there is not such a strong case for it to apply to political satire. How can one be impartial when holding those in power to account through the medium of satire? Is due impartiality sometimes interpreted as 'don't upset the Government?'.[55] Would it be problematic to remove the impartiality requirement for satirical programming whilst retaining it for news? Already Ofcom has stipulated that,

> The approach to due impartiality may vary according to the nature of the subject, the type of programme and channel, the likely expectation of the audience as to content, and the extent to which the content and approach is signalled to the audience.[56]

Audience expectations for political satire should be very different to hard news programming. Given 'audiences aged 16–24 are more likely than other age groups (as a proportion of their BBC TV viewing) to watch BBC comedy programming',[57] satire is an important way to engage young people in political debate. Impartiality should not be a tool which narrows political debate. If it is considered difficult to create effective satire within the confines of impartiality, it should be exempt from the requirement, especially if it is used in a way that helps politicians to avoid scrutiny. Political entertainment which is balanced is rendered somewhat hollow. It is unnecessary and disproportionate in a democratic society where all other media platforms can be partial.

Due Impartiality should consider the power of those who are being satirised, the smaller the impact a political party has on public life the less they are likely to be targets for satirists. Writing jokes about the opposition to counter any satire written about the Government nullifies the point of the satire, pricks itself rather than the pomposity of those in power.

One contributor considered it was impossible to square impartiality with satire, two others said it 'hamstrings' satire. The misinterpretation of the impartiality requirement affects satire and political comedy, creating a superfluous search for elusive right-wing contributors and an omission of left-wing contributors by default, believing balance must be achieved by a lack of one precluding the other.

Removing the due impartiality requirement in satire, whilst still adhering to the due accuracy requirement, would improve its bite and not affect the impartiality

[55] John Lloyd (Executive Producer).

[56] The Ofcom Broadcasting Code, s 5.

[57] BBC Third Annual Report (Ofcom 25 November 2020) 55 www.ofcom.org.uk/__data/assets/pdf_file/0021/207228/third-bbc-annual-report.pdf.

rule for hard news.[58] As one of the contributors commented, they had to have 'pinpoint' accuracy for HIGNFY. They wanted to avoid being sued, but also, to be effective, satire must be truthful. The checks which are done by lawyers and compliance teams pre-transmission mean that often satire is more accurate than news. There should be a 'satire exception' for satirical programming.

> I do find it a bit chilling that … somehow, at some point, this idea got grafted on from the news into satire that you have to have balance because, no you absolutely do not, you really don't, your job is to attack people in power that's it. (Anonymous, Writer and Performer 09).

[58] The Ofcom Code, s 5 and BBC Guidelines, s 3. Participants noted how their content had to be factually accurate.

8

Conclusion

> There was a time when institutions like the BBC were full of privileged, upper middle-class people, who came from very wealthy backgrounds. And we all deplored that as being a terrible thing. What that gave them was an absence of fear, because, who cared if they got fired? They'd be all right. What you now have is people who, from the ground up managed to make their way into these venerated institutions and attracted themselves a very nice salary, and they have got a very expensive flat in London that they can just about afford and losing their job would be catastrophic. And what that means is they are terrified, and they won't ever make a brave decision. And they won't commission something that makes them draw in breath quite abruptly. I am not saying we should go back, I might be saying that, because actually, in this world where money is everything, having people who have money in those positions would give them an awful lot more editorial courage.
> (Anonymous, Writer and Performer 09).

When most of the interviewees discussed making editorial decisions, it was clear that black letter law such as the Communications Act 2003 plays little to no part in their thought process. Some senior participants, such as Lord Michael Grade, Ric Bailey and the long-running producers of HIGNFY referred to the Parody Exception, the issues with using Parliamentary Footage in satirical shows, and to some other specific regulatory or legal aspects of broadcasting regarding flash frames and defamation. This is probably because the sections of the Communications Act 2003 relevant to programme making are written into the Code and into in-house editorial guidelines. No aspects of the right to freedom of expression or a concern about the target's rights to privacy or reputation were raised by the writers.

Most in production rarely refer to the Code when deciding on the appropriateness of programme material. An in-depth knowledge of the soft law of regulations plays very little part for those working in production. It was surprising how many contributors have not read the Code, and how dismissive of the Code those who had not read it were. Therefore, one can conclude that the regulations are not considered by writers or many in production as a fundamental authority when making editorial choices or as a reference point for decision making.

Knowing the regulations would be a useful tool for everyone. It would help writers argue for the inclusion of content. Writers could make an informed decision on that elusive line of acceptability. Those lower down in the pecking order would be able to question how the person in editorial control interpreted and applied the rule and argue against it if they felt the decision was over-censorious.

This would help boost the creation of provocative and challenging content, which in turn would protect the interests of both writers and audience.

Protecting the audience's right to receive information and ideas was rarely a consideration; however, when important societal issues are ignored by political comedians and producers because they do not know the rules, this has effect on the audience. As regulation is there to protect the audience, it would be a good thing if the audience could be protected from those in production erring on the side of caution, especially when considering the transmission of material which is legal and compliant with the Code.

Broadcasters should give more support to those in editorial positions and writers to feel that they can take risks and fail. More emphasis should be given to the 'due' in due impartiality rather than attempting political balance within programming. There should be easier referral routes and producers should feel supported in their decisions to refer material. A more robust defence of productions and performers would enable production teams and creatives to feel braver. This would help alleviate performers' concerns about being cancelled by a broadcaster because of negative audience reaction. As John Lloyd said, part of creating is making mistakes, being an explorer. The BBC especially is in a unique position to take risks because of the way it is funded, but some people are fearful of messing up or causing events described by many as 'a fuss'. The BBC has a requirement laid down in the Charter that it should not be worried about programme failures. Its services should be distinctive from those provided elsewhere and should take creative risks, even if not all succeed, to develop fresh approaches and innovative content. There needs to be a culture where failure is acceptable but that is unlikely to happen when the BBC chastises itself over defendable content.

Ofcom research concludes the audience understands that programme content is subjective, especially around comedy, and audiences also consider freedom of expression is important. The producers understand that the context of comedy helps to mitigate offence. Ofcom research indicates much of the audience is tolerant of, indeed expects, offence in comedy. Yet threats of a social media storm or a media backlash created by a newspaper republishing a few disgruntled Tweets seem to be shifting the power away from the performer/broadcaster and giving it to that vociferous minority on social media. Are these opinions given due weight or are they over-valued? The Heckler's Veto seems to be effective in the minds of the writers, but the audience is often more robust than programme makers give them credit for. This robustness should be a compelling argument to keep contentious programming rather than allowing a minority of the audience credibility in demanding resignations over contentious content especially when it does not breach the Code. As one contributor notes, the number of those who do not complain should be considered, audience figures should give a broadcaster an idea of how many people saw or heard the material and did not complain compared to how many watched it or heard it and were moved to complain (rather than those who were motivated to complain by a newspaper column).

When there are inconsistent lines drawn for the limits of harm and offence or due impartiality it muddies the waters for the writers.

> I think it's the arbitrariness, that one joke is okay one week and then another week it is not okay. Sometimes that's very difficult to get your head around why. Is it because it is that one individual person, have we got a different lawyer? And [performer's name removed] will often say that, when they say 'oh, you can't say this', he'll say, 'oh, have we got a different lawyer? Why's this not okay now?'. Different lawyers, different opinions, [...] it's like when we have lawyers that keep saying we can't say things for various reasons, we say, 'what legal firm do we have this week? Cowardly, Cowardly and Custard?'. (Christine Rose, Writer).

It would be more appropriate to judge contentious content, which could include apparently partial content, against its compliance to the Code or to broadcasters' in-house editorial guidelines rather than make a subjective judgement at an early stage. This might encourage more producers to feel able to take risks. When all the content, especially the more contentious material, has been through the compliance process and the editorial justification for transmission has been decided, then it should be defended by the broadcaster. Broadcasters should use their editorial justification and compliance processes to protect their performers and their output when there is a media storm over programming. This would help producers and writers or performers to be braver when creating content which provokes and challenges an audience because they would know they can rely on the backing of the broadcaster. In turn this can remove some of social media's power, leaving the broadcaster more able to withstand social media storms. The policies and regulations should ultimately decide what can or cannot be said, but as seen, often there is a lack of interest in the Code and rules are misinterpreted. Rather than looking to the Codes as restrictive in nature, a better knowledge of them can be used to enhance a compelling argument to keeping contentious material. The alternative to this is that less challenging material is broadcast and this could have the knock-on effect of changing audience expectations. When Ofcom carries out its next audience research it might need to realign the regulatory boundaries as audiences become used to seeing less contentious material on broadcast platforms. This is problematic as it would lead to a decreasing circle of self-censorship and to less innovative comedy which avoids socio-political content.

Producers should rely more on the Code which would give them the tools to defend provocative and challenging content which complies with the Ofcom Code. This would create a more effective buffer between the broadcaster and disgruntled audience members. This too would add more distance between public service broadcasters and the Government. If the BBC were to have the backing of Ofcom when they decide not to uphold audience complaints into compliant programming, it could give them greater protection from a Government or media backlash.

Pushing boundaries in socio-political work gives creative people the ability to challenge orthodox ideas, to shake up the mainstream, change perceptions and promote critical thinking. Casting back to the first half of this book, considering those innovators in literature and the stage, where would culture and art be without taboo-breaking innovators such as DH Lawrence, Joe Orton, George Bernard Shaw and Shelagh Delaney? Consider how the 1737 Licensing Act censored material written about social issues and important political events; nothing could be written about politics or politicians. Radical writers had to produce and stage their plays for private viewing only because they would not get them passed by the Lord Chamberlain. Theatre managers relied on recycling Shakespearean plays to keep their licences rather than being able to champion new talent which tackled contemporary themes.

Biting, shocking, offensive and provoking satire can be made in the UK under the current Code. It can be done, yet the interviews illustrate that many are too concerned about potential consequences. The lack of regulatory knowledge makes it difficult to challenge decisions and, by doing so, find the legal boundaries. As Trevor Barnes had noted, someone needs to overstep the line sometimes to know where the line is; but few are willing, probably because it might impact on their career, even though it is only the most serious of breaches which end with a sanction. Those who do not know the rules have created their own constraints to such an extent that they rarely get close to the legal limits of expression allowed on broadcast media, let alone push at them.

Few in editorial positions consider their decisions to remove content as acts of censorship. Rather they decide if content was funny enough to counter the potential level of offence and then be transmitted. It is a balancing act. As one executive producer said, something being funny makes it worth 'fighting for', the funnier it is (rather than its lawfulness or regulatory compliance) is a big factor. However, 'funny' is subjective and so a problematic way to measure the suitability of content for broadcast. The funnier the producer considers contentious content, the more likely it is to be 'referred up' the chain. If it is not considered funny enough, rather than refer up or refer to the guidelines, contributors will discuss the issue with their peers or rely on their own judgement, or just cut the content because repeatedly referring content is time consuming. As a producer can be held accountable for a mistake, which might breach the regulations or cause a media storm, it is sometimes easier to say 'no' to contentious content. The edges are smoothed away.

Some writers are frustrated as it seems to them the regulations are applied in a haphazard manner making it difficult for them to judge where the limits of offensive humour lie. The writers are guided by those in production who might not know the regulations well, this then leads to unnecessary self-censorship. The misinterpretation of due impartiality creates a general nervousness around tackling political content. Some feel the rules on due impartiality mean that the Government is protected from successful satirical attack. The rules limit the opportunities to participate in democratic debate. Satire should be able to give voice to unorthodox and minority views (within the legal limitations) which could benefit audiences, opening their minds to new ideas.

Most participants find the due impartiality rules (as they understand them) to 'hamstring' satire. If political satire is to hold the Government to account and if due impartiality is, as Trevor Barnes notes, acknowledging there is more than one aspect to a political argument, creating satire simply for political 'balance' is unnecessary. In conclusion, knowing the Code would make production teams more confident in dealing with contentious content and help with establishing those all-important editorial justifications needed for transmitting it.

I. The Courts

Those in production would do well to look to the precedents set by the courts. These give a high level of protection to political speech and satire as a form of artistic expression. The jurisprudence of both the ECtHR and domestic courts reflects this. Parallels can be drawn between the deliberations of the court and the deliberations of those in editorial positions when considering the suitability of programme content. On the face of it, it appears the courts are more concerned about the chilling effect of restricting creative content than are broadcast production teams. The Council of Europe believes that the ECHR Article 10 (2) qualification that 'protection of the rights of others' used as a reason to restrict work has 'been interpreted by some governments and jurisdictions in such ways as to prohibit legitimate expressions[.] … Often artists will deliberately create work that challenges those concepts[.]'[1] Such work, where not gratuitously offensive, can have an important role in society. This has been addressed in various jurisprudence regarding satirical and political expression, with the acknowledgement that those in political or public positions should be tolerant of a higher degree of criticism and scrutiny, although this becomes problematic when Article 10 conflicts with either Article 8 or Article 14 rights.[2] This is especially true regarding stereotyping, which might create contempt or discrimination. However, the ruling on the cartoons in *Patricio Monteiro Telo de Abreu v Portugal*[3] indicates that whilst the Court recognises the danger of sexual-stereotyping and the potential chilling effect of women entering the political sphere, the Court still considered it was crucial not to restrict legitimate political criticism.[4]

[1] S Whyatt, *Free to create – Artistic freedom in Europe* (Council of Europe Report, 15 February 2023) 11, rm.coe.int/free-to-create-council-of-europe-report-on-the-freedom-of-artistic-exp/1680aa2dc0.

[2] Article 8 is the right to respect for private and family life, home and correspondence, and Article 14 is the prohibition of discrimination.

[3] App no 42713/15 (7 June 2022).

[4] S Balzaretti, 'Political Satire and Sexist Stereotypes, A critical insight on the case of Patricio Monteiro Telo de Abreu' (*Strasbourg Observers*, 14 September 2022) www.strasbourgobservers.com/2022/09/14/political-satire-and-sexist-stereotypes-a-critical-insight-on-the-case-of-patricio-monteiro-telo-de-abreu-v-portugal/.

II. Media Regulation: Restricting Information and Ideas

One of the main reasons given for historically regulating socio-political content was to protect the reputation of the great and the good, and to protect the audience from offensive content. Instead, it sometimes had a detrimental effect on societal cohesion, political knowledge and progressive ideas. The historical overview in this book shows how incredibly powerful the Stage Licensing Act 1737 was and how its changing rules and enforcers influenced early media laws relating to the compliance of cinema content and political entertainment. This, along with the imposition of taxation, copyright and licensing laws, acted to suppress knowledge and innovation, leading to a more myopic creative output, unpopular with writers and publishers. The biggest issue for creating political entertainment for mass audiences lay with the rules around the representation of living people on stage, screen and even a parody diary. In addition to the law there were societal influences and moral crusaders who felt they spoke for the ordinary person, the silent majority.

III. Social Censure

In a BBC broadcast, the 'Reith Lecture on Freedom of Expression', Chimamanda Ngozi Adichie talked about social censure. She describes this as a 'vicious retaliation, not from the government, but from other citizens,' believing that this retaliation 'portends the death of curiosity, the death of learning and the death of creativity.'[5] She is not alone in her concern, many of the interviewees are concerned about social censure which comes in the form of social media pile-ons, often whipped up by negative press coverage. This explains how gaps in creativity happen outside of legal threats.

There are people who do make ground-breaking programming and there seem to be more who want to make ground-breaking programming. They can do it within the limits of the Ofcom Code and yet the environment in some quarters creates a chilling effect which leads to a censorship by omission. Programming is dulled when production teams and writers find it easier to avoid content which might be time consuming or create a furore and instead create programming which is less challenging and less innovative. Less challenging programming creates fewer opportunities for debate both in the media and in wider society and may protect those already in powerful positions.

[5] Chimamanda Ngozi Adichie: Freedom of Speech 'The Reith Lectures 2022 – The Four Freedoms' (TX: BBC Radio 4, 6 January 2023) www.bbc.co.uk/programmes/m001fmtz.

IV. Power and Protection

The interviews reveal a power play between policy, production companies, broadcasters, producers and writers which became apparent when considering who, if anyone, had freedom of expression within the regulations. Whilst employees, writers and those in production have no protected right for their content to be broadcast, the audience still has a right to receive information and ideas, and the broadcaster has the right to freedom of expression. As a public authority, Ofcom should be more pro-active in protecting the rights of the audience.

Looking at the evolution of political entertainment, protection historically came in the form of patronage but today the idea of patronage is more diverse, not simply a wealthy individual indulging an artistic prodigy. It is likely a publisher, a broadcaster, a producer, and even the audience, all can create fame and financial protection for the writer. The writer might lose a little autonomy, feel a need to produce that which they believe an audience wants to hear or an employer is most likely to broadcast. The writer might do so to protect a steady income, keep a roof over her head, or just write what she expects to be broadcast and not to create a rumpus. Self-protection seemed key to many participants' decision making, both personal and professional, in those working in both creative and editorial roles who were 'lower down' the chain of worry.

The decisions which were taken regarding political entertainment historically, and those which are now taken now in terms of what is broadcast and what is edited out, cannot but affect the audience's right under Article 10 of the ECHR to receive information and ideas. The media decides how to frame socio-political content and so is a powerful force in representing political debate.[6] The modern Ofcom Code is not overly restrictive when compared to earlier laws and regulations, the issue is one of 'over-reach' of application of rules on broadcast satire because of the way those who work within the rules interpret them. This makes it difficult to produce biting satire and happens, not just because of a misinterpretation of the regulations but because 'shy' producers worry about pushing the boundaries, concerned about repercussions from their line managers and their audience for transmitting contentious content. In turn, any editorial decisions based on these misinterpretations or concerns impact on the rights of the audience to enjoy programmes which might challenge convention. The audience loses the chance to consider news and political events from a different perspective.

Contributors believe such opportunities should be created through entertainment as the raising of contentious issues in the space of comedy can lead to public discussion and therefore create a constructive route to healthy debate. If satire is there to provoke and challenge, to make people think critically, then it is important that satirical writers have the freedom to attack the hypocrisy and transgressions of the powerful. As argued by scholars and the courts, the free flow of political

[6] John Street, *Mass Media, Politics and Democracy*, 2nd edn (Basingstoke, Palgrave, 2011) 51-52.

information is essential to a functioning democracy. Concerns about breaching the due impartiality rule, erring on the side of caution, and cutting content which is compliant means that the audience suffers from a narrower form of political engagement.

It is not simply Acts or rules that restrict material, or a fear of social censure but a fear of Government reprisal as well. The Government can cause a chill through veiled threats which today lead to broadcast employees becoming fearful of repercussions.[7] The former Conservative Culture Secretary Nadine Dorries privately expressed how displeased she was with the BBC journalist's handling of an interview with the then Prime Minister Boris Johnson, when the journalist Nick Robinson asked the then PM to stop talking. She is reported to have said 'Nick Robinson has cost the BBC a lot of money'.[8] She sent a tweet to the former BBC Political Editor after Laura Kuenssberg shared views that the PM's authority was 'evaporating'. Dorries later deleted the tweet.[9] These implied the Conservative Government was threatening the amount of money the BBC would get through the licence fee; just as concerning as the Conservative Government's threats to sell Channel 4. Did Dorries wish to cause a chilling effect on their scrutiny of politicians? If a Government threatens a broadcaster's income it would follow that such threats could create a chill when making programmes which hold a Government to account.

BBC comedy has been classed by Ofcom as an 'at risk' genre. Ofcom acknowledges that comedy programmes are important and make:

> a particular contribution to the Mission and Public Purposes … a significant contribution to the BBC's distinctiveness and are less likely to be provided for elsewhere. Many at-risk genres are also important for the BBC's delivery of informal learning, as set out in [the] assessment of Public Purpose 2.[10]

Public Purpose 2 states the BBC has a duty to help everyone learn about different subjects in accessible, engaging, inspiring and challenging ways. Learning about politics should be central, as political expression is 'essential for an engaged, sustainable, democratic public culture'.[11] Satire is a form of political expression and therefore political entertainment should be a crucial element of a public service broadcaster's schedule. Such programming provides political information and is considered a gateway programme which encourages further political

[7] Anonymous (Creative Writer 11).

[8] S Kelner, 'Nadine Dorries' briefing against Nick Robinson and the BBC is an attack on us all' *The iPaper* (26 October 2021) www.inews.co.uk/opinion/nadine-dorries-attack-on-nick-robinson-bbc-attack-us-all-1267153.

[9] J Waterson, 'Nadine Dorries denies inappropriate tweet to Laura Kuenssberg' *The Guardian* (18 November 2021) www.theguardian.com/politics/2021/nov/18/nadine-dorries-denies-inappropriate-tweet-to-laura-kuenssberg.

[10] BBC Third Annual Report (Ofcom, 25 November 2020) 53 www.ofcom.org.uk/__data/assets/pdf_file/0021/207228/third-bbc-annual-report.pdf.

[11] P Baym and JP Jones, 'News Parody in Global Perspective: Politics, Power, and Resistance' (2012) 10 *Popular Communication* 2.

engagement.[12] If there is a culture of fear of upsetting the Government leading to a reduction of funding or keeping the channel in public ownership, and therefore retaining its uniqueness, this is likely to impact on output.

A fear of Government reprisals has scuppered artists' freedom of expression for centuries, leaving audiences sitting through more theatrical productions of Shakespeare than of innovative plays.[13] This seems to be echoed in the current era, not with Shakespeare but with programming which does not push at boundaries and oceans of repeats. The broadcasters are playing safe rather than taking risks.

Today's Ofcom Code is not draconian. The United Kingdom is not an authoritarian country; satirists are not imprisoned or punished for challenging the morals or authority of those in power but there are other more insidious ways that stop creatives producing work including the threat of getting bad press and losing work. Political entertainment is an important medium, as one contributor says, another form of scrutiny.[14] If politicians are self-serving or hypocritical then their shortcomings should be revealed and held up to ridicule. If scrutiny encourages integrity in our politicians, then this would be a good outcome, left unchecked the quality of politics and politicians could descend into a quagmire of corruption.

Changing technology leads to fractured regulation, existing laws are built upon, people in high profile editorial roles may be sympathetic to an incumbent Government. Whoever has editorial control can control the message and can frame an event, she or he can decide what is and what is not debated. Not everything reaches the public domain, as Lord Grade notes,

> Everything you broadcast is a choice … 'do we cut there?', 'do we use that bit or do we cut the sentence there?' (Lord Michael Grade).

Today editorial control starts initially with the writer deciding to write or to self-censor, then to the producer giving back 'notes', then the executive producer, department head, potentially to the compliance department or to editorial policy and as 'high' as the head of the channel or broadcaster. It is apparent that not everyone always consults the Code when they are making difficult editorial decisions. They might worry less about a programme being compliant and more about heading off a potential moral panic, bad press coverage, or a Government reaction.

These events can have the effect of making them stop and erase material or not write what they were about to write.[15] The media is the public watchdog, there

[12] MA Xenos and AB Becker, 'Moments of Zen: Effects of The Daily Show on Information Seeking and Political Learning' (2009) 26(3) *Political Communication* 317.

[13] D Thomas, 'The 1737 Licensing Act and Its Impact' in J Swindells and DF Taylor (eds), *The Oxford Handbook of the Georgian Theatre, 1737–1832* (online edn. Oxford Academic, 3 March 2014) 96.

[14] Ric Bailey (Chief Adviser Politics).

[15] See eg Christine Rose (Creative Writer), Charlie Skelton (Creative Writer) and Robin Ince (Creative Writer/Broadcaster).

to give checks and balances to the Government and State institutions. The media creates a 'public space for the dissemination of information and the expression of opinions since the public cannot possibly gather all the relevant information by themselves' and enables the public to discover if authorities and private enterprise are acting democratically and under the rule of law.[16] Therefore the rights of the audience need to be considered. There is public interest in political satire scrutinising parliamentarians and exposing hypocrisy in public life. Unfortunately, this type of political entertainment is costly and has a short shelf life and so is not commercially attractive to make.[17] Therefore it is right that public service broadcasters should give airtime to satire, they are better placed to take risks than purely commercial broadcasters when there is no financial risk from programme failures. The BBC should fund satire to ensure there is no gap in the market. However, the issue is that the model enabling the BBC to take risks and produce political entertainment, funding via the licence fee, is the same model that puts the broadcaster at risk by upsetting the Government.

V. Policy Solutions

Available solutions to address the problems raised through the misinterpretation and overapplication of the rules are two-fold given the two regulations discussed. Harm and Offence and Due Impartiality require different approaches. First, addressing both, training in the Ofcom Code would seem to be the simplest answer. Whilst it is apparent from the interviews that training is given, this training does not seem to have been completely effective as practitioners do not use the Code when making day to day decisions. The Code is not used as ready source of instruction on the regulations. As Bailey said, some in production did not keep up to date with regulatory reform. If these people, or those who are over-cautious, train others then those mistakes may be repeated. If they are to be trained in the regulations it would be better for Ofcom to do this.

Training should be genre specific to allow producers to understand the justifications in allowing offensive, controversial and partial views in political entertainment. This is especially pertinent because of the political speech defence which should allow a greater level of freedom of expression. They should also read Ofcom research and guidance notes to understand audience expectations are that comedy may be offensive and outrageous, and that some genres exist to challenge the orthodox. Training may help the 'shy producer'. The better the regulations are known the more likely those making the editorial decisions might be to push at the boundaries, and be able to build a justification for doing so; by considering

[16] T Baumbach, 'Chilling Effect as a European Court of Human Rights' Concept' (2018) 6(1) *Media Law Cases Bergen Journal of Criminal Law and Criminal Justice* 92.

[17] Neil Webster (Writer and Producer).

the target of the joke, the point of the joke and how it might be interpreted by the audience.

Such training should be regular and mandatory, otherwise new producers working under established executive producers who do not know the regulations are likely to make similar editorial decisions and the cycle starts again.

The second solution is additional to training and is reliant on the broadcaster standing by its decisions and protecting writers, performers and production teams. Where the contentious programme material has been through the broadcasters' in-house compliance process and deemed justifiable within the context, then the broadcaster should defend it. They should back up their writers and production teams. This would give practitioners more confidence in their output and be more willing to explore beyond the normal boundaries.

Turning to due impartiality, an unintentional consequence of imposing a due impartiality requirement onto political entertainment is that it is misinterpreted and creates a censoring mechanism which has a negative effect on programme content. The solution here should be addressed more directly given the importance of political satire to political debate. This would be to remove the impartiality requirement for political satire because the continual conflation of impartiality with balance destroys political satire and has a debilitating impact on democratic engagement.

VI. Towards a Satire Exception

The issues raised by the interpretation of the regulations on harm and offence and impartiality overlap in part but the solution for the regulations on due impartiality require an approach to avert a balancing, or even an omission, of political content. In a democratic, multi-channel, multi-platform society is there a statutory necessity for broadcast satire to be duly impartial?

To remove the misconception that broadcast satire must be balanced, a solution would be to remove the due impartiality requirement from satirical content and political entertainment in broadcast programming. Currently online news providers and streaming services with audio visual content are not required to adhere to a due impartiality requirement, traditional newspapers with satirical columns, caricatures and cartoons are partial, therefore it seems overly restrictive that satirical content on broadcast media is the only medium which demands due impartiality. The evidence from the interviews is that both the existance of an impartiality requirement for satire, and the (mis)interpretation of the impartiality requirement as balance, creates an undesireable chilling effect on the creation and broadcasting of political entertainment.

This is not an argument for removing due impartiality for hard news, nor that the requirement for due accuracy should be removed from satire, otherwise it would be possible for content to stray into misinformation. There is no pressing social need nor is it proportionate for the State to restrict broadcast political comedy output using a due impartiality requirement. There should be rules laid down to ensure broadcasters inform the audience that the programme content is satirical, through a pre-programme announcement and on the electronic programme guide. The tone of the programme should be such that even if an audience came across it unawares, they could easily still judge it as being an entertainment programme. Currently there are rules where programmes expressing personal views are made clear and these can be extended to this content.[18] Ofcom recognises personal views and these are allowed from:

> the outright expression of highly partial views … to the considered 'authored' opinion of a journalist, commentator or academic, with professional expertise or a specialism in an area which enables her or him to express opinions which are not necessarily mainstream.[19]

If it is not presented as hard news and it is clear to the audience that it is an entertainment programme, then the audience is informed.

VII. Once More Unto the Breach

It should be important for broadcasters to feel confident that their content could be defended robustly from Government interference and that Ofcom would allow them to do so. As has happened through history, media freedoms rest with those in power and those in powerful positions. The Government can manoeuvre people sympathetic to the Government into important editorial positions. Whilst in some ways this is not exceptional, most Chairs of the BBC have had political connections but under the last Labour Government the Chairs were people with a mixture of political affiliations.[20] A former Director General of the BBC, Greg Dyke, donated £50,000 to the Labour Party before taking the position, so political alignment is not new, and they are expected to be impartial in their work as are all employees of the BBC.[21]

It is important that Ofcom remains independent of the Government. Ofcom should be protecting the audience from programmes which cause harm and not need to protect broadcasters from an existential threat from Government.[22] This is especially important as Ofcom's powers have been extended to regulating the internet. In Ofcom's statement on the future of media plurality in the UK, they raised the concerns about accuracy and impartiality for online news leaving aside

[18] BBC Editorial Guidelines, s 4.1.
[19] The Ofcom Broadcasting Code, s 5.10.
[20] History of the BBC, 'Chairmen of the BBC' (n.d.) www.bbc.co.uk/historyofthebbc/research/chairmen-of-the-bbc.
[21] M Tran, 'Greg Dyke resigns from Labour party' *The Guardian* (25 June 1999) www.theguardian.com/media/1999/jun/25/bbc.
[22] Anonymous (Writer 11).

how that might affect political parties' online channels.[23] It is important that an impartiality requirement for political entertainment would not be considered alongside this. It would be unnecessary in a democratic society and, coupled with the way it has been interpreted by practitioners, could be applied in a disproportionate manner. There should be no interference with freedom of expression by a public authority unless the content is illegal, and any restriction should be necessary and proportionate.

Currently some production teams are still thinking in terms of taste and decency when judging political entertainment programme content. This thinking restricts provocative political entertainment, narrowing the audience's experiences and that issue should be addressed.

Broadcasters would do well to discover where the limits lie. After all, boundaries are made to push against, and political entertainment is at its best when it not only punches up at the powerful but also pokes at the audience.

> If you don't have the occasional breach, then you are really not doing your job properly.
>
> Trevor Barnes (Compliance Consultant).

[23] See eg the YouTube Conservatives Channel, www.youtube.com/channel/UCXNSyuKeoiHOld1OS3kHuVg.

BIBLIOGRAPHY

Books

Aldgate, A and Robertson, JC, *Censorship in Theatre and Cinema* (Edinburgh, Edinburgh University Press, 2005).
Attenborough D, *Life On Air: Memoirs of a Broadcaster* (London, BBC Books, 2002).
Barendt et al, *Libel and the Media: The Chilling Effect* (Oxford, Oxford University Press, 2004).
Barendt E, *Freedom of Speech*, 2nd edn (Oxford, Oxford University Press, 2005).
Barwise, P and York, P, *The War Against the BBC: How an unprecedented combination of hostile forces is destroying Britain's greatest cultural institution … And Why you should care* (London, Penguin, 2020).
Bernard Shaw G, *Plays Pleasant and Unpleasant* (first published 1946, Penguin, 2000).
Bourdieu, P, *Outline of a Theory of Practice* (trans: Richard Nice) (Cambridge, Cambridge University Press, 1977).
Briggs A, *The History of Broadcasting in the United Kingdom Volume I: The Birth of Broadcasting* (Oxford, Oxford University Press, 1961).
Briggs A, *The History of Broadcasting in the United Kingdom Volume II: The Golden Age of Wireless* (Oxford, Oxford University Press, 1965).
Briggs A, *The History of Broadcasting in the United Kingdom Volume V: Competition* (Oxford, Oxford University Press, 1995).
BBC Editorial Guidelines (British Broadcasting Corporation, 2019).
BBC Editorial Guidelines (British Broadcasting Corporation, 2025).
Carpenter H, *That Was Satire That Was: The Satire Boom of the 1960s* (London, Victor Gollanez, 2000).
Charmaz, K, *Constructing Grounded Theory: A Practical Guide through Qualitative Analysis* (London, Sage, 2006).
Cockerell, M, *Live from Number 10* (London, Faber and Faber, 1988).
De Jongh, N, *Politics, Prudery and Perversions: The Censoring of the English Stage 1901–1968* (London, Methuen, 2000).
Dutton R, *Mastering the Revels: The Regulation and Censorship of English Renaissance Drama* (London, Macmillan, 1991).
Faulk, BJ, *Music Hall and Modernity: The Late-Victorian Discovery of Popular Culture*, 1st edn (Athens, Ohio University Press, 2004).
Fenwick, H and Phillipson, G, *Media Freedom under the Human Rights Act* (Oxford, Oxford University Press, 2006).
Fielding S, *A State of Play: British Politics on Screen, Stage and Page, from Anthony Trollope to The Thick of It* (London, Bloomsbury Academic, 2014).
Franklin, B *Televising Democracies* (London, Routledge, 1992).
Freedman L, *The Offensive Art: Political Satire and Its Censorship Around the World from Beerbohm to Borat* (ABC-CLIO, 2008).
Gibbons, T, *Regulating the Media* 2nd edn (London, Sweet & Maxwell, 1998).
Gibbons T, *Media Law in the United Kingdom* (Alphen aan den Rijn, Kluwer Law International, 2012).
Glaser, B and Strauss, A, *The Discovery of Grounded Theory: Strategies for Qualitative Research* (Chicago, Aldine, 1967).
Greene, Sir Hugh, *The Third Floor Front: A View of Broadcasting in the Sixties* (London, The Bodley Head, 1969).

Halloran, JD, Brown, RL and Chaney, DC, *Television and Delinquency* (Leicester, Leicester University Press, 1976).
Hardy EG, *The Satires of Juvenal*, 2nd edn (London, Macmillan, 1970).
Hart, RP, *Seducing America: How Television Charms the Modern Voter* (Thousand Oaks, Sage, 1999).
Hewitt M, *The Dawn of the Cheap Press in Victorian Britain.: The End of the 'Taxes on Knowledge,' 1849–1869* (London, Bloomsbury, 2014).
Hood, S and Thabary-Peterssen, T, *On Television*, 6th edn (London, Pluto Press, 1997).
Jacques S, *The Parody Exception in Copyright Law* (Oxford, Oxford University Press, 2019).
Johnson, J, *The Lord Chamberlain's Blue Pencil* (London, Hodder and Stoughton, 1990).
Jones JP, *Entertaining Politics: Satiric Television and Political Engagement*, 2nd edn (Lanham, Rowman and Littlefield, 2010).
Little, L, *Guilty Pleasures: Comedy and Law in America* (New York, Oxford University Press, 2018).
Mack, M, Woodsong, C, MacQueen, K, Guest, G and Namey, E, *Qualitative Research Methods: A Data Collector's Field Guide* (North Carolina, FHI360, 2005).
McGinn, TAJ, *Prostitution, Sexuality, and the Law in Ancient Rome* (New York, Oxford University Press, 2003).
McNamara L, *Reputation and Defamation* (Oxford, Oxford University Press, 2007).
Milton, J, *Areopagitica; A Speech For the Liberty of Unlicens'd Printing, to the Parliament of England* (London, 1644).
Nicholson, S, *The Censorship of British Drama, 1900–1968 Vol. I:1900–1932* (Exeter, University of Exeter Press, 2003).
Orton J, J Lahr (ed) *The Orton Diaries* (London, Methuen, 1986).
Ovid, *Ars Amatoria.*
Oxford English Dictionary, 3rd edn (December 2013).
Palmer, J, *Taking Humour Seriously* (London, Routledge, 1994).
Pattie, D, *Modern British Playwriting: the 1950s* (London, Methuen Drama, 2012).
Platt, L, *Musical Comedy on the West End Stage, 1890–1939* (London, Palgrave Macmillan, 2004).
Ponton, G and Gill, P, *Introduction to Politics*, 3rd edn (Oxford, Blackwell, 1993).
Popa, D and Tsakona, V *Studies in Political Humour: In Between Political Critique and Public Entertainment* (Amsterdam, John Benjamins Publishing Company, 2011).
Potter, J, *Independent Television in Britain Volume 3 Politics and Control 1968–80* (London, Macmillan Press, 1989).
Robertson, JC, *The Hidden Cinema: British Film Censorship in Action 1913–1972* (e-book, 1993).
Robertson, JC, *The British Board of Film Censors: Film Censorship in Britain, 1986–1950* (London, Routledge, 2016).
Rudd, N, *The Satires of Horace and Persius* (London, Penguin Books, 1976).
Shellard, D, Nicholson, S and Handley, M, *The Lord Chamberlain Regrets … A History of British Theatre Censorship* (London, The British Library Board, 2004).
Shuger, D, *Censorship and Cultural Sensibility The Regulation of Language in Tudor-Stuart England* (Philadelphia, University of Pennsylvania Press, 2006).
Stephens JR, *The Censorship of English Drama 1824–1901* (Cambridge, Cambridge University Press, 1980).
Street, J, *Mass Media, Politics and Democracy* 2nd edn (Basingstoke, Palgrave, 2011).
Test, GA, *Satire: Spirit and Art* (Tampa, University Press of Florida, 1991).
Thomas, D, Carlton, D and Etienne, A, *Theatre Censorship: From Walpole to Wilson* (Oxford, Oxford University Press, 2007).
Travis, A, *Bound and Gagged: A Secret History of Obscenity in Britain* (London, Profile Books, 2000).
Watt, G, *The Making Sense of Politics, Media, and Law: Rhetorical Performance as Invention, Creation, Production* (Cambridge, Cambridge University Press, 2023).
Winlow, S, Hall, S and Treadwell, J, *The rise of the Right: English nationalism and the transformation of working-class politics* (Bristol, Bristol University Press, 2016).
Wyndham G, *Facing the Nation: Television and Politics 1936–1976* (London, Bodley Head, 1977).

Edited Books

Boyce, G, Curran, J and Wingate, P (eds) *Newspaper history from the seventeenth century to the present day* (Constable, Sage Publications, 1978).

Bramham, P and Wagg, S (eds) *The New Politics of Leisure and Pleasure* (Basingstoke, Palgrave Macmillan, 2010).

Breed, B, Keitel, E and Wallace R (eds) *Lucilius and Satire in Second Century BC Rome* (Cambridge, Cambridge University Press, 2018).

Collinson, DL, 'Leadership, Humor, and Satire' in RA Couto (ed) *Political and Civic Leadership: A Reference Handbook* (Thousand Oaks: SAGE Publications, Inc. 2010) 1071-80.

Hare, I and Weinstein, J (eds), *Extreme Speech and Democracy* (Oxford, Oxford University Press, 2009).

Kitchin, R and Thrift, N (eds), *International Encyclopaedia of Human Geography Vol 8* (Oxford, Elsevier, 2009).

Lockyer, S and Pickering, M (eds), *Beyond a Joke* (Basingstoke, Palgrave Macmillan, 2005).

O'Mally, T and Nicholas, S (eds) *Moral Panics, Social Fears, and the Media: Historical Perspectives* (New York, Routledge, Taylor & Francis Group 2013).

Strinati, D and Wagg, S (eds) *Come On Down?: Popular media culture in post-war Britain* (1st edn) (London, Routledge, 1992).

Swindells J and Taylor DF (eds) *The Oxford Handbook of the Georgian Theatre, 1737–1832* (Oxford, Oxford University Press, 2014).

Tambini, D and Cowling, J (eds) *New News* (London, IPPR, 2002).

Temperman, J and Koltay, A (eds) *Blasphemy and Freedom of Expression: Comparative, Theoretical and Historical Reflections after the Charlie Hebdo Massacre* (Cambridge, Cambridge University Press, 2017).

Wagg, S (ed) *Because I tell a Joke or Two: Comedy, Politics and Social Difference* (London, Routledge, 1998).

Wayne, M (ed) *Dissident Voices The Politics of Television and Cultural Change* (London, Pluto Press, 1998).

Journal Articles

Alkiviadou N, 'Regulating Hatred: Of devils and demons?' (2018) 18(4) *International Journal of Discrimination and the Law.*

Alonso P, 'Sacha Baron Cohen and Da Ali G Show: A Critique on Identity in Times of Satiric Infotainment' (2016) 49 *The Journal of Popular Culture.*

Bailey, R, 'When journalism and satire merge: The implications for impartiality, engagement and 'post-truth' politics – A UK perspective on the serious side of US TV comedy' (2018) 33(2) *European Journal of Communication* 200.

Barendt E, 'Judging the Media: Impartiality and Broadcasting' (1998) 69(B) *The Political Quarterly* 108.

Baumbach, T, 'Chilling Effect as a European Court of Human Rights' Concept in Media Law Cases' (2018) 6(1) *Bergen Journal of Criminal Law and Criminal Justice.*

Baym, G and Jones JP, 'News Parody in Global Perspective: Politics, Power, and Resistance' (2012) 10(1–2) *Popular Communication.*

Bebber B, 'Till Death Us Do Part: Political Satire and Social Realism in the 1960s and 1970s' (2014) 34(2) *Historical Journal of Film, Radio and Television.*

Beck, D, 'Humorous parodies of popular culture as strategy in Boris Johnson's populist communication' (2023) 26(3) *The British Journal of Politics and International Relations*

Becker A, Xenos MA and Waisanen DJ 'Sizing Up The Daily Show: Audience Perceptions of Political Comedy Programming' (2010) 18 *Atlantic Journal of Communication* 144.

Berry, JM, '*Validity and Reliability Issues In Elite Interviewing*' (2002) 35(4) *PS: Political Science & Politics* 679, 680.

Bicknell, J, 'What is Offensive about Offensive Jokes? (2007) 51(4) *Philosophy Today* 458.

Black, J, On Reflexive Racism: Disavowal, Deferment, and the Lacanian Subject (2020) 48(4) *Diacritics: A Review of Contemporary Criticism* 76.

Black, L, 'Whose finger is on the button? British Television and the politics of cultural Control' (2005) 25(4) *Historical Journal of Film, Radio and Television* 547.

Burch, SD, 'When satire more than closed on Saturday night: Henry fielding and the licensing act of 1737' (2008) 16(75) *Theatre Symposium* 135.

Capelotti, JP, 'Defending laughter: an account of Brazilian court cases involving humor, 1997–2014' (2016) 29(1) *Humor* 25.

Collins P, 'Negotiating Selves: Reflections on 'Unstructured' Interviewing' (1998) 3(3) *Sociological Research Online* 1.

Conolly LW, 'Shaw: Mrs.Warren's Profession and The Lord Chamberlain' (2004) 24(1) *The Annual of Bernard Shaw Studies* 46.

Cushion, S, Lewis, J, Wren, M and Ramsay, GN, 'The impact of interventionist regulation in reshaping news agendas: A comparative analysis of public and commercially funded television journalism' (2012) 13(7) *Journalism* 831.

Cushion, S and Lewis, J, 'Impartiality, statistical tit-for-tats and the construction of balance: UK television news reporting of the 2016 EU referendum campaign' (2017) 32(3) *European Journal of Communication* 208.

Dadlez, EM, 'Truly Funny: Humor, Irony, and Satire as Moral Criticism' (2011) 45(1) *Journal of Aesthetic Education* 1.

Emerson, JP, 'Negotiating the Serious Import of Humor' (1969) 32 *Sociometry* 169.

Fish, SE, 'Normal Circumstances, Literal Language, Direct Speech Acts, the Ordinary, the Everyday, the Obvious, What Goes without Saying, and Other Special Cases' (1978) 4(4) *Critical Inquiry* 625.

Franks, M, 'From Public Library Prankster to Playwright: Joe Orton and Postwar Britain's Nanny State' (2017) 20 *Book History* 394.

Freedman, L, 'Wit as a Political Weapon: Satirists and Censor' (2012) 79(1) *Social Research* 87.

Godioli, A and Young, J 'Special Collection of the Case Law on Freedom of Expression' (Columbia Global Freedom of Expression, 2023).

Godioli A, Young, J and Fiori, BM, 'Laughing Matters: Humor, Free Speech and Hate Speech at the European Court of Human Rights' (2022) 35 *International Journal of the Semiotics of Law*.

Greene, VS, '"Deplorable" Satire: Alt-Right Memes, White Genocide Tweets, and Redpilling Normies' (2019) 5(1) *Studies in American Humor*.

Gunatilleke, G, 'Justifying Limitations on the Freedom of Expression' (2021) 22(91) *Human Rights Review* 108.

Hargreaves Heap, SP, 'Television in a digital age: what role for public service broadcasting?' (2005) 20(41) *Economic Policy* 112.

Hart, RP, and Hartelius, EJ, 'Critical Forum The Political Sins of Jon Stewart Critical Studies' (2007) 24(3) *Media Communication* 263.

Harvey D, 'Law and the Regulation of Communications Technologies: The Printing Press and the Law 1475–1641' (2005) *Australian and New Zealand Law & History Society E Journal*.

Hoffman, LH and Young, DG, 'Satire, Punch Lines, and the Nightly News: Untangling Media Effects on Political Participation' (2011) 28(2) *Communication Research Reports* 159.

Holbert, RL, Tchernev, JM, Walther, WO, Esralew, SE and Benski Young, K, 'Voter Perceptions of Political Satire as Persuasion: A Focus on Perceived Influence, Persuasive Intent, and Message strength' (2013) 57(2) *Broadcast Education Association Journal of Broadcasting & Electronic Media* 170.

Holmes, J and Marra, M, 'Over the Edge? Subversive Humor Between Colleagues and Friends (2002) 15(1) *Humour: International Journal of Humor Research* 65.

Johnson, BG, 'The Heckler's Veto: Using First Amendment Theory and Jurisprudence to Understand Current Audience Reactions Against Controversial Speech' (2016) 21(2) *Communication Law and Policy* 175.

Jones, WR, "People Have to Watch What They Say': What Horace, Juvenal, and 9/11 Can Tell Us about Satire and History (2009) 36(1) *Helios* 27.

Judge, S, and Steel, J, 'Online misogyny and the manosphere: Defending discourses of "free speech" within the alt-right and beyond' (2025) *Ethical Space: International Journal of Communication Ethics* [Preprint].

Katsirea, I, '"Fake news": reconsidering the value of untruthful expression in the face of regulatory uncertainty' (2018) 10(2) *Journal of Media Law* 159.

Kilby, A, 'Provoking the Citizen' (2018) 19(13) *Journalism Studies* 1934.

Kumar, S and Combe, K, 'Political parody and satire as subversive speech in the global digital sphere' (2015) 77(3) *The International Communication Gazette* 211.

LaMarre, HL, Kristen, D, Landreville Young, D and Gilkerson, N, 'Humor Works in Funny Ways: Examining Satirical Tone as a Key Determinant in Political Humor Message Processing' (2014) 17(3) *Mass Communication and Society* 400.

Lassiter, JC, 'Defamation of Peers: The Rise and Decline of the Action for Scandalum Magnatum, 1497–1773' (1978) 22(3) *The American Journal of Legal History* 216–36.

Lintott S, 'Superiority in Humor Theory' (Fall 2016) 7(4) *The Journal of Aesthetics and Art Criticism* 347.

Lloyd, D, 'Some Comments on the British Television Act, 1954' (1958) 23(1) *Law & Contemp Probs* 165.

Matamoros-Fernández, A, Bartolo, L and Troynar, L, 'Humour as an online safety issue: Exploring solutions to help platforms better address this form of expression' (2023) 12(1) *Internet Policy Review.*

Mays, J, 'Teen-Age Culture in Contemporary Britain and Europe' (1961) 338 *The Annals of the American Academy of Political and Social Science.*

McDermott K, 'You Gotta Laugh: Teaching Critical Thinking via Comedy' (2019) (19)2 *Pedagogy: Critical Approaches to Teaching Literature, Language, Composition, and Culture* 339.

Mchangama, J and Alkiviadou, N, 'Hate Speech and the European Court of Human Rights: Whatever Happened to the Right to Offend, Shock or Disturb?' (2021) 21 *Human Rights Law Review.*

Meikle, G, '"Find Out Exactly What to Think – Next!": Chris Morris, Brass Eye, and Journalistic Authority' (2012) 10 *Popular Communication.*

Moran, LJ, 'Dangerous Words and Dead Letters: Encounters with Law and The Love that Dares to Speak its Name' (2001) 23(2) *Liverpool Law Review* 153.

Nottage R, 'Report of the Broadcasting Committee 1949: Some of its Administrative Aspects' (1951) 29(2) *Public Administration* 173.

M Palin, *Diaries 1969–1979: The Python Years* (London, Phoenix, 2007).

Pauwels M, 'Anti-racist Critique Through Racial Stereotype Humour What Could Go Wrong?' (2021) 68(4) *Theoria* 169.

Pérez R, 'Racism without Hatred? Racist Humor and the Myth of "Colorblindness"' (2017) 60(5) *Sociological Perspective.*

Pérez, R and Ward, G, 'From Insult to Estrangement and Injury: The Violence of Racist Police Jokes' (2019) 63(13) *American Behavioural Scientist* 1810.

Polymenopoulou, E, 'Does One Swallow Make a Spring? Artistic and Literary Freedom at the European Court of Human Rights' (2016) 16(3) *Human Rights Law Review.*

Prestidge, J, 'Housewives having a go: Margaret Thatcher, Mary Whitehouse and the appeal of the Right Wing Woman in late twentieth-century Britain' (2019) 28(2) *Women's History Review* 277.

Reynolds, NB, 'Features of Greek Satyr Play as a Guide to Interpretation for Plato's Republic' (2012) 29(2) *Polis: The Journal of the Society for Greek Political Thought,* 234.

Richards, D, 'Elite Interviewing: Approaches and Pitfalls' (1996) 16(3) *Politics* 199–204.

Robertson, G, 'Trial of the Century: Lady Chatterley' (2010) 60(11) *History Today* 41.

Rowbottom, J, 'To Rant, Vent and Converse: Protecting Low Level Digital Speech' (2012) 71(2) *Cambridge Law Journal.*

Saunders, G, 'A Last Hurrah? Joe Orton's Until She "Screams", Oh Calcutta and the permissive 1960s' (2017) 37(2) *Studies in Theatre and Performance* 221.
Scheil, KW, 'Sir William Davenant's use of Shakespeare in The Law Against Lovers (1662)' (1997) 4 *Philological Quarterly* 369.
Seaton, J, 'Brexit and the Media' (2016) 87(3) *The Political Quarterly* 335.
Sienkiewicz, M and Marx, N, 'Appropriating Irony: Conservative Comedy, Trump-Era Satire, and the Politics of Television Humor' (2021) 60(4) *Journal of Cinema & Media Studies* 1.
Spoliar, L, 'Learning from laughter: Implicit Religion, satire, and power in two British TV situation comedies' (2022) 43(1) *Journal of Beliefs & Values* 68.
Staszak JF, 'Other/Otherness' (2008) Publie dans *International Encyclopaedia of Human Geography* Elsevier.
Suter, K, 'The British Satirical Revolution' (2004) *Contemporary Review The Free Library.*
Thorisdottir, H, Jost, JT, Liviatan, I and Shrout, PE, 'Psychological Needs and Values Underlying Left-Right Political Orientation: Cross-National Evidence from Eastern and Western Europe' (Summer 2007) 71(2) *Public Opinion Quarterly.*
Todd, J, 'Satire in Defamation Law: Toward a Critical Understanding' (2016) 35 *Review of Litigation* 45.
Willert, Sir Arthur, 'British News Controls: Foreign Affairs' (1939) 17(4) *Council on Foreign Relations* 712.
Xenos, MA and Becker, AB, 'Moments of Zen: Effects of The Daily Show on Information Seeking and Political Learning' (2009) 26(3) *Political Communication* 317.
Young, DG, Bagozzi, BE, Goldring, A, Poulsen, S and Drouin, E, 'Psychology, Political Ideology, and Humor Appreciation: Why Is Satire so Liberal? (2019) 8(2) *Psychology of Popular Media Culture* 134.
Young, J, 'Dogwhistles, Discrimination, Humour and the Law: Regulating Implicit Messaging' (2025) 11(2) *Open Library of Humanities.*

Parliamentary Sources

Broadcasting Committees

Sykes Broadcasting Committee 1923.
Broadcasting Committee 1949.

Hansard

Blasphemous Libel Bill HC Deb 23 December 1819 Vol 41 col 1543.
State Of The Drama HC Deb 31 May 1832 Vol 13 col 245.
Mr. Bernard Shaw's Play (Licence Refused) HC Deb 27 May 1909 Vol 5 col 1477W.
Censorship Of Plays HC Deb 30 November 1911 Vol 32 col 582.
Cinematograph Films (Unofficial Censorship) HC Deb 08 November 1912 Vol 43 col 1612.
Stage Plays (Offensive Personalities) HC Deb 28 November 1912 Vol 44 col 1490.
Broadcasting (Controversial Matter) HC Deb 05 March 1928 Vol 214 cc 811-2.
Censorship Of Plays (Repeal) Bill HC Deb 25 March 1949 Vol 463 cc 713-715.
House Of Commons Proceedings (Television) HC Deb 10 December 1959 Vol 615 col 741.
Parliamentary Reform HC Deb 15 March 1963 Vol 673 c1749.
Censorship Of Stage Plays HL Deb 7 May 1964 Vol 257 col 1326.
Parliamentary Proceedings (Television) HC Deb 28 May 1965 Vol 713 cc 1072-1119.
Theatre Censorship HL Deb 17 February 1966 Vol 272 cc 1151-68.
Televising of House of Lords Proceedings HL Deb 15 June 1966 Vol 275 cc72-94.

House Of Commons Proceedings (Broadcasting) HC Deb 24 November 1966 Vol 736 col 1638–1706.
Theatres Bill HC Deb 23 February 1968 Vol 759 col 831.
Theatres Bill HL Deb 28 May 1968 Vol 292 cc 1059-1060.
Broadcasting of Proceedings HC Deb 21 November 1969 Vol 791 cc1650-1694.
Permissive Society HC Deb 04 May 1970 Vol 801 col 95.
Proceedings of the House (Broadcasting) HC Deb 19 October 1972 Vol 843 cc467-576.
Proceedings Of The House (Broadcasting) HC Deb 24 February 1975 Vol 887 col 51-163.
Proceedings of the House (Broadcasting) HC Deb 08 March 1976 Vol 907 cc147-1183.
Proceedings Of The House (Broadcasting) HC Deb 16 March 1976 Vol 907 col 1183.
House of Commons (Sound Broadcasting) HC Deb 26 July 1977 Vol 936 cc539.
House Of Commons (Sound Broadcasting) HC Deb 6 February 1978 Vol 943 cc 1105-1135.
House Of Commons (Televising Of Proceedings) HC Deb 15 December 1981 Vol 15 cc 166-7.
Televising Of The House HC Deb 20 November 1985 Vol 87, cc 282–337.
Televising of the House HC Deb 09 February 1988 Vol 127 cc196-264.
Televising Of Proceedings Of The House HC Deb 12 June 1989 Vol 154 col 609–644.
Televising of Proceedings of the House HC Deb 19 July 1990 Vol 176 cc 1234–1263.
Defence and the Armed Forces HC Deb 01 November 2000 Vol 355 col 801.
Business of the House HC 3 March 2016 Vol 606 cc 1120-1121.
Freedom of Expression (Religious Satire) HC Deb 5 December 2016 Vol 618 col 13.

Parliamentary Publications (Date Order)

UK Parliament, Joint Select Committee on Stage Plays (Censorship) Report from the Joint Select Committee of the House of Lords and the House of Commons on the stage Plays (Censorship) (London: Printed for H.M.S.O. by Wyman and Sons, 1909).
Report of the Broadcasting Committee 1949 (His Majesty's Stationery Office 1951).
Broadcasting, &c., of proceedings in the House of Commons Select Committee, in the minutes of evidence taken before the committee (Her Majesty's Stationery Office, 1966).
Report of the Committee on Homosexual Offences and Prostitution (London, Her Majesty's Stationery Office London, 1968).
First Report from the Select Committee on Televising of Proceedings of the House Together with the Proceedings of the Committee, Minutes of Evidence taken in Sessions 1987-88 and 1988-89, and Memoranda Volume I Report and Proceedings of the Committee HC 141–11 (London, HMSO, 1989).
House of Commons Broadcasting Committee The Rules of Coverage First Report of Session 2002–03 HC 786 Published on by authority of the House of Commons London (The Stationery Office Limited, 18 June 2003).
Parliamentary Recording Unit Rules of Coverage (June 2003) Annex 1 {note}.
Parliamentary Recording Unit licence agreements *(n.d.)*.
Licence to use Parliamentary proceedings from the House of Commons for Broadcast (Parliamentary Recording Unit, May 2016 Amendment).
UK Government Guidance, Exceptions to copyright (updated 4 January 2021).

BBC Resources

BBC, 'About the BBC' (n.d.).
BBC, 'About the BBC Mission, Values and Public Purposes' (n.d.).
BBC, 'Richard Sharp: Who is the former BBC chairman?' (BBC, 28 April 2023).

BBC Guidance: Impartiality (BBC, 23 June 2025).
'BBC apologises for Frankie Boyle joke' (*BBC News Online*, 28 April 2010).
Sillito, D, 'BBC Apologises over racial slur used in news report' BBC (9 August 2020).
BBC News Online 'On this Day 18th March 1982' *Judge halts 'obscenity' trial.*
BBC News Online Obituary, 'Mary Whitehouse: Moral crusader or spoilsport?' (23 November 2001).
BBC News Online 'Channel 4 News didn't do itself any favours, says Nadine Dorries' (19 May 2022).
BBC News Online 'Who are the BBC governors?' (28 January 2004).
BBC News Online 'Saudi Arabia to punish online satire "mocking public order"' (BBC Online, 4 September 2018).
BBC News 'Tim Davie: BBC Boss prepared to fire stars who break impartiality rules' (29 September 2020).
BBC Variety Programmes Policy Guide for Writers and Producers (1949).
Chimamanda Ngozi Adichie: Freedom of Speech 'The Reith Lectures 2022 – The Four Freedoms' (TX: BBC Radio 4, 6 January 2023).
BBC Statement on *Heresy* (28 November 2019).
BBC News 'Fawlty Towers: The Germans episode to be reinstated by UKTV' (13 June 2020).
From Seesaw to Wagon Wheel: Safeguarding Impartiality in the 21st Century (BBC June 2007).
BBC News, 'Keith Lemon actor sorry for playing "offensive" black characters' BBC (5 June 2020).
BBC News, 'League of Gentlemen stays on BBC iPlayer after Netflix removal' BBC (11 June 2020).
Editorial Complaints Unit *The News Quiz*, Radio 4, TX date 16 February 2024 (BBC, 29 August 2024).

BBFC Archives

BBFC Annual Report for 1913.
BBFC Annual Report for 1914.

Ofcom Resources

BBC Third Annual Report (Ofcom 25 November 2020).
Audience Expectations in a Digital World (Ofcom, April 2020).
BSC Finding, '*Brass Eye Special*, Channel 4 and S4C, 26 and 27 July 2001, 2235–2310 and 0010-045'.
Ofcom's Annual Report on the BBC 2019/20' (Ofcom 25 November 2020).
Ofcom, Ipsos MORI research, 'Public attitudes towards offensive language on TV and Radio: Summary Report' (Ofcom, September 2021).
Ofcom Attitudes to potentially offensive language and gestures on TV and Radio Quick Reference Guide (Ofcom, September 2016).
Ofcom Broadcasting Code, The (with the Cross-promotion Code and the On Demand Programme Service Rules) December 2020 (Last updated: 12 June 2023).
Ofcom Broadcasting Code, The (with the Cross-promotion Code and the On Demand Programme Service Rules) January 2019.
Ofcom Section Five: Special Impartiality Requirements: news and other programmes (Ofcom, 20 October 2025).

Ofcom Broadcast Bulletins

Ofcom Broadcast Bulletin, Issue 179 *Tramadol Nights* (Ofcom, 4 April 2011).
Ofcom Broadcast Bulletin Issue 254 (Ofcom, 19 May 2014).
Ofcom Broadcast Bulletin 284 (Ofcom, 27 July 2015).

Ofcom Broadcast Bulletin Issue 290 (Ofcom, 12 October 2015).
Ofcom Broadcast Bulletin Issue 292 (Ofcom, 09 November 2015).
Ofcom Broadcast and On Demand Bulletin Issue 313 (Ofcom, 26 September 2016).
Ofcom Broadcast and On Demand Bulletin Issue 363 (Ofcom, 8 October 2018).
Ofcom Broadcast and On Demand Bulletin Issue 395 (Ofcom, 27 January 2020).
Ofcom Broadcast and On Demand Bulletin Issue 400 *Good Morning Britain* (Ofcom, 6 April 2020).
Ofcom Broadcast and On Demand Bulletin Issue 404 (Ofcom, 8 June 2020).
Ofcom Broadcast and On Demand Bulletin Issue 494 *Politicians acting as newsreaders, news interviewers or news reporters* (Ofcom, 18 March 2024).

Ofcom Guidance

Ofcom Guidance Notes: Issue Six: Section Five: Due Impartiality and Due Accuracy and Undue Prominence of Views and Opinions (Ofcom, 22 March 2017).
Ofcom Guidance Notes: Issue Twelve: Section Two: Harm and Offence (Ofcom, 18 July 2017).
Ofcom, *General Guidance* (Ofcom, 16 March 2023).
Ofcom *Guide for services: complying with the Online Safety Act* (Ofcom, 21 May 2025).

Ofcom General Material

Ofcom Report on: The Current Affairs Audit 2005.
Ofcom Sanctions Committee statement on *The Russell Brand Show* (Ofcom, July 2010).
Ofcom Broadcast Standards Complaint Assessment *Heresy* (Ofcom, June 2019).
Decision of the Election Committee on a due impartiality complaint brought by the Conservative Party in relation to Channel 4's Channel 4 News Climate Debate' (Ofcom, 28 November 2019).
Ofcom Broadcast Standards Complaint Assessment *Good Morning Britain* (Ofcom, 2020).
Ofcom, *How Ofcom regulates the BBC* (Ofcom, 22 June 2022).
Ofcom, *Tuning into YouTube: UK's media habits revealed* (Ofcom, 30 July 2025).

Newspaper Articles (Digital archive) Date Order

Bernard Shaw, G et al *Letter to the Editor*, *The Times* Issue 38476 (London, England, 29 October 1907).
Staff Reporter, 'The Riots. Rand Death Roll' *The Sydney Morning Herald* NSW: 1842–1954 (8 July 1913).
Staff Reporter '"Mrs. Wilson's Diary" Withdrawn' *The Times*, *The Times* Digital Archive (26 November 1965).
Staff Reporter 'Wilson Satire Planned' *The Times* (23 June 1967).
Staff Reporter, 'Damages for radio statement' *The Guardian* (28th July 1967).
Wardle, I, 'Precedent set in censorship' *The Times*, *The Times Digital Archive* (22 September 1967).
Staff Reporter, 'Profane poem is republished in newspapers' *The Times* Issue 60055 (London, July 14 1977).
Staff Reporter, 'Trial Cash for Mrs Whitehouse' *The Daily Telegraph* (London, March 29 1982).
Whitehouse, Mary (Letters) 'The Romans in Britain' *The Times* Issue 39436 (London, 30 March 1982).
Staff Reporter, 'The TV club' *The Guardian* (18 May 1989).

Online Newspaper Articles

Addley, E, '"Thatcher loved it": Spitting Image victims on being lampooned' *The Guardian* (28 September 2019).
Bakare, L, 'Channel 4 could be privatised by 2024, says Oliver Dowden' *The Guardian* (13 May 2021).

Busby, M and Bakare, L, 'BBC Three show Famalam criticised for Jamaican "stereotypes"' *The Guardian* (22 August 2020).

Bienkov, A, 'Boris Johnson defends calling black people "piccaninnies" with "watermelon smiles"' *Business Insider US* (1 July 2019).

Cain, S, 'The Late Show with Stephen Colbert to end in 2026 as CBS cancels show' *The Guardian* (8 July 2025).

Caldera, C 'Fact check: Fairness Doctrine applied to broadcast licenses, not cable' *USA Today* (28 November 2020).

Deanes, J 'Regulator Warns against "knee-jerk" legislation' *The Guardian* (23 May 2002).

De Jongh, N, 'Taste of Honey led to end of gay ban' *The Guardian* (25 November 2011).

Duncan, C, 'Boris Johnson hides in a fridge on live TV while dodging interview on eve of election' *The Independent* (11 December 2019).

Ferguson, E, 'Why Chris Morris had to make Brass Eye' The Guardian (5 August 2021).

Gardner, B, 'Exclusive: BBC's new boss threatens to axe Left-wing comedy shows' *The Telegraph* (31 August 2020).

Kelner, S, 'Nadine Dorries' briefing against Nick Robinson and the BBC is an attack on us all' *The iPaper* (26 October 2021).

Koblin, J, Grynbaum, MM and Barnes, B, 'ABC Pulls Jimmy Kimmel Off Air for Charlie Kirk Comments After F.C.C. Pressure' *The New York Times* (17 September 2025).

Luckerson, V, 'How the "John Oliver Effect" Is Having a Real-Life Impact' *Time.com* (10 July 2015).

Mason, R, Sabbagh, D, Stewart, H, Allegretti, A and Walker, P, 'Geoffrey Cox accrued at least £6m from second job while a parliamentarian' *The Guardian* (10 November 2021).

Morris, L, 'All the TV shows removed from Netflix, HBO Max and other platforms over blackface controversy' *Radio Times* (30 June 2020).

Olusoga, D, 'David Olusoga: his Edinburgh television festival speech in full' *The Guardian* (24 August 2020).

Peat, J, 'Jacob Rees-Mogg gets meme treatment after Commons lie-down goes viral' *The London Economic* (4 September 2019).

Rawlinson, K and Siddique, H, 'Police to take no action against Jo Brand over battery acid comments' *The Guardian* (14 June 2021).

Thorpe, V, 'Johnson poised to appoint Paul Dacre Chair of Ofcom' *The Guardian* (3 January 2021).

Tran, M, 'Greg Dyke resigns from Labour party' *The Guardian* (25 June 1999).

Travis, A, 'How Harold censored diary spoof' *The Guardian* (17th September 2000).

Waterson, J, 'UK culture minister hints government may sell Channel 4' *The Guardian* (6 October 2020).

Waterson, J, 'Nadine Dorries denies inappropriate tweet to Laura Kuenssberg' *The Guardian* (18 November 2021).

Other Online Resources

Balzaretti S 'Political Satire and Sexist Stereotypes: A Critical Insight on the Case of Patricio *Monteiro Telo De Abreu v. Portugal*.' (*Strasbourg Observers*, 14 September 2022).

British Library Collection Items 'Lord Chamberlain's report and correspondence about A Taste Of Honey' (Lord Chamberlain's Office: © Crown Copyright. Gerry Raffles: © Gerry Raffles Estate).

Cohen, SB *Keynote speech to the Anti-Defamation League* 'Never Is Now Summit on Anti-Semitism and Hate' (Nevada, 2019).

Council Of Europe online information page on hate speech.

Chortle Magazine 'Comics quit Comedy Central's all-female panel show' (Chortle.co.uk, 27 May 2021).

Chortle Magazine 'Frankie Boyle's New World Order Axed' (Chortle.co.uk, 23 March 2023).

Peter Cook's The Establishment Club (Darkestlondon.dom, 11 March 2013).

Cushion, S, 'BBC bias? The Prescott memo falls well short of the standards of impartiality it demands' (*The Conversation*, 14 November 2025).
Economic and Social Research Council Research Ethics.
Kilby, A, 'The Problem with Satirising the Election' (UK Election Analysis, 2019).
Hickman, T, 'Contempt of Parliament, Political Satire and the Case of the Rt Hon Rees-Mogg MP' (*U.K. Constitutional Law Blog*, 12 September 2019).
Hochschild, JH, *Conducting Intensive Interviews and Elite Interviews* Workshop on Interdisciplinary Standards for Systematic Qualitative Research (Harvard University, 2009).
Meta Oversight Board, 'Providing an independent check on Meta's content moderation'.
Meta Oversight Board, 'Elon Musk Satire' (7 March 2024).
Meta Oversight Board, 'Cartoon Showing Taliban Oppression Against Women' (7 March 2024).
Meta Oversight Board, 'Post in Polish Targeting Trans People' (16 January 2024).
Meta Oversight Board, '"Two Buttons" Meme' (20 May 2021).
Milton, J, 'Areopagitica; A Speech For the Liberty of Unlicens'd Printing, to the Parliament of England' printed in the Year 1644.
Murphy, LW, 'Facebook's Civil Rights Audit – Final Report' (8 July 2020).
Parker, E and Shepherd, C, 'About Edna Welthorpe' A Tribute to Joe Orton (Leicester University, 2017).
Summers, CJ, 'Wolfenden Report' (glbtq Inc, 2015).
Vice, John and Farrell, Stephen *The History of Hansard* (House of Lords *Hansard* and the House of Lords Library, n.d.).
Webb, D, 'Romans Won Whitehouse Nil' (The NCROPA Virtual Archive n.d.).
White, Sharon, Ofcom Chief Executive *The consumer and citizen at the heart* Which? Conference (11 June 2015).
Woodhouse, J, 'TV licences for the over-75s' House of Commons research briefing (21 October 2024).
Young, J, 'Meta, Moderation and the Satire Exception' (*Forhum*, 3 July 2024).
Young, J, 'China Cracks Down on Stand Up' (*Forhum*, 13 June 2023).

Audio-visual Media

Boyle, F, *Prometheus Volume 02, The Promethiad* (3 October 2017).
Frisby, D, *The Ofcom Song – 186 Words Not To Use* (YouTube, 25 September 2022).
Have I Got News For You, BBC (TX 17 May 2019, 21:00).
Gossip and Goddesses with Granny Kumar Episode 3 Radio 4 (TX 24 February 2021).
Iannucci, A, *The Guardian* Podcast on politics and satire (TX 28 January 2020).
Nelson, JQ, Trump celebrates Colbert getting booted by CBS in gleeful Truth Social post' *Fox News* (18 July 2025).
Victoria and Albert Museum Exhibition *Censored! Stage, Screen, Society at 50.*

INDEX

Allen, Shane:
due accuracy and impartiality, 161, 165
harm and offence, 102, 114–15, 125, 131, 132, 137, 139, 143, 145
Allen, Steve N:
harm and offence, 115, 125, 129, 137, 148
alt-right:
weaponisation of freedom of expression, 93
Anderson, Lee, 91
authoritarianism, 14–16, 27, 98–99, 150–51, 170–71, 185

Bailey, Ric, 21, 40, 100, 102, 114, 117, 122, 177, 186
due accuracy and impartiality, 155–56, 157–58, 168, 169
balancing rights, 3, 6, 22, 93–94
editorial balance, 82
courts, 24–32
impartiality requirement, 2, 20–21, 39–41, 100
breaches of, 91
Communications Act 2003, 8
see also due accuracy and due impartiality (Ofcom Code s. 5)
Meta Oversight Board, 35–38
Ofcom, 32–35
see also due accuracy and due impartiality (Ofcom Code s. 5); harm and offence (Ofcom Code s. 2),
socio-political satire, 18, 20–21
Barnes, Trevor, 180–81, 189
due accuracy and impartiality, 166
harm and offence, 131, 133, 139
BBC, *see* **British Broadcasting Corporation**
BBC Editorial Guidelines, 89, 99, 108, 114–15, 123, 150, 153–54, 155
Blair, Tony, 90–91
blasphemy, 46–47, 67, 68, 129
Blasphemous and Seditious Libels Act, 49
***Brass Eye* (TV programme),** 18, 18–19, 173
Brexit, 20, 164–65
British Board of Film Censors (BBFC), 44, 55–57, 63–64, 70
British Broadcasting Corporation (BBC):
BBC Charter, 74, 75, 108–9, 153, 172
editorial control, 71–72, 172
funding and licence fee, 73–74, 184
government control
licence fee threats, 184
self-regulation, 74, 75
That Was The Week That Was (*TW3*), 76–78
The Green Book, 75–76
broadcast media, 38, 39–40
BBFC, 55–57, 70
digital media, 94–95
freedom of expression, 93–94
Independent Broadcast Authority, 44
Lord Chamberlain, 52, 63–64
Mary Whitehouse, 67–69, 70
Ofcom, 43–44, 53, 92–93
regulation, 91–94
Till Death Do Us Part, 62
see also British Broadcasting Corporation; censorship; social media
Broadcasting Standards Commission, 92
Bunting, Jo:
due accuracy and impartiality, 159, 164–66
harm and offence, 118, 121, 124
Burma, 14

cancel culture, 4, 22, 62, 93, 109
Catullus, 44
censorship:
abolition of state censorship (theatre), 3–4
British Board of Film Censors, 44, 55–57, 63–64, 70
cinema/film, 55–57
Henry VIII, 45–46
historical origins, 42–44
Joint Select Committee on Stage Plays (Censorship), 53–54
Joint Select Committee on Stage Plays (Censorship), 53–54, 64
Lord Chamberlain, *see* Lord Chamberlain as censor

national security, 56–57
restrictions on political entertainment, 42–43, 82–84
self-censorship, 2, 4, 7, 14, 22, 40–41, 44, 54, 58, 75, 89, 96, 99, 179
due accuracy and due impartiality, 152, 169
harm and offence, 107, 108, 114, 121–22, 123, 127, 130, 139, 148–49
social media, 146–49
socio-political entertainment, 3–4, 5–6, 40
television, 63–64, 65–66, 66–68
theatre licensing and censorship laws, 50–55
calls for reform, 57–58
'manifest absurdities', 63–64
WWI, 56–57
cinema/film:
censorship, 55–57
Charter of Fundamental Rights of the EU (CFREU), 29
Charles II, 46
licensing publications, 46–47
chilling effect, 4, 9, 12–13, 23–24, 28, 40–41, 43–44, 47, 54, 67, 69, 84, 99, 181, 182
due accuracy and impartiality, 152, 155, 161, 171, 172–74, 174–75
harm and offence, 111, 113, 115, 121, 127, 139, 141, 143, 146, 147
China, 14
compliance and legal departments, 116–19
courts' protection of political speech and satire, 23–24, 40, 181
Criminal Libel Act, 49
Cross-promotion Code, 1
Communications Act (2003), 6, 8, 25, 32, 40, 91–93, 100, 108–9, 110, 151, 153, 177
critical thinking, promotion of, 5, 6, 8, 18, 23, 33–34, 45, 96, 168, 179–80
cultural sensibilities, 18, 46–47, 53, 76, 141–42, 166–67

***Daily Show* (US TV programme),** 19, 171
Davie, Tim, 103, 106, 150, 155, 172
defamation, 15, 45–46, 47, 68–69, 117, 177
Alves da Silva v Portugal, 28
Boyle v MGN Ltd, 33–34
democracy, 1–3, 5–6, 7, 23–24, 97–98, 111–12, 133, 141, 151, 162–63, 183–86
chilling effect of political satire, 40–41
digital democracy, 94–95
ECtHR, 27–28
media and political polarisation, 20
necessity test, 24
role of satire, 12–17, 25–26
televising Parliament, 79, 80, 84
Digital Services Act (EU), 35
dignity, 26, 30, 38, 79, 82–83
human dignity, 109
televising Parliament, 87–90
due accuracy and due impartiality (Ofcom Code s. 5), 6, 7–8, 20–21, 39–40, 91, 107–8, 150–53
GB News' failure to uphold, 91
key rules and principles, 153–55
existential threats, 172–74
impartiality rules and reality, 155–64
political satire and the Opposition, 174–76
right-wing comics, 164–66
risky satire, 166–71
polarisation through newscasting (US), 20

***Entertaining Mr. Sloane* (Joe Orton),** 61–62
European Court of Human Rights (ECtHR), 6, 27–28
Alves da Silva v Portugal, 28
Eon v France, 28
freedom of expression (Art. 10), 3, 21–23
Ofcom Code, 93, 98
Handyside v UK, 25–26, 29–30
Le Pen v France, 31–32
Otto-Preminger-Institut v Austria, 30
Patrício Monteiro Telo de Abreu v Portugal, 28–29, 31
political satire, 27–29, 89–90, 181
religious satire, 29–30
sexuality, 30–31
Sousa Goucha v Portugal, 30–31
stereotyping and discrimination, balancing, 31–32
Vereinigung Bildender Künstler v Austria, 29–30
Evans, Simon, 138–39, 141–42

Facebook, 35, 36–38, 95
fake news, 98–99, 170–71
disinformation/misinformation, 18, 93–94
satirical fake news, 17–18
Farage, Nigel, 85, 91, 121, 159
Federal Communications Commission (FCC) (US):
Fairness Doctrine, 19
political bias, 15–16

Fielding, Henry, 47–48
First Amendment (US Constitution):
FCC's Fairness Doctrine, 19
governmental overreach, 15–16
Heckler's Veto, 141
freedom of expression, 1–3, 21–22, 38–41, 183, 185
ECHR (Art. 10), 3, 21–22, 23, 24–27, 28–32, 93–94, 98, 108–9, 143, 151
HRA 1998, 22, 23–24, 24–25, 98
ICCPR, 24
Meta Oversight Board, 35–38
Ofcom, 16, 32–35, 93–94, 98, 111, 131, 143, 177, 178
press freedom, 49–55
unfettered freedom of expression, 3, 5, 26
see also censorship
Frisby, Dominic, 129, 138, 148, 165

GB News, 79, 91, 115, 172
George III, 48
George VI, 57
Germany, 15
Nazi Germany, 14
Grade, Lord Michael, 1, 102, 155, 177, 185
due accuracy and impartiality, 170, 172–73
harm and offence, 140
gratuitous offense, 112–13, 136, 149
Greek Satyrs, 12–13
Greene, Sir Hugh, 67, 77–78
Grimshaw, Laura, 115–16, 139, 163
grounded theory approach to data gathering, 100–1
Gutenberg printing press, 44–45

harm and offence (Ofcom Code s. 2), 6, 7–8, 107–8
bias considerations, 108
key rules and principles, 108–13
chain of worry, impact of, 119–28
compliance and legal departments, 116–19
court of public opinion, 140–46
framework nature, 113–16
inclusivity and exclusivity, relationship between, 134–37
self-censorship, 148–49
social media, 146–49
subjectivity and ever-shifting lines, 128–34
taboos, 137–40
hate speech limitation, 25–27, 27–28, 32, 36–38
***Have I Got News For You* (UK TV panel show),** 17–18, 118, 144, 147–48, 159, 162, 166, 171, 175–76, 177–78
Heckler's Veto, 7, 141–42, 143, 178
Henry VIII:
censorship, 45–46
Holmes, Jon, 116–17, 122, 125, 136–37
homosexual themes, 58–60, 61–62, 68, 77–78
Horace, 13, 47
Human Rights Act (1998):
freedom of expression, 22, 23–24, 24–25, 93, 98
political satire, 23–24
humour, 12, 27–28, 31–32, 33, 36–37, 107, 127
hypocrisy, 1, 18–19, 23, 38, 53, 132–33, 157–58, 169, 173, 183–84, 186

impartiality, *see* **due accuracy and due impartiality (Ofcom Code s. 5)**
Ince, Robin, 130, 168
Independent Broadcast Authority, 44, 84
Independent Television Authority, 74, 75, 92
Independent Television Commission, 92, 173
International Catholic Association for Radio and Television, 67
International Covenant on Civil and Political Rights (ICCPR), 24
Italy:
defamation, 15
par condicio law, 152

Johnson, Boris, 90–91, 97, 112, 140–41, 158–59, 160, 165–66, 169, 172, 184
Juvenal, 13, 43

Kearse, Leo, 128, 148, 165

***Lady Chatterley's Lover* (D.H. Lawrence),** 61, 68
***Last Week Tonight with John Oliver* (US TV programme),** 19, 163
Lawrence, D.H., 61, 68
libel, 45–46, 49, 66, 68, 70
limitations on freedom of expression, 9, 30, 40–41, 99, 102, 139, 180–81
see also balance
Linehan, Graham, 129, 134, 143, 169

literature, 61, 66
permissive literature, 60–61
Lady Chatterley's Lover, 61, 68
Obscene Publications Act 1959, 60–61
regulating the printed word, 44–47
see also printed material
Lloyd, John, 119, 122–24, 130, 149, 158, 161–62, 168, 178
Lord Chamberlain as censor, 3–4, 43–44
abolition, 65–66
BBFC, influence on, 55–56
beyond theatre, 63–65
homosexual themes, 58–59, 61–62
Joint Select Committee on Stage Plays (Censorship), 53–54
Lady Chatterley's Lover, 61–62
post-WWII role, 57–58
power to stop performances, 50–51
Sexual Offences Act, 61–62
Stage Licensing Act (1737), 47–48
theatre censorship, 43–44, 47–48, 50–53
advisory board, introduction of, 54–55
Joint Select Committee recommendations, 53–54
Theatre Regulation Act (1843), 50
Lucilius, Gaius, 13–14

margin of appreciation, 30, 36
media regulation, 40, 103, 174, 182
Meta Oversight Board (MOB), 27, 35–36
'Cartoon Showing Taliban Oppression Against Women' 37–38
'Elon Musk Satire', 37
'Polish Post Which Targeted Trans People' 38
'Two Buttons Meme', 36–37
morals, protection of, 6, 14, 24, 43, 52, 62, 185

national security, 24
censorship justification, 56–57
National Theatre:
The Romans in Britain, 68–69
National Viewers' and Listeners' Association (NVLA), 67
Nazi Germany, 14
necessity test, 24
'negative space', 13–14
Newman, Andrew, 135–36, 163
newspapers:
Boyle v MGN Ltd, 33–34
defamation, 33–34
government/politician relationships with, 49–50, 112
licensed newspaper industry, 50
Newspapers Stamp Duty Act (1819), 49–50
political independence, 49–50, 112, 178
press freedom, 49–50
right-wing comedians, 164
unlicensed newspapers, 49–50
see also printed material
North, Steve, 137

Obscene Publications Act (1959), 60–61
Obscene Publications Act (1964), 64
Ofcom Broadcasting Code, 6, 43–44, 53, 92–93
balancing rights, 32–35
Boyle v MGN Ltd, 33–34
due accuracy and due impartiality (s. 5), 6, 7–8, 19–21, 39–40
see also due accuracy and due impartiality (Ofcom Code s. 5)
freedom of expression, 16, 32–35, 93–94, 98, 111, 131, 143, 177, 178
Good Morning Britain/Piers Morgan incident, 34–35
harm and offence (s. 2), 6, 7–8
see also harm and offence (Ofcom Code s. 2)
independence, importance of, 188–89
misinterpretation and overapplication of rules, 186–87
Redmond-Bate v DPP, 34–35
regulations on political content, 43–44, 177–81
offensive content, 2, 27, 35, 40, 97–98, 110–11, 128–29, 133, 136, 142, 182
Oftel, 92
On Demand Programme Service Rules, 1
Orton, Joe, 61–62
Entertaining Mr. Sloane, 61–62
Mrs Edna Welthorpe, 62–63
What the Butler Saw, 63
over-reach:
misinterpretation of regulations, 4, 21, 162, 175, 183
over-regulation of content, 4, 98
Ovid, 42–43

Parody Exception, 17–18, 88–89, 177
Parsons, Andy, 118–19, 168
Persius, 13
Peterloo Massacre (1819), 49
Plowman, Jon, 90, 120, 123, 125, 132, 133, 167
poetry, 42–43, 44, 47
see also printed material

polarisation through newscasting, 20, 77
political apathy, 17
political engagement, 2–3, 16–17, 21–22, 70, 98–99, 100, 107, 183–85
political satire, 1–2, 5–6, 9
authoritarian states, 14
balancing rights, 18, 20–21
British TV, 17–18
courts' protection of political speech and satire, 23–24, 40, 181
definition, 8, 17
democracy
chilling effect of political satire, 40–41
role of satire, 12–17, 25–26
democratic backsliding, 15–16
due accuracy and due impartiality (Ofcom Code s. 5)
political satire and the Opposition, 174–76
risky satire, 166–71
ECtHR, 6, 23
political satire, 27–29, 89–90, 181
religious satire, 29–30
HRA 1998, 23–24
importance as political discourse, 15–16, 17–19
Meta Oversight Board, 27, 35–36
'Cartoon Showing Taliban Oppression Against Women' 37–38
'Elon Musk Satire', 37
'Polish Post Which Targeted Trans People' 38
'Two Buttons Meme', 36–37
origins, 12–13
religious satire, 29–30
satire exception, proposal for, 187–88
scrutiny of politicians, 16
politicians:
entertainers, as, 90–91
entertainment, as, 78–81
media relations, 71–78
televising Parliament, 79–81
editorial control, 81–86
rules of coverage, 86–90
power, patronage and protection, 183–84
editorial bias, 185–86
negative impact on creativity, 185
threats to BBC licence fee, 184–86
press freedom, 49–50
printed material:
Church control over, 45
permissive literature, 60–61
printing press, development of, 44–45
seditious libel offence, 45–46
suppression of political speech, 46–47
***Private Eye* (UK satirical news magazine),** 63, 65, 162
propaganda, 2, 73
theatre, 57
public health, 24
public order, 14, 24, 30
Public Order Act (1968), 64

Race Relations Act (1965), 64
Radio Authority, 92
Radiocommunications Agency, 92
regulations on political content, *see* **censorship; Ofcom**
religious satire, 29–30
***Report of the Committee on Homosexual Offences and Prostitution*,** *see* ***Wolfenden* Report**
reputation, 2–3, 6, 10, 24, 30–31, 48, 69–70, 130–31, 166–67, 182
royal reputation, 57
televising of Parliament, 80–81, 82
restrictions on political entertainment, 42–43, 82–84
see also censorship
Roman *satura*, 13–14
Rose, Christine, 115, 121, 122–23, 139–40, 147, 158, 160–61, 179
Rubinstein, Jolyon, 116–17, 118, 166–68, 174

satire, 180–81
British TV, 17–18
courts, 181
definition, 17
importance, 17–19
origins, 12–13
power, patronage and protection, 183–84
editorial bias, 185–86
negative impact on creativity, 185
threats to BBC licence fee, 184–86
satire exception, proposal for, 187–88
see also political satire
satire exception, proposal for, 187–88
Saudi Arabia, 14
Sayle, Alexei, 102, 115, 124–25, 137
seditious libel offence, 45–46, 49
self-censorship, 2, 4, 7, 14, 22, 40–41, 44, 54, 58, 75, 89, 96, 99, 179
due accuracy and due impartiality, 152, 169
harm and offence, 107, 108, 114, 121–22, 123, 127, 130, 139, 149

Sexual Offences Act (1956), 61, 68–69
sexuality, 30–31, 67, 131, 173
  homosexual themes, 58–60, 61–62, 68, 77–78
Shaw, George Bernard, 42
  Mrs Warren's Profession, 51–53
Six Acts, 49
Skelton, Charlie, 101, 138, 143–44, 146–47, 157–58, 169
social censure, 2, 5, 12–13, 182, 184
social media, 7, 12, 14, 22, 95, 109, 130, 140–41, 178–79
  Meta Oversight Board, 35–38
  self-censorship, 146–49
social mores, 2, 53, 109
***Spitting Image* (TV programme),** 15–16, 82–83, 171
Sri Lanka, 14
Stage Licensing Act (1737), 47–48, 64, 99, 182
Star Chamber (UK), 45–46
stereotyping and discrimination, balancing, 31–32, 33–35, 113, 128, 129, 135, 136, 141–43, 181

taboos, 43, 76, 131, 137–38, 149
televising Parliament, 10, 79–81
  editorial control, 81–86
  rules of coverage, 86–90
television:
  censorship, 63–64, 65–66, 66–68
  Independent Television Authority, 74, 75, 92
  Independent Television Commission, 92, 173
  International Catholic Association for Radio and Television, 67
  Television Act (1954), 65
  see also broadcasting media
***That Was The Week That Was* (*TW3*) (UK TV programme),** 76–78
***The Day Today* (UK TV programme),** 18
***The Late Show with Stephen Colbert* (US TV programme),** 15
***The Mash Report* (UK TV programme),** 18
***The Nearly Man* (UK TV drama),** 83–84
***The Romans in Britain* (UK play),** 68–69
theatre:
  'angry young men', 59–60
  homosexual themes, 58–59
    Entertaining Mr. Sloane, 61–62
  Joint Select Committee on Stage Plays (Censorship), 53–54, 64
  Lord Chamberlain's censorship, 50–55
  political theatre, 60
  Stage Licensing Act (1737), 47–48
  Theatre Act (1968), 3–4, 66, 68–69
  theatre licensing and censorship laws, 50–55
    calls for reform, 57–58
    'manifest absurdities', 63–64
    WWI, 56–57
  Theatres Act (1843), 51
Thoday, Jon, 102, 126–27, 163–64, 171
Tik Tok, 95
***Till Death Do Us Part* (UK TV comedy),** 33, 62, 68, 132–33
Trump, Donald, 15–16, 150, 170–71, 174

understanding editorial decisions, 99–100
  data-gathering, 100–1
    timeline, 105–6
  due accuracy and due impartiality (Ofcom Code s. 5), 107–8, 150–53, 153–55
    existential threats, 172–74
    impartiality rules and reality, 155–64
    political satire and the Opposition, 174–76
    right-wing comics, 164–66
    risky satire, 166–71
  ethical considerations, 104–5
  harm and offence (Ofcom Code s. 2) rules and principles, 107–8, 108–13
    chain of worry, impact of, 119–28
    compliance and legal departments, 116–19
    court of public opinion, 140–46
    framework nature, 113–16
    inclusivity and exclusivity, relationship between, 134–37
    self-censorship, 148–49
    social media, 146–49
    subjectivity and ever-shifting lines, 128–34
    taboos, 137–40
  participants, 101–4
United States:
  Daily Show, 19, 171
  Donald Trump, 15–16, 150, 170–71, 174
  FCC
    Fairness Doctrine, 19
    political bias, 15–16
  First Amendment (US Constitution)
    FCC's Fairness Doctrine, 19
    governmental overreach, 15–16
    Heckler's Veto, 141
  Last Week Tonight with John Oliver, 19, 163
  polarisation through newscasting, 20
  The Late Show with Stephen Colbert, 15
***Unspun* (UK TV programme),** 18, 161, 163–64

Walpole, Robert, 47–48, 51, 57, 64, 80–81
Webster, Neil, 157–58, 167, 169
Whitehouse, Mary, 62, 66–69, 70
Wilson, Harold, 64–65, 68
Wilson, Richard, 131, 134, 144, 147, 166
***Wolfenden* Report,** 58–59

X, 95

YouTube, 94–95

www.ingramcontent.com/pod-product-compliance
Ingram Content Group UK Ltd.
Pitfield, Milton Keynes, MK11 3LW, UK
UKHW020811290926
15470UKWH00003B/1098

9 781509 988662